SPECTRUM

Language Arts

Grade 6

Dr. Betty Jane Wagner

 McGraw-Hill
Consumer Products

Author

Betty Jane Wagner

Professor
Reading and Language Department
National-Louis University
Evanston, IL

Editorial Reviewer Board

Illustration
Steve McInturff

McGraw-Hill
Consumer Products

*A Division of The **McGraw·Hill** Companies*

Send all inquiries to:
McGraw-Hill Consumer Products
8787 Orion Place
Columbus, OH 43240-4027

Printed in the United States of America

ISBN 1-57768-476-1

1 2 3 4 5 6 7 8 9 10 GRAY 05 04 03 02 01 00

Table of Contents

Mechanics ....

Usage ....

Special Problems

Grammar ....

Parts of Speech   pages

Sentences

Writer's Handbook ....

1 Capitalization: Sentences, Titles, Days, Months, People

To capitalize or not to capitalize? Writers need to know how to answer this question about the words they write.

.... **Did You Know?** ....

The first word of a sentence is capitalized.

> **P**lease sign your name on the line at the bottom.

The names of people and pets are capitalized. So are people's initials and titles.

> **D**avid **J**acobson   **B**uck   **M**r. **A**lfonso **G**arcia, **J**r.

Words used to name relatives are capitalized *only* when the words are used as names or as part of names. They are not capitalized when preceded by a possessive pronoun, such as *my*, *your*, or *his*.

> Will **D**ad pick up **M**other at the train station?
> I like staying with my grandmother.

The names of days, months, and holidays are capitalized, but the names of seasons are not.

> On **M**onday, **M**arch 12, Sasha will interview the mayor.
> Our family always has a picnic on **I**ndependence **D**ay.

The pronoun *I* is capitalized.

> Michael and **I** went to the video store.

....

Show What You Know

Circle the twenty-three letters that should be capitalized.

galileo was an Italian astronomer and physicist. he was born in Italy on february 15, 1564. in 1609 galileo built his first telescope. i heard about galileo when i went to a planetarium with my father. the guide also talked about the edwin p. hubble Space Telescope, which was released on sunday, april 15, 1990. he spoke of the mission that made repairs on the telescope in 1993. col. richard o. covey and dr. n. jan davis were part of the crew that repaired the telescope.

Score: _____   Total Possible: 23

Proofread

Read the newspaper article. The writer left out 32 capital letters. Use the proper proofreading mark to show which letters should be capitalized.

Example: tuesday, april 5

Pet Party a Huge Success

On saturday, october 21, mr. and mrs. Howard c. jahn, jr., hosted an unusual event at their home to benefit a local animal shelter. they invited their friends to a costume party and competition—for their pets! Dozens of animals came to the party dressed as everything from donald duck to sherlock holmes. the Jahns' dog dodger, outfitted as count dracula, greeted the guests. First prize went to dr. caroline t. Sturgis's cockatoo claude for his Batman costume. "claude is very honored—i think," said Dr. sturgis. The jahns' nephew, mr. sidney K. abert, accompanied by his cat delilah, said, "This is the best party that uncle Howard and aunt Stella have had since New year's eve."

Practice

Imagine that you have just met this girl and her dog. Write a short paragraph describing the meeting.

_____

_____

_____

_____

_____

_____

_____

Tips for Your Own Writing: Proofreading . . . .

Choose something you have written recently. Check your writing, asking yourself this question: Did I capitalize the first word in every sentence, all names, and the pronoun _I_?

 *W*as the answer to the question "Yes"? Capital!

2 Capitalization: Places, Documents, Groups

Check the capitals—Declaration of Independence (document) for Americans (people) in Washington's White House (places).

Did You Know?

The names of specific places and things—cities, states, countries, divisions of the world, regions of the United States, streets, parks, and buildings—begin with a capital letter.

> He flew from **B**oston, **M**assachusetts, to **P**aris, **F**rance.
> The **W**hite **H**ouse is located at 1600 **P**ennsylvania **A**venue.

The names of historic documents begin with a capital letter.

> The **M**agna **C**arta was written in 1215.

The names of races, nationalities, religions, and languages begin with a capital letter.

> Many **C**ubans speak **S**panish and **E**nglish.

Show What You Know

Read the paragraph. On the lines, write the names that should have capital letters. Be sure to capitalize the words when you write them.

José Ubico was born in el salvador, a small country in central america. Ten years ago, he came to the united states, fleeing from the war in his homeland. José settled in los angeles where other salvadorans lived. José, who spoke spanish, learned english as well. One summer he went to washington, d. c., to see its many historic sights. His favorites were the jefferson memorial and the national archives museum where he saw copies of the constitution and the bill of rights.

1. _____   7. _____
2. _____   8. _____
3. _____   9. _____
4. _____   10. _____
5. _____   11. _____
6. _____   12. _____

Score: _____   Total Possible: 12

Proofread

Here is part of an essay about a world-famous building. The writer forgot to capitalize fifteen words. Use the proper proofreading mark to show which letters should be capitalized.

Example: south america

Every year, people from all over the world—americans, Japanese, british, chinese—

come to see the taj mahal. It was built on the jumna River in agra, india, by Shah Jahan,

the mogul emperor of India (1592–1666). The domed, white marble building is both an

islamic monument and a tomb for the emperor's beloved queen, Mumtaz Mahal.

During his reign, Shah Jahan expanded india's territory in the far east. He also made

islam the state religion and placed the country's capital in Delhi. But today he is

remembered for constructing one of the world's most beautiful buildings—the Taj mahal.

Practice

Look at or imagine a map of your state. Choose a place that you think is interesting, unusual, or fun. Write a short paragraph telling about the place. Explain why a visitor to your state should plan to see this place.

_____

_____

_____

_____

_____

_____

Tips for Your Own Writing: Proofreading ....

Choose a piece of your own writing and give it to a partner to proofread while you proofread your partner's paper. Look for the names of places and things. Check to see whether your partner capitalized the names. Use proofreading marks to show what should be changed.

 Remember ... a name always wears a cap! A capital letter, that is.

3 Capitalization: Titles

Just as names of people are capitalized, names or titles of books and other materials are also capitalized.

·············· Did You Know? ··············

The first, last, and key words in the title of a book, magazine, movie, play, story, report, poem, painting, or song are capitalized.

The articles *a*, *an*, and *the*; the conjunctions *and*, *or*, *nor*, and *but*; and short prepositions such as *at*, *in*, and *of* are not capitalized unless they are the first or last words of the title. Notice that the titles of books, magazines, movies, and plays are italicized. When handwritten, these titles are underlined.

Jayne's favorite book is ***A Wrinkle in Time.***
My mother likes to read the magazine ***The New Yorker.***
Last night we watched the movie ***Close Encounters of the Third Kind.***
A local theater group put on the play ***A Raisin in the Sun.***
Henry read aloud the story "**T**he **F**ox and the **C**row."
The title of my report is "**L**incoln as a **C**ountry **L**awyer."
Tanya memorized the poem "**S**topping by **W**oods on a **S**nowy **E**vening."
The painting "**H**ouse by the **R**ailroad" is by Edward Hopper.
The entire chorus joined in the song "**O**h, **W**hat a **B**eautiful **M**orning!"

Show What You Know

Circle each word that should begin with a capital letter.

the kids' world almanac of baseball

sarah, plain and tall

"under a telephone pole"

raiders of the lost ark

"nothing gold can stay"

the little house on the prairie

tales and legends of india

"ramona and the three wise persons"

born on the fourth of july

"song of the open road"

Score: _____   Total Possible: 35

Proofread

Here is part of an article about how to write a report. The writer did not properly capitalize the nine titles in the article. Use the proper proofreading mark to show which letters should be capitalized.

Example: "the fall of the house of usher"

where to find information

After seeing the painting "a woman in Black at the opera," you have decided to write

your report on the artist Mary Cassatt and call it "an american artist in Paris." You have

some general information about Cassatt from encyclopedias, such as *world book* or

Encyclopaedia britannica. Now, where else should you look? Read any books about the

artist, such as *an american impressionist* or *mary cassatt.* Check the indexes of magazines,

such as *art and history* and *American artists,* that might have articles about her.

Practice

What is your favorite book or movie? Write a short summary of the book or movie and then explain why you like it. Give your paragraph a title. Remember to underline the title of the book or movie in the summary.

_____

_____

_____

_____

_____

_____

_____

_____

Tips for Your Own Writing: Proofreading ....

Look at several pieces of your own writing. Do they have titles? Did you use any titles within the copy? Check to see whether you capitalized the titles correctly.

 Titles name books or other materials. Capitalize the key words in their names.

4 Capitalization: Direct Quotations

The first word of what I say is always capitalized. But if what I say is in parts, then it's a case of sometimes a capital and sometimes no capital.

·························· Did You Know? ··························

A <u>direct quotation</u> shows a person's words. A writer puts quotation marks before and after the quotation. The first word in the quotation is always capitalized.

> "**T**his award is a great honor," said Ms. Tannoy.
> She exclaimed, "**N**o one was more surprised than I was."

In a <u>divided quotation</u>, words such as *she said*, called speaker's tags, are in the middle of the quotation. The first word in the first part of the quotation is always capitalized. But the first word in the second part is capitalized *only* if it begins a new sentence.

> "**T**his award is a great honor," said Ms. Tannoy. "**T**hank you for giving it to me."
> "**T**his award," said Ms. Tannoy, "is a great honor."

Show What You Know

Read the sentences. Circle the twelve words that should begin with a capital letter.

Cara asked, "so what are we going to do our group report on?"

"i think," said Wayne, "we should do our report on the Squealing Wheels."

"oh, no," groaned Ahmed, "not that awful rock group again!"

"the Wheels are great," Wayne insisted. "they've had three number-one hits."

"let's vote," Cara interrupted. "all those for the Squealing Wheels? All those

against? Okay, no Wheels. Any other suggestions?"

"if we want to do a music topic," Rachel offered, "how about focusing on a

particular trend, like the return to acoustic performances?"

"that's a good idea," said Cara. "what do you guys think?"

"it's okay, with me," said Ahmed, "if it's okay, with Wayne."

Wayne grumbled, "yeah, all right. But I still say the Wheels are the best."

Score: _____   Total Possible: 12

Proofread

**Here are some famous quotations. They are missing six capital letters.
Use the proper proofreading mark to show which letters should be capitalized.**

Example: Eleanor Roosevelt said, "no one can make you feel inferior without your consent."

1. "and so, my fellow Americans," said John F. Kennedy, "ask not what your country

can do for you; ask what you can do for your country."

2. Gertrude Stein said, "a rose is a rose is a rose is a rose."

3. "what's in a name?" asked Romeo. "that which we call a rose by any other name

would smell as sweet."

4. "always do right," said Mark Twain. "This will gratify some people and astonish the rest."

5. "in spite of everything, I still believe," Anne Frank said, "that people are really good

at heart."

Practice

**Work with a partner. Think of three questions to ask
each other. Write your partner's answers as direct
quotations. Try writing one of the answers as a
divided quotation. When both of you are finished,
check each other's writing for correct capitalization.**

Tips for Your Own Writing: Proofreading ....

The next time you write a story, make sure to write a conversation for two or more of your characters.
Capitalize the first word in each quotation and the first word in the second part of a divided
quotation only when it begins a new sentence.

*What do sentences and quotations have in common? Their first words are
always capped.*

5 Capitalization: Friendly and Business Letters

The first words in certain parts of letters, such as greetings and closings, need capital letters.

.... Did You Know? ....

There are two kinds of letters: friendly letters and business letters. Each kind of letter has its own form, but both letters have a greeting and a closing. The first word in a greeting is capitalized. So are any names or titles used in the greeting. Only the first word in a closing is capitalized.

Friendly Letter

1296 Meadow Drive
Glenview, IL 60025
August 17, 2000

Dear **T**eresa,
   I have been home for a week, but it seems much longer! I really miss you and Rico. I had such a good time staying at your ranch.

             Your friend,

             Carolina

Business Letter

1296 Meadow Drive
Glenview, IL 60025
December 2, 2000

Appleby, Incorporated
1348 Forest Avenue
Houston, TX 77069

Dear **S**ir or **M**adam:
   I am returning the sweater you sent. I ordered a Large and received a Small. Please send me the correct size.

             Sincerely yours,
             Carolina Ramirez
             Carolina Ramirez

Show What You Know

Circle each word that should begin with a capital letter.

1. dear aunt katherine,

2. your patient cousin,

3. hope to hear from you soon,

4. dear mr. oglethorpe:

5. sincerely,

6. dear customer service department:

7. yours truly,

Score: _____   Total Possible: 14

Proofread

Here are two short friendly letters. There are five missing capital letters in each. Use the proper proofreading mark to show which letters should be capitalized.

Example: My aunt kathy will arrive in may.

---

129 Wickam Way
Hillville, NJ 08505
April 28, 2000

dear uncle fred,

    mom told me that you fell down the

back steps and sprained your ankle. I'm

sending you several of my favorite books

to help pass the time.

        your nephew,

        Wilson

4490 Main Street
Weston, IA 50201
may 4, 2000

dear wilson,

    The books arrived, and i have already

read one. Thank you for thinking of me. A

sprained ankle is painful and boring!

        love,

        Uncle Fred

Practice

Think of a school or community problem. Write a letter to the editor of your local paper explaining the problem and your solutions to the problem. Write a draft of the body of your letter on the lines below. Then, using the business form, write the entire letter on a separate sheet of paper.

_____

_____

_____

_____

_____

Tips for Your Own Writing: Proofreading . . . .

Look at a letter or note you have written recently. Check to see that you capitalized the appropriate words in the greeting and closing.

 A phone call is nice, but a letter is better!

Lesson

6 Review: Capitalization

A. Use the proper proofreading mark to fix thirty missing capital letters.

last saturday, which was august 23, my brother bill married suzanne. it's about time, too, because everyone has been working on that wedding since valentine's day! my sister jenny was the maid of honor, and i was an usher. it was hot, crowded, and uncomfortable. when rev. benson finally introduced mr. and mrs. william j. krupski, i wanted to cheer. of course, mom was crying, but then so were dad, aunt shirley, uncle dave, and lots of other people. maybe they were just glad it was over, as i was!

Score: _____   Total Possible: 30

B. Use the proper proofreading mark to show fifteen words (names of places, buildings, groups, religions) that should begin with capital letters.

In northwest cambodia, not far from its border with thailand, lies the ruined city of angkor. From about 880 to about 1225, angkor was the capital of the mighty Khmer Empire. The city has several temple complexes, all larger than the egyptian pyramids, that were built to honor hindu gods. The greatest of these temples is angkor wat. Its vast stone walls are covered with scenes from hindu mythology. Angkor was abandoned about 1434, and the capital was moved to phnom penh. Rediscovered by french missionaries in the 1860s and now regarded as one of southeast asia's great masterpieces, Angkor has begun to attract many tourists from the west.

Score: _____   Total Possible: 15

C. Write the titles from the title and paragraph below in the blanks on the following page, adding capital letters where they are needed. If the title is in italics, also underline it.

that versatile writer: edgar allan poe

Edgar Allan Poe wrote his first book *tamerlane and other poems* in 1827 when he was 18. He soon began writing fiction. Five of his stories were published in a newspaper, the *philadelphia saturday courier,* and a sixth story won a $50 prize. Poe then became editor of a magazine, the *southern literary messenger.* His story "the murders in the rue morgue" is considered to be the first classic detective story. Some of his poems, such as "the raven," are still well-known today.

16

1. _____

2. _____

3. _____

4. _____

5. _____

6. _____

Score: _____   Total Possible: 6

D. Use the proper proofreading mark to add five capital letters where needed.

"senator Brock," the reporter asked, "do you know Hiram M. Douglas?"

"no, I do not," said Senator Brock. "the name is unknown to me."

"but look at this picture," insisted the reporter. "isn't that you and Douglas?"

Score: _____   Total Possible: 5

E. Use the proper proofreading mark under five lowercase letters that should be capitalized.

1422 Bristol Road

Columbus, OH 43221

may 22, 2000

dear kaitlin,

thank you for the birthday present. It was very clever of you to remember

how much I liked Tina Weems's CD *Sweet Weems* and to give me a copy of

my own. Isn't Tina supposed to have a new CD next month?

your friend,

Tyesha

Score: _____   Total Possible: 5

REVIEW SCORE: _____   REVIEW TOTAL: 61

7 Punctuation: Sentences, Abbreviations, and Initials

Periods can be used to end a sentence, but they also let you know that a word is an abbreviation. That little dot is a valuable mark.

.... Did You Know? ....

A period is used at the end of a sentence that makes a statement.

> Football is a popular sport.

A period is used after abbreviations for titles, the months of the year, and the days of the week.

Doctor—Dr.	Mister—Mr.	Senator—Sen.
October—Oct.	January—Jan.	December—Dec.
Friday—Fri.	Wednesday—Wed.	Monday—Mon.

A period is used after initials in names.

> Susan Brownell Anthony—Susan **B.** Anthony
> Booker Taliaferro Washington—Booker **T.** Washington

Show What You Know

Read the paragraph below. First, add periods at ends of sentences where needed. Then, change each bold word to an initial or abbreviation by adding a period and drawing a line through the unnecessary letters. Circle each period.

Early on **Saturday**, the first of **November**, Joseph **Andrew** Simon got into his car.

Mr. Simon is a teacher at Lyndon **Baines** Johnson High School. Every **Monday** and

Wednesday in **September** and **October**, he taught exercise classes for some heart

patients of Dr. **Pablo** Gonzalez These classes were held at Dwight **David** Eisenhower

Elementary School The classes were so popular that other programs hired him. Every

Tuesday and **Thursday** morning, he worked at Gerald **Rudolph** Ford University

Professor Althea **Jane** Perkins sponsored the program. **Senator** Gutierrez and **Reverend**

Tanaka participated in that class Now each Saturday in November and **December**, Mr. Simon

will be coaching a wheelchair basketball team in the James **Francis** Thorpe fieldhouse.

Score: _____   Total Possible: 23

Proofread

Read these notes for a report. Use proper proofreading marks to add nine missing periods.

Example: Dr. Bashir

  Margaret H Thatcher was born on Oct. 13, 1925 Mr and Mrs Alfred Roberts were her parents. The family lived in Grantham, Lincolnshire, England. After graduating, Margaret became a tax attorney and eventually was elected to Parliament in 1959 Becoming a member of Parliament is similar to being a senator in the United States government. Margaret Thatcher became the first woman leader of Britain's Conservative Party on Feb 11, 1975 Four years later on May 3, 1979, she was elected Prime Minister She resigned that post in Nov of 1990.

Practice

Write notes to summarize the events of the school week. Write your notes in complete sentences, and use abbreviations when possible.

1. _____

_____

2. _____

_____

3. _____

4. _____

5. _____

Tips for Your Own Writing: Proofreading ....

Look for lists, notes, and other informal writing you have done. Check your writing to make sure you put a period at the end of sentences that are statements, and after initials, abbreviations, and each title.

Remember . . . periods put an end to statements and abbreviations.

8 Punctuation: Other Abbreviations

Don't be fooled—there are some abbreviations that do not use periods!

.... Did You Know? ....

Two-letter postal abbreviations for state names do not have periods. See page 160 for a complete list.

Tennessee—TN   California—CA
Idaho—ID   New York—NY

Abbreviations for metric measurements do not have periods.

meter—m   kilogram—kg   milliliter—mL
liter—L   gram—g   kilometer—km

Initials for the names of organizations or companies do not use periods.

American Broadcasting Companies—ABC
Boy Scouts of America—BSA

Some terms that are made up of more than one word are known by their initials. These do not use periods.

videocassette recorder—VCR
gross national product—GNP

Show What You Know

Write the abbreviations or initials for the following items.

1. Indiana _____

2. milligram _____

3. Texas _____

4. centimeter _____

5. Illinois _____

6. Nevada _____

7. Maine _____

8. Washington _____

9. kiloliter _____

10. Florida _____

11. National Basketball Association _____

12. recreational vehicle _____

13. American Heart Association _____

14. World Health Organization _____

15. Eastern Standard Time _____

16. Environmental Protection Agency _____

17. decimeter _____

18. most valuable player _____

19. North Dakota _____

20. Unidentified Flying Object _____

Score: _____   **Total Possible: 20**

Proofread

Proofread this part of a report and change the bold words to abbreviations. Write the abbreviations on the lines below the report.

Hurricanes sweep the Gulf of Mexico during the summer months. The whirling storms can measure 200 to 300 **miles** (320 to 480 **kilometers**) in diameter. The eye of
1   2
a hurricane travels at a speed of 10 to 15 **miles per hour,** or 16 to 24 kilometers per
3
hour. The cloud forms may rise 10,000 **feet** (3048 **meters**) high and cover thousands of
4   5
miles. One of the costliest hurricanes to strike the United States was Hurricane Andrew, which hit the Bahamas and headed **northwest** to **Florida** and **Louisiana** in 1992.
6   7   8

1. _____   5. _____

2. _____   6. _____

3. _____   7. _____

4. _____   8. _____

Practice

Find out about a storm in your state or imagine one that could hit. Write some notes using abbreviations. Your notes should be in complete sentences.

_____

_____

_____

_____

_____

_____

Tips for Your Own Writing: Proofreading ....

Look at some of your math papers or science reports to find examples of measurements. Check to see that you wrote the metric and customary measurement abbreviations correctly.

 Abbreviations save time and space when you are taking notes or making lists.

9 Punctuation: End Marks

"What does this say this is confusing" Can you read those sentences? Punctuation marks will make them clear! *"What does this say? This is confusing."*

.... **Did You Know?** ....

A period is used at the end of a sentence that makes a statement.

Machines help us with many daily tasks.

A period is used at the end of a sentence that gives an order or makes a request.

Turn on the dishwasher.

A question mark is used at the end of a sentence that asks a question.

How many machines do you use each day?

An exclamation point is used at the end of a statement, order, or request that expresses strong feeling.

That machine is awesome!
Pull that plug right now!

Show What You Know

Put the correct punctuation mark at the end of each sentence. Circle any periods you add so they will be easier to see.

Do you think robots will replace the workforce I doubt it However, many of tomorrow's jobs will be performed by robots Think about the advantages this will bring for humans They can do work that is dangerous for people to do Noise, heat, smoke, and dust do not bother them Neither does the freezing cold of outer space A built-in computer controls a robot's actions so it can be programmed to do many difficult jobs

The word *robot* comes from the Czech word *robota*, which means "drudgery" What does *drudgery* mean It's work that is repetitive and tiresome Robots don't care what the task is They can work twenty-four hours a day at a steady pace Best of all, they never make mistakes How super Robots never get bored and they never complain They are truly special

Score: _____   Total Possible: 17

Proofread

Use proofreading marks to add twelve end punctuation marks where they are needed.

Example: I love to swim.

Hiking is one of the most enjoyable forms of exercise. Walking is a form of hiking Almost anyone can do it. All you really need is comfortable clothing and very comfortable walking shoes Shoes are probably the most important hiking tool. You will be on your feet a lot, so take care of them Get properly fitting shoes to avoid blisters and sore feet It's also wise to check the weather report before you start. You can then select the correct type of clothing

Find a special place to walk It can be on a sidewalk in a park, a trail in the forest, or a path in the country What can be better than walking along in a wooded area Nothing on earth As you walk, the sights and sounds of nature are all around you You hear the leaves rustling. Are you listening to the birds What beautiful sounds

Practice

There are many kinds of exercise. What is your favorite? Write a paragraph about your favorite exercise that will convince your friends it is a great activity.

_____

_____

_____

_____

_____

Tips for Your Own Writing: Proofreading ....

Select a story you have recently written. Check to see if you put periods after sentences that are statements, orders, or requests, question marks after questions, and exclamation points after sentences that express strong feelings.

Punctuation is the key to others understanding what you write. Use the right marks when you write!

10 Punctuation: Sentences

Sentences that run into each other need end punctuation. Use end punctuation marks to separate them.

.... **Did You Know?** ....

Two or more sentences written as though they were one sentence are hard to read. Correct use of end punctuation and capital letters will help you write better sentences.

> **Incorrect punctuation:** Sundials, water clocks, and hourglasses were the earliest timekeepers they were made from natural materials in the A.D. 1000s, mechanical clocks were invented in China.
>
> **Correct punctuation:** Sundials, water clocks, and hourglasses were the earliest timekeepers. They were made from natural materials. In the A.D. 1000s, mechanical clocks were invented in China.

A comma cannot be used as an end mark. Two sentences separated by only a comma are incorrectly punctuated.

> **Incorrect punctuation:** Sundials tell time by measuring the angle of the shadow cast by the sun, hourglasses do not.
>
> **Correct punctuation:** Sundials tell time by measuring the angle of the shadow cast by the sun. Hourglasses do not.

Show What You Know

Add periods where they are needed to correct the punctuation in this paragraph. Then circle the words that should be capitalized.

Early European mechanical clocks were huge the gears of the mechanical clocks often occupied whole rooms they had no dials or hands but marked the time by ringing a bell these clocks, like other early clocks, were inaccurate by 1400, the mechanical timekeeper had become a part of everyday life almost every town had an enormous "town clock."

Score: _____   Total Possible: 10

Proofread

The paragraph below has four places where the punctuation is incorrect. Correct the sentences by using proper proofreading marks to add four end punctuation marks and four capital letters.

Example: Seals are interesting animals they are found in many parts of the world.

Harbor seals spend most of their time on floating ice chunks or land bearded seals enjoy spending their time in the same way. Harbor seals weigh between 100 and 150 pounds. They are usually about five feet in length. The weight of the larger bearded seals can be up to 1,500 pounds they can grow to be twelve feet long. Harbor seals like to play in groups bearded seals are happy spending time alone. Seals have generally poor hearing, but their sight is good. Bearded seals have big, brushlike whiskers harbor seals have small, delicate ones.

Practice

Choose a pair of the animals in the picture and write a paragraph comparing them. How are they alike? How are they different? When you are finished, reread your paragraph to check for sentences that are missing end marks.

_____

_____

_____

_____

_____

_____

Tips for Your Own Writing: Proofreading ....

The next time you write a report, check for sentences that need end marks. Read the sentences aloud to listen for mistakes in end punctuation.

 Punctuation marks will help mark "the end" of sentences.

11 Punctuation: Sentence Fragments

"When I got on the bus." Is this a sentence? Add the missing parts to make a complete sentence.

.... Did You Know? ....

A sentence fragment is a group of words that is not a sentence. A *fragment* is a part of a sentence.

Fragment: Until it got dark.
Sentence: We played baseball until it got dark.

Fragment: After we ate dinner.
Sentence: After we ate dinner, we did our homework.

Show What You Know

Rewrite the paragraph to eliminate the sentence fragments. You can do this by adding the fragment to the beginning or end of the sentence it should be part of.

Itaipú, the most powerful electricity-producing dam in the world, is in Brazil. Paraguay and Brazil built the dam on the Paraná River. Which is in an area of dense tropical vegetation. The dam is 633 feet high and 5 1/2 miles long. After the dam was completed in 1991. The total cost of building it was determined to be $18 billion. The dam contains enough building materials to build a city for four million people. Because the water running over the dam sounds like music. It is called Itaipú, which means "singing dam" in Portuguese.

_____

_____

_____

_____

_____

_____

Score: _____   Total Possible: 3

Proofread

Eliminate the three sentence fragments by adding the fragments to the beginning or end of a sentence.

George Washington Carver helped save farm industry in the South by showing farmers how to rotate crops. Which means to plant different crops from year to year. Through his bulletins and speeches. Carver taught farmers many things. He spent many years researching peanuts. Which was one of his great achievements.

1. _____

_____

2. _____

_____

3. _____

_____

Practice

Write a paragraph that tells what you believe to be the most exciting summer Olympic sport to watch. Give reasons for your choice. Be sure to use complete sentences.

_____

_____

_____

_____

_____

Tips for Your Own Writing: Proofreading ....

Choose a favorite piece of your writing. Reading your work aloud can help you find sentence fragments. Some writers find it helps to "hear" problem sentence fragments if they read their papers "backwards," starting with the last sentence first.

 Remember to make sentences "whole"—no parts or fragments allowed.

Lesson

12 Review: Punctuation

A. Read these notes. Use the proper proofreading mark to add ten missing periods after sentences, abbreviations, and initials.

In an address to Congress in 1961, Pres Kennedy called for a commitment to land a man on the moon before the end of the 1960s *Apollo 8* was launched on Dec 21, 1968 Astronauts James A Lovell, William Anders, and Frank Borman were on board The spacecraft reached the moon on Tues the 24th and proceeded to make ten orbits around the moon Splashdown occurred early on Fri the 27th of Dec

Score: _____   Total Possible: 10

B. Write an abbreviation for each bold term.

In math class today we used formulas to change measurement systems. We changed **miles** (_____) to **kilometers** (_____) and **feet** (_____) to **meters**
\ 1 \ 2 \ \ \ \ \ \ \ \ \ \ \ \ \ \ \ \ \ \ 3
(_____). Then we used the map scale to measure the distance of the Oregon Trail
\ \ \ 4
from Independence, **Missouri** (_____), to Fort Walla Walla, **Washington**
\ 5
(_____). Finally, we calculated the travel time on the trail for a wagon and a
\ \ \ 6
recreational vehicle (_____). We discovered that the **miles per hour** (_____)
\ \ \ \ \ \ \ \ \ \ \ \ \ \ \ \ \ \ \ 7 \ 8
were very different!

Score: _____   Total Possible: 8

C. Use the proper proofreading marks to add seven missing end punctuation marks to these directions.

Have you ever made homemade clay These directions will help you create a small quantity of clay. Take one cup of warm water, one cup of salt, and two cups of cooking flour Mix the ingredients together Squeeze the wet flour until it is smooth and does not stick to your fingers. It's ready for modeling You can create any type of sculpture you wish You may also want to add food coloring to various batches to make colorful figures of clay Have fun

Score: _____   Total Possible: 7

D. **The paragraph below has three incorrect sentences. Correct the sentences using proper proofreading marks to add three end punctuation marks and three capital letters.**

For many years, people in the United States used streetcars to travel in cities. At first, streetcars were called horsecars because they were pulled by horses. Later, streetcars were powered by steam in the 1800s, people began trying to use electric power, but making electricity was considered to be too expensive. In 1888 a machine was invented that made electricity inexpensively. In that same year, the first electric-powered streetcars were put into use they quickly replaced the steam-powered streetcar. With the invention of the gas engine, electric streetcars were soon replaced by buses and cars. By 1930 the streetcar had begun to disappear from city streets. Interest in streetcars revived in the 1970s streetcars use less energy per person and create less pollution than automobiles.

Score: _____   **Total Possible: 6**

E. **Find and circle five sentence fragments. Then rewrite the paragraph by adding each fragment to the end of a sentence.**

Garrett A. Morgan invented the gas mask. Morgan had to prove that his mask would work. Before people would use it. He showed a man going into a small tent. That was filled with smoke. The man stayed in the tent. For about twenty minutes. Next, the man went into a small room filled with poison gas. He stayed for fifteen minutes and was fine. When he came out. In 1916 Morgan used his gas mask to rescue more than twenty workers. Who were trapped in a smoke-filled tunnel in Cleveland.

_____

_____

_____

_____

_____

Score: _____   **Total Possible: 5**

REVIEW SCORE: _____   **REVIEW TOTAL: 36**

13 Punctuation: Commas I

Commas are the road signs writers use to separate things so they are easier to read.

.... Did You Know? ....

Commas are used to separate three or more items in a series. Put a comma after each item except for the last one.

> Rolls, bagels, scones, and muffins are displayed in the bakery.
> Customers can see, smell, and admire the different kinds of bread.
> I bought carrot muffins, rye rolls, blueberry scones, and onion bagels.

Commas are used after introductory words such as *yes, no,* and *well.*

> Yes, that bakery makes the best sourdough bread in the city.
> Well, you have to get there early before the bread is gone.

An appositive follows a noun and gives more information about the noun. In the examples below, the appositives are in bold type. Commas are used to set off appositives from the rest of a sentence.

> Mr. Schultz, **the bakery owner,** is very proud of his breads.
> My favorite is pumpernickel, **a sour rye bread.**

Commas are used in direct address. Commas separate the name of the person spoken to from the rest of the sentence.

> Do you have any wheat bread, Mr. Schultz?
> Jerry, I put a loaf aside just for you.
> You know, Mr. Schultz, you are a wonderful man!

Show What You Know

Read the paragraph. Add fourteen commas where they are needed.

Dogs come in all sizes shapes and colors. The American Kennel Club the official dog breeding organization recognizes 130 breeds in seven categories. For example, sporting dogs include pointers setters and retrievers. Collies sheepdogs and corgis are considered herding dogs. Ben my boxer is classified as a working dog. But to me, Ben is a companion. When I say, "Ben come," he always comes. Well maybe he doesn't *always* come. But he certainly comes when I say, "Dinner Ben." Yes *dinner* is definitely a word he knows!

Score: _____   **Total Possible: 14**

Proofread

Add eleven commas to this conversation where they are needed. Use the proper proofreading mark to show where each comma should be placed.

Example: Well, are you ready to begin?

"Lionel, I've got the telescope, two blankets, and some hot chocolate. Let's go outside and look at the moon the stars and the planets."

"Well I don't know, Lucy. Will there be any snakes, spiders, or bats out there?"

"No, I don't think so Lionel. Annie Callahan my next-door neighbor goes out star-gazing every night. So does Harry Thoreaux, your dentist. Last night he saw a meteor. Wouldn't you like to see a meteor Lionel?"

"Yes, Lucy I would. But only if I don't have to see any rats roaches or worms!"

"Then I suggest you look up Lionel, rather than down!"

Practice

Write a paragraph in which you describe your favorite foods to a friend. In the first sentence, list at least three different foods. Then describe them. Use your friend's name in at least one sentence.

_____

_____

_____

_____

_____

_____

Tips for Your Own Writing: Proofreading ....

Choose a piece of your own writing and ask a partner to proofread it, checking for commas between items in a series and with introductory words, appositives, and direct address.

 Commas separate things to make your writing as clear as a bell.

14 Punctuation: Commas and Sentences

Use the correct road signs (commas with words) to combine short sentences into a larger one.

.... Did You Know? ....

Sometimes two or more sentences are written as though they were one sentence without space or punctuation between them.

> An anteater has powerful front claws it uses its claws to tear open ant nests.

One way to correct the punctuation is to put an appropriate punctuation mark at the end of the first sentence and capitalize the first word of the second sentence.

> An anteater has powerful front claws. It uses its claws to tear open ant nests.

Another way to correct the punctuation is to put a comma at the end of the first sentence and add an appropriate conjunction, such as *and*, *but*, or *or*, at the beginning of the second one.

> An anteater has powerful front claws, **and** it uses its claws to tear open ant nests.

Show What You Know

Read the following paragraph. Add commas and periods where they are needed. Underline the conjunctions, and circle any words that should be capitalized.

Last summer I visited my grandparents they live near Corpus Christi, Texas. I saw many new and interesting things but one of the most unusual things I saw was an armadillo. One night my grandfather took me into the backyard and he pointed to an animal in the bushes by the garage. The animal had a pointed snout and rabbitlike ears but strangest of all, it looked as if it were covered in armor. It was an armadillo and it was looking for insects and frogs to eat. Its name means "the little armored one" in Spanish its armor helps protect it from enemies. It can pull in its feet and nose or it can roll into a ball. I watched the armadillo for a long time but it didn't roll into a ball.

Score: _____   Total Possible: 16

Proofread

Correct the eight sentences by adding a comma and a conjunction to each sentence. Use the proper proofreading mark to show where each comma and the conjunction should be placed.

Example: Summer vacations can be boring or fun, ^{but} mine was a lot of fun.

An aardvark is an odd-looking animal it is also called an ant bear. *Aardvark* comes from the Afrikaans language it means "earth pig." You might have to look very closely an aardvark does look a little like a pig. However, it has a long, sticky tongue it also has large, rabbitlike ears. An aardvark cannot see very well it has good hearing. It has long, sharp claws it uses them to burrow dens and open ant and termite nests. Maybe aardvarks are shy maybe they do not want to get sunburned. You can look for them during the day they come out only at night.

Practice

Look up information about an animal whose name begins with an *a*. Write a paragraph about the animal. What does it look like? Where does it live? What does it eat? Try to use commas and conjunctions to combine some of your sentences.

_____

_____

_____

_____

_____

_____

Tips for Your Own Writing: Proofreading ....

Look at a story that you have written. Check to see if you have sentences that need separating. Use end punctuation or commas and conjunctions to correct the punctuation. Remember, commas alone cannot be used to combine sentences.

 Your thoughts may run together, **but** don't let your sentences do that!

Lesson
15 Punctuation: Commas After Phrases and Clauses

Sentences are easier to read and understand when commas are used to set off phrases and clauses at the beginning of the sentences.

.... Did You Know? ....

A comma is used after a long prepositional phrase at the beginning of a sentence. A comma is not necessary if the prepositional phrase is very short. A prepositional phrase is a group of words that begins with a preposition such as *at, in, on,* and *of.*

> On a beautiful August morning, Mark went climbing.
> At noon he reached the mountain peak.
> In 1998 Mark climbed his highest peak.

A comma is used after a subordinate clause at the beginning of a sentence. A subordinate clause is a group of words that begins with a subordinate conjunction such as *after, although, before, if, unless, when,* and *while.* Even though the clause has a subject and a verb, it cannot stand alone as a sentence.

> After he got to the top, Mark sat down to rest.
> While he was resting, he admired the view.

Show What You Know
Add seven commas where they are needed in this paragraph.

After La Salle explored the area the French claimed the land in 1682 and called it Louisiana. After the French and Indian wars in the 1700s France had to give Louisiana to Spain. In 1800 Spain had to give Louisiana back to France. Although Napoleon I wanted an American empire he wanted money more. In 1803 he decided to sell Louisiana. For about $15 million the United States could buy the land. When President Thomas Jefferson heard about the offer he was delighted. Before Napoleon could change his mind Jefferson bought the land. With one bold, decisive stroke the United States doubled in size.

Score: _____   Total Possible: 7

Proofread

Read this paragraph and add four commas that are needed. Use the proper proofreading mark to show where each comma should be added.

Example: After grapes have been dried, they're called raisins.

    If you want something good to eat, have some raisins. For a long, long time I didn't like raisins. But one day there wasn't anything else to eat, so I popped a few raisins in my mouth. As I chewed I realized, hey, these are good! Now I eat them all the time. At lunch I have a box for dessert. After a long day at school I have a box as a snack. When I get the urge to munch I go for the raisins. Without a doubt, I am now a raisin raver.

Practice

Describe what is happening in these pictures. Write your description on the lines below. Try to begin some of your sentences with subordinate conjunctions or prepositions.

_____

_____

_____

_____

_____

_____

_____

_____

Tips for Your Own Writing: Proofreading ....

The next time you write a report, check to see if you used any long phrases or clauses to introduce sentences and used commas to set off those phrases and clauses from the rest of their sentences.

 Think of commas as places to pause briefly.

16 Punctuation: Commas II

Commas are used to make sentences as clear and easy to read and understand as possible.

.... **Did You Know?** ....

A comma may not be required in a sentence, but it may be needed to avoid confusing the reader. Remember, the purpose of all punctuation marks is to help a reader easily read and understand what is written.

I didn't know whether to wait for Henry was very late.
I didn't know whether to wait, for Henry was very late.

When he called Henry apologized to me.
When he called, Henry apologized to me.

Henry brought his raincoat and his umbrella was in his briefcase.
Henry brought his raincoat, and his umbrella was in his briefcase.

Show What You Know

Read the paragraph below. Add nine commas where they are needed to avoid confusion.

Because the director was new students were reluctant to get involved in the jazz band. But when the director called James was eager to try out for first trumpet. However, before he could answer James had to ask Elliot's advice. To James Elliot is the expert on music. To be successful groups must play music that appeals to many people. Soon after they played the jazz band was declared a success. It got good reviews from everyone but the *Chronicle* critic was particularly kind. Whether amateur or professional musicians like to be applauded and appreciated. When the jazz band finished its concert series the musicians were sorry it was over.

Score: _____   Total Possible: 9

Proofread

To avoid confusion, add a comma to each bold sentence in the paragraph below. Use the proper proofreading mark to show where each comma should be added.

Example: When the Wright brothers began,flying was still a dream.

Orville and Wilbur Wright became interested in airplanes in 1898. **They began by testing kites and gliders were the second step in their program.** They flew their gliders from a beach near Kitty Hawk, North Carolina. **By the time they had finished their glider tests numbered more than 700.** The men had to solve many problems. **For example, because engines were heavy planes could not get off the ground.** The Wrights designed and built a small, lightweight engine for their plane. On December 17, 1903, Orville was the pilot of the first successful airplane flight. **When he landed the plane was already part of history.**

Practice

Can you think of sentences in which the lack of a comma can cause a misreading? Read the examples below. Then, write at least one sentence of your own, once with and once without a comma.

Examples: After cleaning up my sister took a nap.

After cleaning up, my sister took a nap.

_____

_____

_____

_____

Tips for Your Own Writing: Proofreading ....

Exchange one of your papers with a partner. Proofread each other's writing to see whether punctuation marks, especially commas, were used in ways that will help a reader easily understand the writing.

 Clear up confusion! Use commas!

17 Punctuation: Semicolons and Colons

Semicolons and colons look a lot alike. Semicolons separate sentences. Colons come before lists, after the greeting in a business letter, and in numbers used to tell time.

························· **Did You Know?** ·························

A semicolon (;) can be used when combining two related sentences.

I rushed to the shelf; the book was already gone.

A semicolon also can be placed before a conjunction such as *besides, however, nevertheless, moreover,* and *therefore,* when combining two related sentences. A comma should be placed after those conjunctions. When using a conjunction such as *and, but,* or *or,* place a comma, not a semicolon, before the conjunction.

The book is very popular; **therefore,** it is hard to find.
I rushed to the shelf, **but** the book was already gone.

A colon (:) is used before a list of items. Usually, the colon follows a noun or pronoun. Do not use a colon after a verb or a preposition that introduces a list.

I looked for these books: a mystery, a biography, and an almanac.
The library has books, magazines, CDs, and audiocassettes.

A colon is also used between the numbers for hours and minutes in time.

The library opens at 9:00 A.M. and closes at 5:30 P.M.

A colon is used after the greeting in a business letter.

Dear Ms. Sloan:

Show What You Know
Read the paragraph. Add semicolons and colons where they are needed.

At 900 P.M. I watched a program about Pompeii. Pompeii was a Roman city in southern Italy it was located near a volcano, Mt. Vesuvius. The people thought Vesuvius was extinct however, they were wrong. On August 24, A.D. 79, Vesuvius proved it was active it erupted suddenly and violently. Thick layers of ash and rock buried these towns Herculaneum, Stabiae, and Pompeii. In 1748 Pompeii was excavated. These public buildings were found in the city center temple, council chamber, assembly hall, courthouse, and market.

Score: _____   Total Possible: 6

Proofread

Two semicolons and three colons are missing in the paragraph below. Use proper proofreading marks to show where each semicolon or colon should be placed.

Example: Caroline's alarm didn't go off at 7ˆ00 A.M.ˆ;it was the beginning of a bad day.

    Caroline sat fuming on the school bus; it was stuck in traffic on the highway. She tried to stay calm however, she was afraid she would be late for school. The deadline to sign up for the ski trip was this morning at 915. It was now 8:45. Mentally, Caroline made a list of things she could do: cry, scream, walk, or laugh. She tried to breathe deeply she tried to focus on a happy thought. No happy thoughts came to mind; nevertheless, she did feel a little better. It was now 905. There was nothing she could do; all the spots for the ski trip would be filled by the time she got to school. Caroline wrote the following notes return new ski hat, take up bowling, and sign up for special school activities earlier next time!

Practice

Imagine that you are having a party. Using complete sentences, write an invitation in which you tell your guests the kind of party, the date, the time, the place, and any other information you think they should know. Use colons and semicolons.

_____

_____

_____

_____

_____

Tips for Your Own Writing: Revising ....

As you write your next report, think about the structure of your sentences. Are there any related sentences that you could combine using either a semicolon, or a semicolon and a conjunction? Are there any lists that you could rewrite using a colon?

 Despite its name, a semicolon is not just half a colon. It's half a colon plus a comma!

18 Review: Commas, Colons, Semicolons

A. Add twelve commas that are needed in the paragraph below. Use the proper proofreading mark to show where each comma should be placed.

Hey I'm home Mom! Wow, I'm out of breath! I ran all the way because I didn't want to miss *Beanie and Frank* my favorite TV show. Tonight Beanie is finally going to tell Frank, Chloe and Spike her big secret. Sure, I can set the table now. The show doesn't start for ten minutes. Mom, will you please get Joey Donna, and the dog out of here? No take the dog with you Joey! Donna that little whiner, really gets on my nerves. Okay, I'm finished. Mom if I can just watch this show the one I've been waiting to see, all by myself, I promise I'll wash dry, and put away the dishes after dinner without being asked. Thanks Mom.

Score: _____   Total Possible: 12

B. Correct the punctuation by either making two separate sentences or combining them with a comma and a conjunction (and, but, or). Write the sentences on the lines.

1. Other people may prefer roses or orchids I like sunflowers best.

_____

2. Sunflowers turn their heads to face the sun they also look like little suns.

_____

3. They have large heads of yellow flowers the heads contain many small black seeds.

_____

4. Sunflowers grow in people's gardens they are grown as a crop.

_____

5. The seeds are processed for vegetable oil they are used as bird food.

_____

6. Birds may like to eat sunflower seeds so do people.

_____

Score: _____   Total Possible: 6

C. Add two commas where needed in this paragraph. Use the proper proofreading mark to show where each comma should be added.

In the mid-nineteenth century, the main overland route to the Northwest was the Oregon Trail. From Independence, Missouri, people walked 2,000 miles to reach the Williamette Valley in Oregon. In 1836 a group of missionary families made the long trip on the trail. When people back East read the reports of the trip many of them decided to go to Oregon, too. By 1846 more than 6,000 people had used the Oregon Trail. After gold was discovered in California in 1848 fewer people made the trek to Oregon. Soon the trail was all but forgotten.

Score: _____   Total Possible: 2

D. Add five commas where they are needed to make the sentences less confusing to read. Use the proper proofreading mark to show where each comma should be added.

When the storm hit Maya was working at home. She waited patiently for the storm would soon be over. Maya held her dog and her cat hid under the bed. By the time the storm had finished the power lines were down. Inside the house was dark but safe.

Score: _____   Total Possible: 5

E. Add either one semicolon or one colon to each sentence in the paragraph below. Use proper proofreading marks to show where they should be added.

Every day at 615 A.M., the alarm clock goes off and Jenny gets out of bed. She always does the same things wash face, brush teeth, get dressed, and eat breakfast. Jenny always eats a bowl of cornflakes she always drinks a glass of milk. Jenny laughs about her routine however, she has no intention of changing it.

Score: _____   Total Possible: 4

REVIEW SCORE: _____   REVIEW TOTAL: 29

19 Punctuation: Quotation Marks and Dialogue

Quotation marks signal that someone is talking. Use them to find out who said what!

.... Did You Know? ....

Dialogue, only a speaker's actual words, is set off from the rest of a sentence by a comma and quotation marks. A speaker's tag, such as *Ana Maria said*, is not enclosed in quotation marks.

> "Oh, look! They have posted roles for the play," Ana Maria said.

If the speaker's tag is placed before the dialogue, a comma is placed after the last word of the tag to separate it from the dialogue.

> Ana Maria said happily, "I'm going to be Dorothy."

When the speaker's tag interrupts dialogue, quotation marks are placed around each part of the quotation. The interrupting speaker's tag is separated from the quoted words by commas.

> "Yes, he is," continued Ana Maria, "and Theo's the Cowardly Lion."

Show What You Know

Rewrite the four sentences below. Enclose the dialogue within quotation marks. Separate with commas the speaker's tag from the dialogue.

1. Ana Maria asked Are you coming to the dress rehearsal after school, Jason?

_____

2. Yes replied Jason but I will be late.

_____

3. I left my costume at home he continued and I have to pick it up.

_____

4. I think we are going to be great Jason concluded as he ran toward home.

_____

Score: _____   Total Possible: 4

Proofread

Read the play review below. Use proper proofreading marks to add the missing quotation marks and commas. Ten commas or quotation marks need to be added.

Example: "I wonder how everyone liked the play," said Ana Maria.

The sixth-grade class of Elm Place School performed in a production of *The Wiz.*

The following comments were made by parents attending the play:

"I really enjoyed the play" said Mrs. Fiore.

Mr. Moreno agreed, saying, "Yes, the kids did a terrific job.

You're right," said Mr. Goldberg, and the best performer was my son, Jason."

"Oh, no," said Mr. Moreno the best performer was my daughter, who played Dorothy.

I disagree said Mrs. Fiore. "The best performer was my son, Aaron, who played the Scarecrow."

The parents laughed. They agreed that all the performers were wonderful.

Practice

Write a short dialogue that you may have had with a friend about an event in your town. Begin a new paragraph each time the speaker changes.

_____

_____

_____

_____

_____

_____

Tips for Your Own Writing: Proofreading ....

Choose a story you have written that contains dialogue. Exchange papers with a partner. Check your partner's writing for opening and closing quotation marks, commas that separate the speaker's tag from the dialogue, and new paragraphs each time the speaker changes.

 The reporter asked, "May I quote you?"
"Sure," I replied, "if you enclose my comments in quotation marks."

20 Punctuation: Dialogue–Commas and End Marks

Commas and periods always go within closing quotation marks. No questions asked. Exclamation points and question marks are open to question, aren't they?

.... **Did You Know?** ....

Commas and periods are *always* placed inside closing quotation marks.

"Until 1996**,**" the sports fan said, "the Los Angeles Lakers held the record for the most team wins in a single season**.**"

Question marks and exclamation points are placed inside the closing quotation marks if they are part of the quotation.

Her friend asked, "How many games did the Lakers win in one season**?**"

Question marks and exclamation points are placed outside the closing quotation marks if they are *not* part of the quotation.

How exciting to hear, "The Bulls broke the Lakers' record"**!**

....

Show What You Know

Add a total of twenty-nine quotation marks, commas, and end punctuation where they are needed in the sentences.

How excited Jan was when she heard the sportscaster say, Last night the Chicago

Bulls broke the team record for games won in a single season

The Bulls broke the record she shouted as she ran into my room.

I asked calmly, What record did they break

Jan asked How could you not know? Don't you pay attention to sports

No I replied. I don't pay much attention to sports

How could I have known that Jan was about to give me a crash course in sports

trivia when she said, Come over here and sit down

The Chicago Bulls just won seventy games for this season Jan explained and that's

the most games ever won in a single season by an NBA team

Score: _____   **Total Possible: 29**

Proofread

Read this conversation between two sportscasters. Use proper proofreading marks to add eleven missing quotation marks, commas, and end punctuation marks.

Example: I told my family "There is absolutely no sport as exciting as basketball!"

Bart said Listen to the crowd shouting!" The Chicago Bulls had just won their seventy-second game of the 1995–1996 season. "Who would have believed that we would be sitting here tonight announcing that the Chicago Bulls have established a new record for the most games won in a single season

"Yes," said Bob. "it wasn't too long ago that people were asking whether the Bulls could break the record

Now that the Bulls have won their seventy-second game, said Bart people are asking me whether the Bulls' record can be broken"

Bob replied, "Only time will tell."

Practice

Think about an exciting sports event you have participated in or seen. Write a dialogue between you and a friend in which you talk about the event. Remember to start a new paragraph each time the speaker changes.

_____

_____

_____

_____

_____

_____

Tips for Your Own Writing: Proofreading ....

The next time you write a story, include some dialogue. Make sure you place all periods and commas within closing quotation marks, and question marks and exclamation points outside quotation marks in quoted material.

In or out—"Watch your quotation marks and end punctuation!"

Lesson

21 Punctuation: Direct and Indirect Quotations

Adam said, "Take it directly from me. This is a direct quotation." He then added that an indirect quotation restates something that was said.

.... Did You Know? ....

A <u>direct quotation</u> is the exact words someone said or wrote. A direct quotation is enclosed within quotation marks.

> Abraham Lincoln said, **"A house divided against itself cannot stand."**

An <u>indirect quotation</u> is a restatement or rephrasing of something said or written. An indirect quotation is *not* enclosed in quotation marks.

> Abraham Lincoln said that **a house in which there is no unity cannot withstand pressure from outside forces.**

An indirect quotation is often introduced by the word *that*, and a comma is not used to separate the speaker's tag from the indirect quotation.

> Abraham Lincoln said **that** a house in which there is no unity cannot withstand pressure from outside forces.

Show What You Know

Decide whether each sentence includes a direct or an indirect quotation. If a sentence includes a direct quotation, add quotation marks where they are needed. If a sentence is an indirect quotation, write *indirect* on the line.

1. In one speech, Abraham Lincoln commented, The ballot is stronger than the bullet. _____

2. Lincoln said in a campaign speech that no one would ever consider him a person

who would become a President. _____

3. What is conservatism? is a question Lincoln once asked. _____

4. Discouraged by news during the Civil War, Lincoln noted in 1861, If McClellan is not

using the army, I should like to borrow it for a while. _____

5. Lincoln stated that persons must stand firm in their important basic beliefs. _____

6. In a letter to the editor, Lincoln noted that he supported giving the privileges of government

to all those who helped bear the burdens of being involved in government. _____

Score: _____   Total Possible: 9

46

Proofread

Read the article about Lincoln. It contains eight errors in punctuation involving direct and indirect quotations. Use proper proofreading marks to correct the errors.

Example: Mrs. Rainbucket said, How about grabbing an umbrella? Mr. Hailstorm said that We could expect wet weather.

Abraham Lincoln attended school less than a year but actually wrote his own math book. He said, There were some schools, so called, but no qualification was ever required of a teacher, beyond readin', writin', and cipherin', to the Rule of Three.

One book that made a lasting impression on Abe was *Life of Washington.* Of this book he said, I recollect thinking then, boy even though I was, that there must have been something more than common that those men struggled for.

Lincoln became a lawyer simply by reading law books to familiarize himself with the law. He said that, "If someone is resolutely determined to make a lawyer of himself, the thing is more than half done already."

Practice

Imagine that you are a reporter who interviewed Abraham Lincoln during the Civil War. Write an article, using direct and indirect quotations.

_____

_____

_____

_____

_____

_____

_____

Tips for Your Own Writing: Proofreading ....

See if you can find a piece of your own writing that includes direct and indirect quotations. Make sure the speaker's tags are separated from direct quotations with commas, both opening and closing quotation marks are used, quotation marks with indirect quotations were avoided, and indirect quotations were introduced by the word *that*.

 *K*nowing who said what and what was said puts a reader in the know!

22 Punctuation: Titles

If you use quotation marks, you won't go wrong
When writing the name of a poem, story, report, or song.
But for names of newspapers, magazines, books, and movies it's wrong.
Use underlining to mark them bold, dark, and strong.

.... Did You Know? ....

The titles of short written works, such as reports or articles, short stories, songs, and poems, are enclosed in quotation marks.

> "Secrets of the Maya" (magazine article)
> "The Celebrated Jumping Frog of Calaveras County" (short story)
> "America the Beautiful" (song)
> "Southbound on the Freeway" (poem)

The titles of long works, such as books, magazines, newspapers, plays, and movies, are underlined in writing. In printed materials, the names appear in italic type.

> Missing May, or in printed type *Missing May* (book)
> Time for Kids, or in printed type *Time for Kids* (magazine)
> Miami Herald, or in printed type *Miami Herald* (newspaper)
> Oklahoma!, or in printed type *Oklahoma!* (play)
> The Lion King, or in printed type *The Lion King* (movie)

Show What You Know

Add quotation marks or underlining to the titles in these sentences.

1. In 1932 Pearl Buck won a Pulitzer Prize for her book The Good Earth.

2. The Muddy Puddle is a nonsense poem by Dennis Lee.

3. On April 18, 1995, the last issue of the newspaper the Houston Post was published.

4. Langston Hughes is best remembered for his poetry including Mother to Son.

5. My Favorite Things is a song from the play The Sound of Music.

6. Did you see the article There's a Sense of Urgency about Amphibian Census in the Chicago Tribune?

Score: _____   Total Possible: 12

Proofread

Read this article about children's literature. The writer used quotation marks and underlining incorrectly for six titles. Use proper proofreading marks to correct them.

Example: "Winnie the Pooh" is my favorite book, and I Remember is my favorite poem.

Literature has long entertained children. Children have been amused by poems such as "Whistling" from Jack Prelutsky's book "Rainy Rainy Saturday." They have cheered for Wilbur the Pig as they read Charlotte's Web, by E. B. White. Mr. White was not only a children's author but also the founder of the magazine "The New Yorker."

Children have even delighted in movies based on literature. In 1939 L. Frank Baum's book The Wonderful Wizard of Oz was made into the movie "The Wizard of Oz." In the movie, Dorothy sang the song Somewhere Over the Rainbow. The movie Aladdin was based on the short fairy tale "Aladdin and the Wonderful Lamp." In 1996 Roald Dahl's book "James and the Giant Peach" was adapted into a movie. Literature will always be a rich source of entertainment for children, both young and old.

Practice

Imagine you are a reviewer of books for very young children. Write a paragraph naming two books, stories, or poems that you like and tell why you like them.

_____

_____

_____

_____

_____

Tips for Your Own Writing: Proofreading ....

Select a piece of your own writing that includes titles. Check your writing to make sure that you have underlined titles of books and movies or placed the titles of poems and stories in quotation marks.

Titles of books, magazines, newspapers, and movies = underlining. Titles of stories, poems, reports, and songs = "quotation marks."

23 Punctuation: Friendly and Business Letters

Are you sending a friendly or a business letter? The only major differences are that business letters have an inside address, and the greeting is followed by a colon.

.... Did You Know? ....

A friendly letter and a business letter both have distinct parts. The only difference in punctuation is following the greeting. A comma is used in a friendly letter and a colon in a business letter.

Friendly Letter

Heading ⟶ 8001 Colt Drive
Boise, ID 83709
September 7, 2000

Dear Katy, ◄ **Greeting**
  Did you really rent a hot-air balloon? It must have been fun, but a bit frightening.
  Please write and tell me about your adventure. ◄ **Body**

Sincerely, ◄ **Closing**
Glissaia ◄ **Signature**

Business Letter

Heading ⟶ 854 Station Drive
Dunwoody, Georgia 30338
September 7, 2000

Balloons, Inc.
45 Martina Way
Dunwoody, Georgia 30338 } **Inside Address**

Dear Ms. Bouchard: ◄ **Greeting**
  What is the cost for 100 balloons in bunches of ten? } ◄ **Body**

Sincerely, ◄ **Closing**
Glissaia Shon ⟵ **Signature**
Glissaia Shon **Printed name**
Event Manager ◄ **Title**

Show What You Know

Add punctuation where it is needed in this friendly letter to correct the four errors.

248 Sexton Drive
Mettawa Illinois 60045
September 2 2000

Dear Karin
  We made a hot-air balloon for our school play by attaching a plastic cloth to a cardboard box, and filling the cloth with helium-filled balloons. It looked great!
        Your friend
        Madrena

Score: _____   **Total Possible: 4**

Proofread

Correct the punctuation in this business letter. Use proper proofreading marks to correct the five errors.

Example: Sea Isle⁁City, FL 34746

---

513 Elm Wood Place
Kansas City, Missouri, 64112
August 23 2000

Country Music Association
One Music Circle South
Nashville Tennessee 37203

Dear Music Director

Our band, Country Nights, has played together for more than eight years. We have recently written and performed a new song that we think you will like. The song "Days into Nights" is recorded on the enclosed tape. Please let us know if you are interested in this song and others we have written.

Sincerely

Mitch Fellfield

Mitch Fellfield
Manager, Country Nights Band

Practice

Think about a musical group that you would like to see perform. Write the body of a business letter to the group asking if they will be performing somewhere near you. Ask about prices, dates, and locations of the upcoming performances. On another sheet of paper, write your letter adding all the necessary parts.

Tips for Your Own Writing: Proofreading ....

Choose a letter you have recently written. Check the letter to make sure it has the correct parts and is correctly punctuated.

 Greetings to friends, use a comma in a letter. Greetings in business letters: use a colon.

Lesson

24 Review: Punctuation

A. Use proper proofreading marks to add commas and quotation marks to each sentence. You will need to make sixteen corrections.

1. Homer wrote "Your heart is always harder than a stone.

2. Absence," Sextus Propertius wrote, makes the heart grow fonder.

3. In *Othello,* Shakespeare wrote My heart is turned to stone.

4. And what my heart taught me wrote poet Robert Browning I taught the world.

5. But it is wisdom to believe the heart, wrote George Santayana in one of his poems.

Score: _____   Total Possible: 16

B. Read the conversation below. Use proper proofreading marks to add end punctuation and quotation marks where they are needed. You will need to make nineteen corrections.

How did Vice-President Harry Truman feel when he heard Mrs. Franklin D.

Roosevelt say, Harry, the President is dead

He gave a clue, when he said to the press, I felt like the moon, the stars, and all

the planets had fallen on me

Harry Truman, our teacher said, took over the presidency during World War II after

President Roosevelt died from a stroke

She then asked us, How did Truman indicate that he knew the job of being

President would be difficult

His comments to the press, Mai answered, showed that it would be difficult to

replace Roosevelt

Score: _____   Total Possible: 19

C. Use proper proofreading marks to add quotation marks to all direct quotations below. You will need to make sixteen corrections.

1. My younger brother asked, How many planets are there?

2. I told him that there were nine planets, and Earth was one of them.

3. Then he asked me if Earth was the largest planet.

4. No, I told him, Jupiter is the largest planet, and Earth is very small in comparison.

5. He continued to question me, asking, Is Earth the smallest planet?

6. I explained that Pluto was the smallest planet.

7. But Earth is the best planet, he said.

8. Yes, it is, I agreed, because only on Earth can plants and animals live.

9. Then he told me that Earth was the best planet because I lived here.

10. I laughed and said, No, Earth is the best because we both live here.

Score: _____   Total Possible: 16

D. Use proper proofreading marks to correct the nine errors in the paragraph below. Be sure to underline the names of books, plays, movies, newspapers, or magazines. Enclose the names of poems, articles, stories, or songs in quotation marks.

My partners and I are preparing a presentation about the Mississippi River. Jessica is reading a passage from Mark Twain's book Life on the Mississippi. Matt and Carlos are singing the song Ol' Man River from the play Show Boat. Sonia is reading part of the article The Great Flood of 1993 that appeared in the October 1993 issue of National Geographic World. I am providing background information and closing the presentation with a poem that my partners and I wrote. It is called The River of History.

Score: _____   Total Possible: 9

REVIEW SCORE: _____   REVIEW TOTAL: 60

25 Usage: Verbs—Froze, Shook, Rang

Verbs, or action words, come in different forms. Which form do you use?

.... **Did You Know?** ....

A <u>verb</u> is an action or being word in a sentence. It tells what happens or what is. The form that you use depends upon the action that is being described. For example, the <u>past</u> form of a verb describes a past action. It usually consists of one word. The <u>past participle</u> form consists of the past form that is used with a helping verb such as *have, has, had, was,* or *were.*

Look at the present, past, and past participle forms of each of the troublesome verbs below. Then read the sentences that follow. They show correct usage for each form of these verbs.

Present	Past	Past Participle
Today they **freeze**.	Yesterday they **froze**.	They **have frozen**.
Today they **shake**.	Yesterday they **shook**.	They **have shaken**.
Today they **ring**.	Yesterday they **rang**.	They **have rung**.

We **froze** peach ice cream on the Fourth of July.
Dad **had frozen** the hamburger meat that he cooked on the grill.

We **shook** the whole way home after seeing the action movie.
The city residents **had been shaken** by the disasters that occurred.

Tina **rang** the dinner bell for the members of the camp.
She **has rung** that bell every evening for twenty years.

Show What You Know

Underline the correct form of each verb in parentheses.

Carlos was worried. He was sure he had (froze, frozen) the ice cream dessert long
1
enough. But would it be ready for the club members thirty minutes from now? Carlos

took the pan out of the freezer and (shook, shaken) it lightly. Well, no ripples disturbed
2
the surface—a good sign! Just then the phone (rang, rung): Dana was sick and couldn't
3
come. After the phone had (rang, rung) four more times, the meeting was off. Too
4
many members were sick or busy. "I (froze, frozen) that dessert for nothing," said
5
Carlos. "But this has not (shook, shaken) my confidence. I know I made a tasty treat!"
6

Score: _____   Total Possible: 6

Proofread

The following TV editorial uses the verb pairs *froze/frozen*, *shook/shaken*, and *rang/rung*. Each verb form is used incorrectly once. Using the proper proofreading marks, delete each incorrect word and write the correction above it.

Example: The people were ~~shook~~ by the accident.
(shaken written above shook)

The people of this county have froze through one of our worst winters, and earthquakes have shook our homes. We cannot blame nature on politicians. But we can blame them for failing us. In a recent session, the state legislature frozen funds for earthquake relief. This act shaken our faith in the government.

Just one week ago, we rung in a new year. Let us resolve to shake up the government. Politicians, take notice: we have rang the alarm!

Practice

You may notice that the verbs in this lesson describe sensory actions. Write a strong sensory sentence for each verb in each pair. Use the same topic within each pair, but vary the sentences enough to make them interesting.

froze/frozen

_____

_____

shook/shaken

_____

_____

rang/rung

_____

_____

Tips for Your Own Writing: Proofreading ....

Choose a piece of your own writing. See whether you find any of the three verb pairs from this lesson and if you used the correct form of each verb.

Froze, shook, and rang can stand by themselves, but frozen, shaken, and rung need a little help.

Lesson

26 Usage: Verbs–Swam, Tore, Took

Some verbs don't conform to the patterns we expect. Swam, swum? Tore, torn? Took, taken? *How do you know which is right?*

····························· Did You Know? ·····························

The <u>past</u> form of a verb describes a past action. It usually consists of one word. The <u>past participle</u> form consists of the past form that is used with a helping verb such as *have, has, had, was,* or *were.*

Look at the present, past, and past participle forms of each of the troublesome verbs below. Then read the sentences that follow. They show correct usage for each form of these verbs.

Present	Past	Past Participle
Today they **swim**.	Yesterday they **swam**.	They **have swum**.
Today they **tear**.	Yesterday they **tore**.	They **have torn**.
Today they **take**.	Yesterday they **took**.	They **have taken**.

The bluefish **swam** together in a vast school off the coast.
They **have swum** along this coast for hundreds of years.

"You **tore** the jacket!" gasped the actress.
The curtain **was torn** from the stage in the scuffle that followed.

"I think you **took** more than your share," complained the hungry camper.
But she **had taken** exactly what was her due.

Show What You Know
Write the word that best completes each sentence.

The bluefin tuna _____ at its unfortunate prey. Then it _____
1(tore, torn)   2(swam, swum)
swiftly toward another victim. That helpless fish had _____ one of its fins badly. A
3(tore, torn)
sea bass had _____ a large shrimp for its dinner. The shrimp had _____
4(took, taken)   5(swam, swum)
by lazily and carelessly. The hunter of the sea was no longer hungry, so it

_____ no more victims.
6(took, taken)

Score: _____   Total Possible: 6

Proofread

The following radio script uses the verb pairs *swam/swum*, *tore/torn*, and *took/taken*. Using the proper proofreading marks, delete four incorrect words and write the correction above each one.

swam
Example: We ~~swum~~ for an hour.

NARRATOR: Here comes our hero, Pam Pekinese. Pam has swum across the lagoon

in record time. (*Sound effect for swimming.*)

PAM: I have swam my last mission! It's true that I'm the world's greatest

swimming Pekinese, but I have took all I can take! See? Those playful

dolphins torn two of my favorite hair ribbons. Yap, yip.

MEL MYNAH: You didn't expect any dolphins you swam by to pass up a chance to

tease you? They did the same thing when you swum by them last

week.

NARRATOR: Tune in next week for "Strange Animals Do Strange Things."

Practice

Write a brief description of a giant squid attacking a boat at sea. Use all the verb pairs presented in this lesson. Choose other words carefully to give the story a strong sense of action.

_____

_____

_____

_____

_____

_____

Tips for Your Own Writing: Proofreading ....

Choose a sample of your own writing. Look for *took/taken*, *swam/swum*, and *tore/torn*. Check to see that you used a helping verb with *taken*, *swum*, and *torn*.

If you swam through this lesson without hitting a snag, you have swum well!

27 Usage: Verbs—Wrote, Stole, Began

Troublesome verbs refuse to conform. You have to learn them one by one—or two by two!

.... Did You Know? ....

The <u>past</u> form of a verb describes a past action. It usually consists of one word. The <u>past participle</u> form consists of the past form that is used with a helping verb such as *have, has, had, was,* or *were.*

Look at the present, past, and past participle forms of each of the troublesome verbs below. Then read the sentences that follow. They show correct usage for each form of these verbs.

Present	Past	Past Participle
Today they **write**.	Yesterday they **wrote**.	They **have written**.
Today they **steal**.	Yesterday they **stole**.	They **have stolen**.
Today they **begin**.	Yesterday they **began**.	They **have begun**.

"Where is the poem that I **wrote?**" bellowed Milton.
The weary poet **had written** many stanzas last night.

Someone **stole** Hannah's gym shoes.
My favorite sneakers **were stolen** from the gym, also.

The mourning dove **began** its sorrowful song.
The birds **had begun** their chorus at 4:30 in the morning!

Show What You Know

Read the paragraph. Underline the correct form of each verb in parentheses.

In an ancient land called Sumer, scholars (wrote, written) on clay tablets with a
1
stylus. The stylus was a tool that made wedge-shaped marks in wet clay. Young

students (began, begun) their education by learning to write with this tool. Why did the
2
Sumerians develop this type of writing? One reason was that they had (began, begun)

to record laws. Writing down a code of laws allows a society to apply laws equally. For
3

example, Sumerian judges could punish any powerful person who (stole, stolen) goods
4
the same as anyone else who had (stole, stolen). Soon, people found easier ways to
5
write. Keepers of records have not (wrote, written) on clay tablets for centuries!
6

Score: _____   Total Possible: 6

Proofread

The following interview uses the verb pairs *wrote/written, stole/stolen,* and *began/begun.* Each verb form is used incorrectly once. Using the proper proofreading mark, delete each incorrect word and write the correction above it.

began
Example: We ~~begun~~ our day early.

INTERVIEWER: Tell us what you have wrote lately, Pete.

PETE PORTER: Well, Zara, I have been writing an epic poem about the dawn of the computer age. Some critics might claim that I stolen the idea from Beryl Brinkley, but that's not true.

INTERVIEWER: Critic Natalie Naster claimed that you had stole the rhymes. But enough of that. You written ten short poems last year, didn't you?

PETE PORTER: Right. But now I have began to create epic poetry!

INTERVIEWER: Fascinating. When you begun your career, we had no idea you'd write epic poetry. We look forward to your new poem.

Practice

Imagine the dispute between poets Pete Porter and Beryl Brinkley. Write a short letter that one of these poets might write to the other one. Include the verbs presented in this lesson.

_____

_____

_____

_____

_____

_____

Tips for Your Own Writing: Proofreading ....

Choose a story you have written. See whether you find any of the three verb pairs from this lesson. Make sure you used a helping verb when necessary.

 "Wrote/written, stole/stolen, began/begun—
Learning verbs in pairs can be lots of fun!"

28 Usage: Verbs—Blew, Sank, Fell

Studying past forms of verbs in pairs gives us clues to solving verb mysteries. Elementary, my dear Watson!

.... Did You Know? ....

The <u>past</u> form of a verb describes a past action. It usually consists of one word. The <u>past participle</u> form consists of the past form that is used with a helping verb such as *have, has, had, was,* or *were.*

Look at the present, past, and past participle forms of each of the troublesome verbs below. Then read the sentences that follow. They show correct usage for each form of these verbs.

Present	Past	Past Participle
Today they **blow.**	Yesterday they **blew.**	They **have blown.**
Today they **sink.**	Yesterday they **sank.**	They **have sunk.**
Today they **fall.**	Yesterday they **fell.**	They **have fallen.**

The wind **blew,** slapping rain across the deck.
Fiercer gales **had blown** before.

One storm last fall **sank** a freighter ten miles off the coast.
But no ship of mine **has** ever **sunk.**

In a shocking crash, the main mast **fell** to the deck!
It **had fallen** so suddenly, no one could sound a warning.

Show What You Know

In each pair of sentences, draw a line to match each sentence with the verb form that it should use.

The BBW Story (Big Bad Wolf)

1. The BBW had a reputation to keep up: he ____ houses down.   blown
   This wouldn't be the first straw hut he had ____ away.   blew

2. But when the pigs heard him, their hearts had ____ to their toes.   sank
   Before hiding, they ___ their valuables into the well.   sunk

3. What was the outcome? The house had ___—no big deal.   fallen
   "We really ___ for that huff-and-puff story," said Pig Junior.   fell

Score: _____   **Total Possible: 6**

Proofread

The following is an imaginary diary entry by a sailor in the 1700s. The writer used the verb pairs *blew/blown*, *sank/sunk*, and *fell/fallen* incorrectly six times. Using the proper proofreading mark, delete each incorrect word and write the correction above it.

Example: The sun ~~sunk~~ below the horizon.
<small>sank</small>

At about 9:00 A.M., a gust of wind blown suddenly, shaking the ship to its keel.

Just then the second mate fell to the deck. Others had fell, too, so great was the jolt.

The tempest blew, and then it had blew some more. Another dreadful gust hit. "Have

we sank for good?" cried the first mate. "The enemy never sunk this scow," shouted

Captain Cruz, "nor will Mother Nature now!" When the wind had fell, we knew that

the ship had not sunk.

Practice

Imagine that you are at sea on a boat like the one in the picture. Suddenly, an intense storm blows up. Describe the experience, using strong action verbs and vivid descriptive words. Also, use the three pairs of verbs presented in this lesson.

_____

_____

_____

_____

_____

_____

_____

Tips for Your Own Writing: Proofreading ....

Review a report you have written. Look for the words *blew/blown*, *sank/sunk*, and *fell/fallen*. Check the sentences to see that you have used a helping verb with *blown*, *sunk*, and *fallen*.

You neither sank nor fell in this lesson, nor have you sunk or fallen! If you blew your own horn, then you have blown it for good reason.

Lesson

29 Usage: Verbs—Lie/Lay, Rise/Raise

Many writers have trouble with these tricky verb pairs. See whether you can beat the averages!

························· **Did You Know?** ···························

The following word pairs have related meanings that invite confusion. Read on to learn how to use them correctly.

Lie means "to be at rest or recline." *Lay* means "to put or to place (something)."

> Beth just wanted to **lie** on the beach for a whole week.
> You should **lay** your beach towel on the sand away from the surf.

Rise means "to move in an upward direction." *Raise* means "to lift (something)" or "to move something higher."

> The moon should **rise** in the early evening, according to the script.
> Jenny tugged on the rope to **raise** the cutout moon in the theater set.

Show What You Know

Correctly fill in each blank with one of these words: *lie, lay, rise, raise.*

A Night in Camp

I am happy as I _____ on the air mattress, gazing at the brilliant, starry sky. I
                    1

feel I could grab the low, oval moon and _____ it here beside me. Instead, I
                                          2

_____ very still. No noise disturbs the quiet. No breeze rustles the leaves above.
     3

Nearby, I see smoke _____ lazily from the dying campfire. It curls and twists up to
                      4

the leafy ceiling of tree limbs. Hypnotized, I watch it _____ higher and then
                                                          5

disappear. When I _____ my head a little, I see that the embers have at last died
                    6

out. I want to wake up before dawn so that I can see the sun _____. All is well in
                                                               7

camp. This is the life!

Score: _____   **Total Possible: 7**

62

Proofread

The following bread recipe uses the verbs *lie/lay* and *rise/raise* incorrectly four times. Using the proper proofreading mark, delete each incorrect word and write the correct word above it.

Example: Does the cookbook l̶a̶y̶ ^lie^ on the table?

Della's Old-Fashioned Bread

1. Mix the yeast, sugar, and warm water in a small bowl. Put the bowl in a warm place

for the yeast to raise.

2. In a separate bowl, mix the flour and salt. Lie this bowl aside for now.

3. After ten minutes, mix everything together in a large bowl. Make a ball of dough.

4. If the dough will lay in your hand without sticking, it is just right. If not, add flour.

5. Put the dough on your board. Rise your hand and push your palm into the dough. Raise

your hand and repeat the action. (This action is called "kneading" the dough.)

Practice

Look at the drawing. What time of year does it suggest? Write a brief story or description in response to this picture. Use the verb pairs *lie/lay* and *rise/raise*.

_____

_____

_____

_____

_____

_____

_____

Tips for Your Own Writing: Proofreading ....

Choose a piece of your own writing. Look for the verbs *lie* and *lay.* Check to see that *lie* is used when you mean "to be at rest" and *lay* when you mean "to put or place." Look for other troublesome word pairs such as *rise* and *raise.*

✏ *Don't lie down on the job, don't lay your troubles down, and don't raise your voice. Just rise to the occasion! Get it?*

30 Usage: Verbs—Can/May, Let/Leave, Teach/Learn, Bring/Take

With some confusing verb pairs, we just have to learn and remember the difference. It's hard work, but the payoff is appropriate usage!

.... Did You Know? ....

The following word pairs have related meanings that invite confusion.

Can means "to be able to (do something)." *May* means "to be allowed or permitted to (do something)."

> **Incorrect:** "**Can** I be excused?" asked Carmen.
> **Correct:** "**May** I be excused?" asked Carmen.

Let means "to allow." *Leave* means "to depart" or "to permit something to remain where it is."

> **Incorrect:** "**Leave** me go!" begged the caged animal's eyes.
> **Correct:** "**Let** me go!" begged the caged animal's eyes.

Teach means "to explain" or "to help (someone) understand." *Learn* means "to gain knowledge."

> **Incorrect:** Please **learn** me how to tie a square knot.
> **Correct:** Please **teach** me how to tie a square knot.

Bring means "to fetch" or "to carry toward (oneself, something, or someone)." *Take* means "to carry in a direction away from (oneself, something, or someone)."

> **Incorrect:** **Bring** your mom to that countryside restaurant.
> **Correct:** **Take** your mom to that countryside restaurant.

Show What You Know
Underline the correct form of each verb in parentheses.

1. (Can, May) I speak six languages? Yes, (can, may) I show you now?

2. (Leave, Let) me just say this before I have to (leave, let).

3. Teachers want to (teach, learn) their pupils. Pupils want to (teach, learn) from them.

4. (Bring, Take) your lunch, but (take, bring) me the extra money.

Score: _____   Total Possible: 8

Proofread

The following report contains the verbs presented in this lesson. In six places, those verbs are used incorrectly. Using the proper proofreading mark, delete each incorrect word and write the correction above it.

Example: ~~Leave~~ Let us do the work.

The Chinese write their language in a different way than people write their languages in the West. They do not use an alphabet, if you may imagine that. Instead, the Chinese learn a unique character for every word. There are about fifty thousand characters in all. Imagine having to learn all those characters or having to learn them to someone else. In fact, educated Chinese can read thousands of characters. This knowledge will leave them read a newspaper easily.

Can I tell you one more thing? I am studying Chinese, and I will bring you to my class if you'd like. Just be sure to take an open mind with you.

Practice

Write one sentence for four of the verbs introduced in this lesson. Then use a dictionary to find definitions for these verbs that are different from the ones presented here. Write a sentence for each different definition you find.

_____

_____

_____

_____

_____

_____

Tips for Your Own Writing: Proofreading ....

The next time you write a story or report, be aware of how you can use *can* and *may*. Remember, *can* means "to be able to" and *may* means "to be allowed to."

May I congratulate you on this lesson? You can *now ace these difficult verbs!*

Lesson
31 Review: Verbs

A. The following is a fictional account of an expedition to the South Pole. Underline the correct form of each verb in parentheses.

The expedition consisted of Woods, Danner, and Abaji, the captain. On December 1,

the crew (began, begun) its trek inland across the ice shelf. The first mishap occurred
        1

that very day. One of the dogs lost its footing and (fell, fallen) into the icy water.
                                                              2

Though it (swam, swum) to safety, the dog (shook, shaken) all over and was badly
         3   **4**

chilled. That night, the wind (blew, blown) with a terrible force. Earlier, it had
                               5

(blew, blown) down one of the tents in camp. The crew soon learned that a gust had
 6

(tore, torn) this tent beyond repair. The very next day, they watched helplessly as one
 7

of the supply sleds (sank, sunk) into a crevasse. Weighted down with food, it had
                     8

(sank, sunk) with terrifying speed. Hungry and engulfed by bitter cold, the party
 9

(fell, fallen) into despair.
 10

Three days later, all but one had (froze, frozen) to death. This was Captain Abaji,
                                   11

who (wrote, written) in his diary every day. His last entry was "We have (fell, fallen).
    12   **13**

Here I have (wrote, written) the truth: we perished with courage."
              14

Score: _____   Total Possible: 14

B. Decide whether the underlined word in each sentence is used correctly. If it is, put a C above the word. If it is not, write the correct word above the underlined word.

Brett had <u>stolen</u> a candy bar from his sister Ann's lunch box. He <u>taken</u> it without
          1   **2**

thinking about his action. As he <u>torn</u> off the wrapper, he realized what he'd done.
                                  3

Though the candy looked tasty, Brett <u>began</u> to feel very ashamed. He <u>wrote</u> a note of
                                     4   **5**

apology to put in Ann's lunch box with the candy bar. Just then, Ann came into the

kitchen. Brett was <u>froze</u> in his tracks.
                   6

Score: _____   Total Possible: 6

C. In each blank, write a verb from the list. Some verbs may be used more than once. Some may not be used at all.

raise	rise	take	bring	let	leave	can	may	lie	lay

Clyde's Bad Break in Show Biz

MS. DÍAZ: Please _____ something to school for your demonstration speech.
1

LOU: _____ I bring my pet snake Clyde? It will _____ quietly in one
2 3

place and not bother a soul. We'll only have to worry if we see it

_____ its tail.
4

MS. DÍAZ: But _____ your snake bite?
5

LOU: Maybe. But I'll tell Clyde: "You _____ not bite!"
6

MS. DÍAZ: Thanks, but I cannot _____ Clyde come to school. You will have to
7

_____ your talented snake at home.
8

Score: _____   Total Possible: 8

D. Write the verb in the parentheses that correctly completes each sentence.

1. (rang, rung) The year is 1905. The school bell has just _____. The teacher

_____ that bell by hand at the same time yesterday.

2. (teach, learn) The one-room schoolhouse is full of youngsters eager to _____.

The school has one teacher. She will _____ students of all ages.

3. (lie, lay) The students sit down and _____ their hands together on their desks.

No one will slouch or _____ down in this schoolroom!

4. (rise, raise) To ask a question, students must _____ their hands. The teacher

says, "Yes, Maude (or Clarence), you may _____."

5. (bring, take) There is no lunchroom. Students _____ cold food from home to

school. They _____ the leftovers home after the closing bell rings.

Score: _____   Total Possible: 10

REVIEW SCORE: _____   REVIEW TOTAL: 38

32 Usage: Adjectives

✏️ *Writing—and life—would be dull without comparisons. We have rules in English for how to compare using adjectives.*

.... **Did You Know?** ....

Adjectives—words that modify nouns or pronouns—use different forms when used to make comparisons. The <u>comparative</u> form of an adjective is used to compare two things.

> This fish is **larger** than that one.   Sara is **more talkative** than Li.

The <u>superlative</u> form of an adjective is used to compare more than two things.

> The Siberian tiger is the **largest** member of the cat family.
> The **most talkative** person I've ever known is Kareem.

Did you notice two of the adjectives end with *-er* or *-est* and the other two adjectives use *more* or *most?* Short adjectives usually add *-er* or *-est*. Longer adjectives usually add *more* or *most.*

Most adjectives are *regular:* they follow the above patterns in forming their comparatives and superlatives. But a few adjectives are *irregular:* they form their comparatives and superlatives in different ways.

Regular Adjectives	Comparative Adjectives	Superlative Adjectives
good	better	best
bad	worse	worst

The only way to learn these irregular forms is to memorize them.

. . . .

Show What You Know

Rewrite each adjective in bold type. Write it in the blank in either the comparative or superlative form.

1. On the tennis court, Mei is a **powerful** opponent. Is she _____ than Jo?

2. But Jo has a **strong** backhand. It may be _____ than Mei's.

3. They are both **good** players. But which one is the _____ player?

4. Their match was a **long** one. It was the _____ match in the tournament.

5. It was also **exciting.** It was the _____ match I saw all week.

Score: _____   Total Possible: 5

Proofread

In the following report, underline the five adjectives that are used in their comparative or superlative form. For each of the four forms used incorrectly, use the proper proofreading mark to delete it and write the correction above it.

Example: A car moves ~~more slow~~ than a train.
(slower written above)

The pyramid is a basic form in geometry. Human beings have built pyramids as

tombs or places of worship throughout history. Of all the pyramids in the world, the

taller one is King Khufu's Great Pyramid in Egypt. It rises more than 450 feet (137

meters). Some people consider this the beautifulest as well as the largest pyramid.

Native Americans also built many pyramids. American pyramids had a stair-stepped

side and a flat top. The completest one today is the Temple of Inscriptions at Palenque,

Mexico. Though quite beautiful, this structure is much more short than Egypt's Great

Pyramid.

Practice

Write a story using at least five comparative or superlative adjectives.

_____

_____

_____

_____

_____

_____

Tips for Your Own Writing: Proofreading ....

The next time you write a description in a story, be sure you use -*er* or *more* with adjectives when comparing two things, and -*est* or *most* with adjectives when comparing more than two things.

When comparing two, use two letters (-er); when comparing three or more, use three letters (-est).

33 Usage: Adverbs

*A*dd spice to your writing with adverbs—especially adverbs of comparison.

.... **Did You Know?** ....

Adverbs—words that modify verbs, adjectives, or other adverbs—use different forms when used to make comparisons. The <u>comparative</u> form of an adverb is used to compare two actions.

>Deb arrived **later** than Heather.
>Bill shuffled his test papers **more noisily** than Tyrone.

The <u>superlative</u> form of an adverb is used to compare more than two actions.

>Jewel climbed the **highest** of all.
>Of all the students, Ernesto worked the **most rapidly**.

Short adverbs add *-er* or *-est.*

Most adverbs that end in *-ly* form their comparatives and superlatives using *more* and *most.* A few that do not end in *-ly* also use *more* and *most.*

>I eat olives **more often** than Mom, but Dad eats them the **most often.**

Most adverbs are *regular:* they follow the above patterns in forming their comparatives and superlatives. A few adverbs are *irregular.*

>**Regular:**   The Badgers played **badly** in the play-offs.
>**Comparative:** The Tigers played **worse** than the Bears.
>**Superlative:**   Of all the teams, the Lions played the **worst.**

. . . .

Show What You Know

Rewrite the adverb in the bold type. Write it in the blank in either the comparative or superlative form.

1. Our hockey team skated **badly.** We skated _____ than we usually do.

2. The coach arrived at the rink **late.** The goalie arrived _____ of all.

3. Carl missed the goal **frequently.** He also shot _____ than others.

4. Our fans cheered **noisily.** Of all the schools' fans, we cheered the

_____.

Score: _____   **Total Possible: 4**

Proofread

In the following school newspaper article, underline the eight adverbs that are used in the comparative or superlative form. For the four forms used incorrectly, use the proper proofreading mark to delete the word and write the correction above it.

             easier

Example: That race is ~~more easy~~ than this one.

    The Science Club sponsored a Turtle Derby last Thursday. Three candidates—Ralph, Ed, and Trixie—lined up at the starting gate. At the pop of a balloon, they were off! Trixie moved slowly to start. But Ralph moved more slowly than Trixie. Ed moved the more slowly of the three. (It was clear that Trixie took the race seriouser than Ralph.)

    When interviewed, a spectator, Perry Plum, said: "Trixie started badly, but Ed started worse than she did. Ralph started the baddest of the three." Not everyone agreed. Tilly Towson said, "I rate Trixie pretty high, Ed higher than Trixie, and Ralph the highest of all!"

    So who won? The turtle who tried most hard—Trixie, of course.

Practice

Look at the picture. Write a description of the skier's run down the ski slope. Use at least two adverbs in their comparative or superlative form.

_____

_____

_____

_____

_____

_____

_____

Tips for Your Own Writing: Revising ....

Choose a piece of your own writing. Exchange it with a partner to find the adverbs. Then, look for places to use adverbs that compare. Revise your writing.

What have you done superbly? *Then think of something you did* more superbly, *and finally, something you did the* most superbly *of all!*

34 Usage: Adjective/Adverb

*H*ere is some advice: Don't mix up your adjectives and adverbs.

.... **Did You Know?** ....

Some adjectives and adverbs look and sound nearly alike. Often, the only difference is that the adverb has the ending *-ly* added.

> My head sank into the **soft** pillow.
> I padded **softly** down the hall to avoid waking my mom.

An adjective modifies or describes a noun or a pronoun. It also tells which one, what kind, or how many. An adjective fits into both blanks in this sentence: The _____ dog was very _____.

An adverb modifies or describes a verb, an adjective, or another adverb. It also tells when, how, where, or to what extent. Most adverbs end in *-ly* and can be moved to several places in a sentence.

In English, there are many of these similar adjective/adverb pairs. Here are a few more examples: *quiet/quietly, deep/deeply, sad/sadly, bright/brightly, dark/darkly.*

● ●

Show What You Know
Write the word that completes each sentence.

1. In May 1980, Mount Saint Helens in Washington exploded _____. (loud, loudly)

2. Previously _____, this volcano had not erupted in 123 years. (quiet, quietly)

3. It raised a very _____ mushroom cloud like a bomb blast. (dark, darkly)

4. Hot ash spread _____ outward from the blast. (rapid, rapidly)

5. In nearby areas, it piled up _____, almost like snow. (deep, deeply)

6. _____ and featherlight, the ash created a breathing hazard. (Soft, Softly)

7. We must _____ report the deaths of many wild animals. (sad, sadly)

8. A _____ count revealed that 60 people died. (late, lately)

Score: _____   **Total Possible: 8**

Proofread

Read Tim's report about his recent visit to a wetlands area. Pay careful attention to his use of adjectives and adverbs. For each of the six that have been used incorrectly, use the proper proofreading mark to delete the word and write the correction above it.

                                   quickly

Example: I walked across the street ~~quick~~.

Last month, I spent a busily week with my cousin Daneale in Peachtree City. We had an easily time finding things to do. Peachtree City has lakes, wetlands, bicycle paths, and recreational areas. You could walk into some wetlands on strongly constructed walkways. You started in bright light, but this changed to shady and then to dimly light as the canopy of leaves thickened. The air smelled of cypress trees and wet earth. It was a time for quietly observation. At the end of the walk, Daneale and I saw a water moccasin. At least, that's what we think it was, but we didn't look too close. To be honest, I was a bit scared. I squeezed Daneale's hand tight.

Practice

Write a sentence for the adjective and the adverb in each of the following word pairs. Express the same idea in both sentences. Here is an example:

weak: I felt weak after running five miles.

weakly: I weakly lifted the weights after my run.

close: _____

closely: _____

prompt: _____

promptly: _____

sad: _____

sadly: _____

Tips for Your Own Writing: Proofreading ....

Look at a story you have written. Circle the adjectives and underline the adverbs. Then, check the adjectives, using this sentence: The _____ (noun) is very _____.

 A strong *effort will be* strongly *rewarded.*

35 Usage: Good/Well, Bad/Badly

Good and well *are as tangled as a plate of spaghetti! Read on to untangle them.*
(Thank goodness bad *and* badly *are pretty straightforward.)*

.... **Did You Know?** ....

Good and *bad* are adjectives. Use them to modify nouns or
pronouns. Sometimes they follow the verb. *Well* and *badly* are
adverbs. Use them to modify verbs, adjectives, or other adverbs.

> I helped Raoul choose a **good** book.
> I feel **good** about the food we collected for homeless people.
> Mrs. Choy told me that Raoul read **well** in class.
> We had a **bad** thunderstorm last night.
> The weather forecaster predicted **badly**.

The word *well* is a special problem. It usually functions as an
adverb, but it can be an adjective when it is used to mean "healthy."
Usually, the adjective *well* follows a linking verb such as *am*.

> **Adverb:**   Marita sang **well** at her concert last night.
> **Adjective:** "I am **well**," replied Ms. Slocum.

Remember that *good* is *always* used as an adjective. Also, remember
that "feeling good" describes a state of mind, while "feeling well"
describes someone's health.

. . . .

Show What You Know
Underline the correct word in each word pair in parentheses.

   Weightlessness is a potential health problem in space travel. Muscles can weaken

(bad, badly) if astronauts fail to exercise enough. Another (bad, badly) effect is that the
     1   2

heart may get larger. On the other hand, some astronauts say that weightlessness

makes them feel (good, badly). It brings on a mood of contentment. Scientists have
            3

found ways to help people cope with weightlessness. So, if you should meet an

astronaut, ask, "How are you? Are you (good, well) today?" Maybe she or he will
                                    4

answer, "I'm fine. I have coped (good, well) with weightlessness."
         5

                                        Score: _____   **Total Possible: 5**

Proofread

Bonita Bower's campaign speech has been published. It has five errors in it. Using the proper proofreading mark, delete each incorrect word and write the correction above it.

Example: The runner ran ~~good~~ *well* in the race.

Good evening. I'm running for mayor. During the last election, I was defeated

bad. But since then, I have talked to many people from all walks of life. And I feel well

about that. I've learned that we must all take an interest in city government.

I support conservation. As mayor, I will educate my staff to use supplies wisely. If

we do good at this, I will not request an increase in office budgets for two years.

I also want to improve public transportation. Service isn't always very well. People

who work far from home and don't drive are getting a badly deal.

Please vote for me, Bonita Bower, next Tuesday. I promise to do a good job!

Practice

Look at the picture. Have you ever thought about how difficult it must be to perform simple, daily tasks in space? Use your imagination to think of a way that this young astronaut could solve his problem. Use the word pairs introduced in this lesson.

_____

_____

_____

_____

_____

_____

Tips for Your Own Writing: Proofreading ....

Choose a piece of your own writing. Look for the words *good, well, bad,* and *badly.* Make sure that you used *good* and *bad* to describe nouns and pronouns, and *badly* to describe verbs, adjectives, and other adverbs. Pay particular attention to the word *well.*

 Did you do well *in this lesson? Then you should feel* good *about it!*

36 Usage: Accept/Except, Loose/Lose, Than/Then

*W*ords that sound alike or are spelled similarly can trap you. Don't get caught!

·················· Did You Know? ··················

Because the following word pairs are similar in spelling and pronunciation, writers tend to confuse them. Be careful to use each word in the appropriate context.

Accept means "to take or receive (something)" or "to consent to (something)." *Except* means "other than."

> I'd like to **accept** your invitation to address your computer club.
> Any day of the week **except** Monday is all right with me.

Loose means "not fastened" or "not tight." *Lose* means "to be unable to find" or "to fail to keep."

> The chain has come **loose** from my bicycle's back wheel.
> The wheel wobbled and I started to **lose** my balance.

Than introduces the second part of a comparison. *Then* means "at that time" or "afterward."

> New Jersey has a larger land area **than** Connecticut.
> We went to Connecticut, and **then** we went to New Jersey.

Show What You Know

Underline the word in parentheses that correctly completes each sentence in the paragraphs below.

"I (accept, except) the challenge," responded the game-show contestant. "Just this

¹
one try, and (than, then) I'll stop."

²

The host read the question: "What nations have more land (than, then) the U.S.?

³
Uh-oh. I think Rachel's microphone came (loose, lose). Let's try again. Rachel? (Buzzer.)

⁴
The correct answer is Russia, (than, then) Canada, (than, then) China. So sorry, Rachel,

⁵   ⁶
but you (loose, lose). You won't get any prizes, (accept, except) the play-at-home game."

⁷   ⁸

Score: _____   Total Possible: 8

Proofread

The following story contains words presented in this lesson. Five of them are used incorrectly. Using the proper proofreading mark, delete each incorrect word and write the correction above it.

accept

Example: I ~~except~~ your invitation.

One day, Lucy's pet parakeet flew away. After two weeks of looking for it, Lucy's

mom told her that she'd have to except her loss. "It is painful to loose a pet like

Teresa," said Lucy sadly. "I should never have let her loose from her cage."

Than one day Lucy was visiting her cousin Dee in a nearby town. They heard a

"tap, tap, tap" on the kitchen window. Dee exclaimed, "I believe it's Teresa!"

Dee's mom said, "This is the wildest pet story I've ever heard."

"Accept for Juan's snake story," suggested Dee. "Juan claimed that when his pet

snake got lose, it came out of the wall in his neighbor's apartment!"

Practice

Write sentences for each of the word pairs presented in this lesson. Use your imagination to create interesting sentences.

_____

_____

_____

_____

_____

_____

Tips for Your Own Writing: Proofreading ....

Scan a piece of your writing looking for the words in this lesson. Use _then_ for "next"—_than_ for "compare"; _accept_ for "receive"—_except_ for "not"; _loose_ for "not tight"—_lose_ for "no win."

Accept _the fact that English words are sometimes tricky to spell (except when you know all the spellings)!_

Lesson 37 Usage: Principle/Principal, There/They're/Their, Its/It's

*H*omophones are words that sound alike but have different spellings and meanings. The words in this lesson are homophones.

.... **Did You Know?** ....

Because the following words sound the same and look alike, writers tend to confuse them. Context is the best clue as to which word to use in a sentence.

Principle means "a basic rule or belief." *Principal* means "most important" or "main." It also means "the chief or main person."

> This science experiment demonstrates the **principle** of inertia.
> Mrs. Monetti's **principal** objection was the noise.
> Mrs. Monetti is the **principal** of our school.

There means "at that place." *They're* is a contraction for "they are." *Their* means "belonging to them."

> The people in Lake Landis really like it **there**.
> **They're** having a wonderful festival in July.
> Have you seen **their** brochure for the festival?

Its is the possessive form of *it*. *It's* is a contraction for "it is."

> The bird fluffed up **its** feathers.
> You know **it's** going to be a cold day.

Show What You Know

Underline the word in parentheses that correctly completes each sentence in the paragraph below.

Today I'll demonstrate the (principle, principal) of osmosis. (Its, It's) the
                                    1   2
(principle, principal) lesson that we'll cover this week. Osmosis is the movement of one
            3
solution to another when (they're, their) separated by a membrane. A plant absorbs
                                      4
most of (its, it's) water by the process of osmosis. Would the lab groups please pick up
          5
(there, their) notebooks and follow me? If you will gather around Table 2, you will see
      6
that a demonstration is set up (there, their).
                                      7

Score: _____ **Total Possible: 7**

78

Proofread

In Talia's report, use the proper proofreading mark to delete each of the six incorrect words and write the correction above it.

Example: They forgot ~~there~~ *their* books.

Dragonflies are among the most beautiful insects. Because their principle food is insects, their helpful, too. They can eat there own weight in insects in a half hour.

It's hard to believe, but a dragonfly lives almost it's entire life in a wingless form called a nymph. The beautiful, gauzy-winged flier that we know represents only a few weeks to a few months of this insect's life. Dragonflies live for several years.

No insect can fly as fast as a dragonfly. They're are reports of these fliers darting as fast as a car on the highway—60 mph! No wonder they can catch so many insects.

Some extinct ancestors of today's dragonfly were huge. They had wingspans of almost three feet. Its hard to imagine that!

Practice

Look at the picture. How would you react to seeing a giant dragonfly? Write a description of this dragonfly as if you were seeing it in real life. Try to use the words introduced in this lesson.

_____

_____

_____

_____

_____

_____

Tips for Your Own Writing: Proofreading ....

Search for any of these troublesome words—*principal/principle, there/they're/their, its/it's*—in a piece of your own writing. Determine whether you have used the words correctly.

Don't forget the apostrophe! It's a small mark, but its presence can make all the difference.

Lesson
38 Review: Adjectives, Adverbs

A. In the following movie review, underline the correct form of the adjective in each set of parentheses.

For a *really* (good, best) film, see *Danada Square* by director George Chan. It is a
1
(more sentimental, sentimentaler) movie than Chan's previous film, *Run Home! Danada*
2
Square tells the story of a young Asian-American woman who starts a business in a

shopping center. She encounters many difficulties, including prejudice. But the

(baddest, worst) part of all her troubles is conflict with the landlord of her store. Of
3
course, this (bad, worst) person is the villain of the movie. Of Chan's four films, I think
4
that this is the (goodest, best) one.
5
On the other hand, *Damage in Kuala Lumpur* is the (baddest, worst) movie I've
6
seen in years. It's a disaster movie about three high-rise towers in that Asian capital.

The (taller, tallest) of the three, called the "Black Tower," has a bomb scare. Then the
7
"Green Tower," which is (taller, tallest) than the "White Tower," catches fire. So it goes.
8
Stay away from this movie and save your money!

Score: _____   Total Possible: 8

B. In each sentence in the paragraph below, underline the correct form of the adverb in parentheses.

Ziggy Zales hit (low, more low) in yesterday's opening match. He hits the
1
(most low, lowest) of any tennis player that I can recall. Laura Farfone delivers the
2
(most fast, fastest) serve of any tennis player. Her serve is definitely (fast, faster) than
3   **4**
that of champion Maria Rivera. Some people think tennis moves (more quickly,
5
quicklier) than baseball. Laura slept (badly, bad) before the tennis match. But Ziggy
6
slept (more badly, worse) than Laura.
7

Score: _____   Total Possible: 7

C. Choose the word from the parentheses that correctly completes each sentence and write it in the blank.

1. The defense attorneys were certain that their case was very _____. (strong, strongly)

2. "I _____ object!" exclaimed the lawyer. (strong, strongly)

3. The main witness for the defense related a _____ story. (sad, sadly)

4. She _____ wiped her tears away, which was a nice touch. (sad, sadly)

5. The attorney wants a _____ conclusion to this trial. (prompt, promptly)

6. "The court will reconvene _____ at ten o'clock," said Judge Wu. (prompt, promptly)

Score: _____   Total Possible: 6

D. Read Marla's report on "Weird Planets." There are twelve errors. Using the proper proofreading mark, delete each incorrect word and write the correction above it.

The more we know about the principle planets in our solar system, the more normal our planet Earth seems. Earth has eight planet cousins, and their really weird!

Consider Mercury, the planet closest to the sun. A day on Mercury is 88 Earth days long. One side of Mercury faces the sun for 88 days in a row, getting bad burned at 800°F. The opposite, shady side must loose heat for those 88 days. Its frigid!

Saturn is beautiful, accept it is deadly. It has the largest and most visible rings, which circle it's middle like a belt. You wouldn't want to vacation their: Saturn's winds blow at speeds of 1,000 mph. That's about five times faster then a severe tornado's winds.

But the weirdest planet is Uranus. This planet violates the principal by which the other planets rotate like tops. Instead, Uranus spins oddly on its side. (If I were Uranus, I wouldn't feel very good after eons of this motion.) Uranus should except the "weirdest planet" award!

Score: _____   Total Possible: 12

REVIEW SCORE: _____   REVIEW TOTAL: 33

81

39 Usage: Plural Nouns

 *One, two, three—how many? Two or more means "use the plural."*

.... **Did You Know?** ....

A singular noun names one person, place, thing, or idea. A plural noun names two or more persons, places, things, or ideas.

Plural nouns are formed in the following ways:

- **most nouns, add *-s.***

     girl**s**   friend**s**

- **nouns ending in *s, sh, ch,* or *x,* add *-es.***

     box**es**   church**es**

- **nouns ending in *y* preceded by a consonant, change *y* to *i* and add *-es.***

     body—bod**ies**

- **nouns ending in *y* preceded by a vowel, add just *-s.***

     toy—toy**s**   boy—boy**s**

- **some nouns ending in *o,* add *-s.* Some ending in *o* preceded by a consonant, add *-es.***

     radio**s**   echo**es**

- **many nouns ending in *f* or *fe,* change the *f* to *v* and add *-es* or *-s.* Some nouns ending in *f,* add only *-s.***

     calf—cal**ves**
     knife—kni**ves**
     chief—chief**s**

- **a few nouns, make *no* change between the singular and plural.**

     sheep   moose

- **a few nouns form the plural irregularly.**

     goose—geese
     child—children

Show What You Know

Write the plurals of the underlined words on the lines.

1. the echo of two banjo   _____

2. recipe: ten ripe cherry and two tomato   _____

3. some essay challenge your belief   _____

4. the report "Wolf and Fox"   _____

5. a new play, "Do Sheep Have Tooth?"   _____

Score: _____   Total Possible: 10

Proofread

Read Dino's story. He has formed seven plurals incorrectly. Using the proper proofreading mark, delete each incorrect plural and write the correct word above it.

Example: I read three ~~storys~~ today.
(stories)

My ~~friendes~~ and I wanted to have a computer club. We're crazy about ~~computeres~~.

We started inviting everyone we thought would like to join. We decided not to have a

president because we don't like the idea of having bosses. Instead, we have two

~~chieves~~: a chief program chairperson and a chief refreshment chair. They will have no

~~vetos~~ over club ~~decisiones~~.

Thinking up a clever name wasn't easy. In the end, we chose "~~Torpedos~~." Why?

Because sometimes torpedos come after you, figuratively speaking, when you carelessly

key in a mistake!

Practice

Write a brief story about an afternoon "lineup" on the radio. Include plural nouns in your writing.

_____

_____

_____

_____

_____

_____

Tips for Your Own Writing: Proofreading ....

If a plural form you want to use in your writing is not shown in this lesson, look the noun up in the dictionary. Most dictionaries list irregular plurals. Otherwise, add *-s* or *-es* to the noun.

Adding -s is a good bet for forming a plural, but it won't always be right.

Lesson

40 Usage: Possessive Nouns

It's mine! It's mine! Possessive nouns show ownership.

.... **Did You Know?** ....

A <u>possessive noun</u> shows ownership of a noun that follows. Remember: a noun is a word that names a person, place, thing, or idea.

The following rules show how to form the possessive of nouns:

If the noun is singular, add an apostrophe and *s*.

> I'm going to my sister**'s** new office.
> Cass**'s** job is public relations director of the national fair.

If the noun is plural and ends in *s*, add an apostrophe only.

> This national fair is the cities**'** showcase.

If the noun is plural and does not end in *s*, add an apostrophe and *s*.

> The fair has a children**'s** pavilion.

Show What You Know

On the line, write the correct possessive form of each underlined noun.

1. <u>birds</u> adaptations for flight   _____

2. a <u>bird</u> wing   _____

3. an <u>ostrich</u> story   _____

4. an <u>ibis</u> story   _____

5. <u>owls</u> quiet hunting flights   _____

6. <u>mice</u> chances when a hawk is near   _____

Score: _____   **Total Possible: 6**

Proofread

Read Marianne's report. Using the proper proofreading mark, delete each of the five incorrect possessive nouns and write the correction above it.

Example: What is your ~~cousins's~~ ^{cousin's} name?

In ancient Greece, many myths were told and later written down. One such myth is about Icarus, who was Daedalus' son. Daedalus was a marvelous builder and inventor. But he had been imprisoned in a maze for a crime. Daedalus saw a way to escape. He made wings for himself out of birds's feathers and some wax. Using the wings, Daedalus was able to fly out of the maze.

Icarus was so excited by the wings's power and the thrill of flying that he ignored his father's warning. He used his fathers wings and flew higher and higher. He got too close to the suns burning rays and melted the wax that held together his wings. He fell to his death.

Practice

Look at the picture. Imagine that you are the rabbit and that you are being hunted by the owl. What emotions would you feel? What strategies would you devise to outwit this bird of prey? Write a paragraph of the rabbit's thoughts below. Use some possessive nouns in your paragraph.

_____

_____

_____

_____

_____

Tips for Your Own Writing: Proofreading ....

Choose something you have written recently. Check any possessive nouns you used to make sure you have used apostrophes correctly.

 You've done another day's _work. Or is it two_ days' _work?_

41 Usage: Plural/Possessive

With plurals and possessives, you don't always hear the difference, but you can see it.

.... **Did You Know?** ....

A <u>plural noun</u> names two or more things, persons, places, or ideas.
A <u>possessive noun</u> shows ownership of a noun that follows.

Sometimes we have difficulty deciding whether a noun is plural, possessive, or both. The following guidelines will help you:
Some plural possessive nouns end in an apostrophe only.

      houses' colors   cities' population

Irregular plurals form the possessive by adding **'s**.

      women**'s** club   mice**'s** hole   sheep**'s** wool

All singular possessive nouns end in **'s**. Remember that a singular noun names one thing, person, place, or idea. Every singular noun forms the possessive by adding **'s**, regardless of the noun's ending.

      girl**'s** dress   school**'s** playground

To distinguish singular possessives from plural possessives ending in **'s**, you must know the irregular plurals for words, such as *mice* or *children*.

....

Show What You Know

Is the underlined word a singular possessive, a plural possessive, or a plural? Write *SP*, *PP*, or *P* on the line.

1. We found Mr. <u>Jackson's</u> golf ball in our backyard.   _____

2. "It bounced and skidded through several <u>neighbors'</u> yards."   _____

3. "I will be playing in the <u>men's</u> tournament next week!"   _____

4. "Although I've golfed for three <u>years</u>, this is my first tournament."   _____

5. Mr. Jackson hit the ball, and it bounced off Mrs. <u>Karas's</u> house.   _____

6. Perhaps they should warn the <u>spectators</u> at the tournament!   _____

                                            Score: _____   **Total Possible: 6**

Proofread

Read Matthew's report about the saber-toothed cat. It contains six errors in plural and possessive nouns. Using the proper proofreading mark, delete each incorrect word and write the correction above it.

Example: That ~~houses'~~ house's shutters should be painted.

About twelve thousand years' ago, the last of the saber-toothed cats died. You may know this creatures name as *saber-toothed tiger,* but it wasn't actually a tiger. The cats' name comes from the long, sharp front teeth that it possessed. A saber is a kind of sword.

It is many scientists' belief that the saber-toothed cat used its teeths razor-sharp edges to prey upon thick-skinned animals such as mastodons. A mastodon was a hairy animal similar to an elephant. It, too, is now extinct.

Today we know much about the saber-toothed cat's story because many of these animals were trapped in the La Brea tar pits in California. The tars ability to preserve body material has provided a rich source of fossils. Probably the animals were drawn to the pits in the first place because mastodons bodies had been trapped there.

Practice

Pretend that you have stumbled upon the fossil of an extinct animal. Write a description of your discovery using some plurals and possessives.

_____

_____

_____

_____

_____

Tips for Your Own Writing: Proofreading ....

Exchange something you have written recently with a partner. Scan for any possessive nouns. Then, be sure that an -' or -'s was added to show possession.

 Don't let plurals' pitfalls snag you!

42 Usage: Contractions

Here's a hint for identifying contractions: look for the apostrophe and see whether any letters have been omitted.

···················· Did You Know? ·····················

A <u>contraction</u> is a word formed by combining two words and omitting one or more letters. We show the omission of letters by inserting an apostrophe. One type of contraction combines a pronoun and verb.

she + is = she's	I + am = I'm
who + is = who's	we + are = we're
I + have = I've	he + will = he'll
you + have = you've	they + will = they'll

Another type of contraction combines a verb and the negative word *not*.

are + not = aren't	will + not = won't

Do not confuse contractions with possessive pronouns. For example, the contraction *you're* sounds like the possessive pronoun *your*.

You're sorry that you lost **your** videocassette.

Show What You Know

In the paragraph below, write the contraction for each underlined word or group of words above the word or words.

<u>We are</u> disturbed about plans for the new superhighway. <u>It is</u> supposed to cut
1   2

through the forest preserve. If the road is built, some animal populations <u>will not</u>
3

survive. They <u>cannot</u> tolerate the increased noise and air pollution. <u>We have</u> formed a
4   5

citizen committee to work for a change. <u>Who is</u> interested in becoming a member?
6

<u>I am</u> in charge of next month's meeting. Please <u>do not</u> forget to sign our petition
7   8

before you leave.

Score: _____   Total Possible: 8

Proofread

Read the following tour guide to a historic house. Help the editors make seven corrections. Using the proper proofreading mark, delete each incorrect contraction and write the correction above it.

Example: I'll
~~I~~ be home by dark.

Welcome to the Elisa Bentley house. Wont you come in? You're first stop is the

vestibule, a small entry room. Notice the hand-painted wallpaper from about the 1800s.

Its' really quite rare. Next, youll enter the formal parlor. Of course, this house had no

electricity, and w'eve tried to preserve that feeling by using low lighting. Notice the

Regency style of decoration. Is'nt it exquisite! The master bedroom is next. Here we'l

see a hand-carved, four-poster bed. Ms. Bentley was most particular about the condition

of her bed. Please return to the front of the house. Your tour has ended.

Practice

Imagine that you will write a guide for your room or some other room that you know well. Follow these steps:

1. Allow yourself time to walk through the room (at least in your mind) and notice details.

2. Decide which details are worth writing about and which ones should be left out.

3. Write the guide to the room just as if you were walking around it, noticing the details.

_____

_____

_____

_____

_____

Tips for Your Own Writing: Proofreading ....

Remember that a contraction stands for two words. It must have an apostrophe. A possessive pronoun never uses an apostrophe.

 _If_ you'll _try hard, you_ won't _fail to understand contractions._

43 Review: Plurals, Possessives, Contractions

A. In each sentence, form the plural of the word in parentheses and write it in the blank to complete the sentence.

1. Today's _____ have a wide variety of software. (computer)

2. Our software usually comes in _____ that we call *packages*. (box)

3. You can play many _____ on the computer. (game)

4. My screen saver shows little _____ gliding through the water. (torpedo)

5. I've also seen screen savers that show _____ exploding. (tomato)

6. Many people used to regard computers as _____. (toy)

7. But _____ in offices find that software makes workers productive. (boss)

8. Software can teach you fingering for _____ or tuning for pianos. (banjo)

9. Some do-it-yourself packages tell how to repair _____ on houses. (roof)

10. Packages even instruct _____ on building thermal homes. (beginner)

11. And some packages tell farmers how to raise calves and _____! (goose)

12. You could probably tell many more _____ about unusual software. (story)

Score: _____   **Total Possible: 12**

B. In the paragraph below, write the possessive form of each underlined word above it.

I couldn't help laughing at <u>Dad</u> accident. He dabbed red paint on both of his
            ₁

<u>sleeves</u> cuffs. He "had a <u>sheep</u> face"—meaning he looked sheepish. I couldn't wait to
₂   ₃

see the <u>kids</u> reaction when they came in. "It was my <u>hands</u> fault," said Dad. "They're
            ₄   ₅

clumsy."

Score: _____   **Total Possible: 5**

C. **Read this explanation of the naming of the computer object we call a** *mouse.* **If an underlined possessive or plural noun is used correctly, write C above it. Otherwise, write the correction there.**

Have you wondered where computer <u>objects'</u> names come from? A *bug* is
  1
so named because a real insect interrupted several <u>circuits</u> electron flow in an
  2
early computer. But perhaps the <u>mouses</u> name is the most humorous. It's not
  3
difficult to guess the <u>name's</u> origin. A <u>computers</u> mouse has a long "tail" and a
  4 5
smooth, rounded shape. How strange it would be if the computer mouse looked like a
goose. Would we now have "<u>geese</u>-driven" software programs?
  6

Score: _____ Total Possible: 6

D. **Read the following science report. It contains eight errors. Using the proper proofreading mark, delete each incorrect contraction and write the correction above it.**

Large birds of prey are very territorial. This means that they wont tolerate other
large birds living nearby, especially if the other birds' diets are similar to theirs. They
want to avoid competition with the other birds.

Large crows and owls, for example, do not mix well. The spring is an especially
tough time of year, because their trying to raise their young. If youre lucky enough to
live in an uncrowded area that has many large trees, you may see this bird drama
played out above you're own head.

Large owls are very powerful creatures, and most birds dont bother them. But
crows are very social—this means that they're accustomed to living closely with each
other. And they rely on each other, too. When crows feel threatened, theyl'l call all
other crows within earshot. (Wer'e used to the sound of crows. They're very noisy
birds.) In this way, many crows can gang up on an owl. In the end, its quite possible
for the crows to win.

Score: _____ Total Possible: 8

REVIEW SCORE: _____ REVIEW TOTAL: 31

91

44 Usage: Simple Past Tense

"It was the best of times, it was the worst of times." How do we tell about things that happened in the past?

.... Did You Know? ....

Tenses of verbs tell whether an action or a state of being took place in the past, the present, or the future.

We use the <u>past tense</u> of a verb to talk or write about something that happened in the past. The <u>simple past tense</u> consists of one word that describes a past action. Many verbs form the simple past tense by adding *-d* or *-ed* to the present tense.

Present Tense	Simple Past Tense
Today they ask.	Yesterday they ask**ed**.
Today they play.	Yesterday they play**ed**.
Today they climb.	Yesterday they climb**ed**.

Other verbs form the simple past tense <u>irregularly</u>: sometimes by changing spellings, sometimes by not changing at all.

Present Tense	Simple Past Tense	Present Tense	Simple Past Tense
make	made	buy	bought
choose	chose	drink	drank
know	knew	hit	hit
feel	felt	cut	cut

Show What You Know

In the blank, write the correct past tense of the verb in parentheses to complete the sentence.

1. Clara _____ to paint her house this summer. (decide)

2. The store manager _____ a good brand of paint. (recommend)

3. Then Clara _____ many cans of that paint. (buy)

4. Next, she _____ the old paint off the exterior of her house. (scrape)

5. To reach the high spots, she carefully _____ on a strong ladder. (climb)

6. Then Clara _____ the paint on the outside walls. (brush)

7. That evening she _____ her freshly painted home. (admire)

Score: _____   Total Possible: 7

Proofread

Using the proper proofreading mark, delete each of the twelve incorrect past-tense verbs and write the correct word above it.

asked
Example: Yesterday I was ~~ask~~ to a party.

Last May our town celebrated its centennial, or one-hundredth, anniversary. We maked a lot of preparations. A cleanup committee wash and brushd all public buildings. Members of the fire department clumb on high ladders to put up flags and bunting.

At last the celebration started. The high point was when Mayor Lopez askt Olga Janssen—at 105, our oldest citizen—what she rememberd about the old days. "How I usd a churn to make butter and playd dominoes with my cousins," said Mrs. Janssen.

At the end, we all drunk a ginger ale toast to the town's next century. We knowed most of us wouldn't be here for the next celebration, but we feeled happy to be at this one. To officially close our celebration, the mayor hitted a large bell with a mallet.

Practice

Rewrite the story in Show What You Know, describing Clara's painting experience. Add descriptive details. When the story is finished, underline all the past-tense verbs.

_____

_____

_____

_____

Tips for Your Own Writing: Proofreading ....

If you need help with past-tense verbs, use the dictionary. A dictionary entry for an irregular verb usually lists the past-tense form right after the main entry. For any verbs that give you trouble, write them in your journal or writing folder where you can find them easily.

 The only time you can control time is when you change verb tense!

45 Usage: Subject-Verb Agreement I

You don't want your subjects and verbs to fight with each other. Make sure they agree!

·························· **Did You Know?** ·····························

The **present tense** form of a verb is used to talk or write about something that is happening now. In the present tense of most verbs, the only form that changes is the one used with *he, she,* or *it.* This form adds either *-s* or *-es.* By using the appropriate form of the verb with the subject, we make the subject and verb agree in number. A verb with an *-s* ending is used with *he, she, it,* or other singular subjects, and a verb without an *-s* ending is used with all other subjects.

A **conjugation** is a table of the forms that a verb takes in a particular tense. Below are conjugations of two verbs in the present tense.

Present Tense of *Live*		Present Tense of *Fix*	
I live	we live	I fix	we fix
you live	you live	you fix	you fix
he, she, it live**s**	they live	he, she, it fix**es**	they fix

Most verbs ending in *s, sh,* or *ch* add *-es* in the present form for *he, she,* or *it.*

· ·

Show What You Know

If the subject and verb in each sentence agree, put a **C** above the underlined verb. If they do not agree, write the correct present-tense form of the verb above the underlined verb.

1. My older sister Karin <u>fixes</u> cars.

2. She washes and <u>wax</u> them, too, for a small fee.

3. Karin <u>works</u> on cars most Saturdays.

4. She often <u>start</u> working at 7:00 in the morning.

5. Mom isn't very good with cars, so she sometimes <u>watch</u> Karin.

6. Karin only <u>wish</u> she could make more money fixing cars.

7. I think Karin is too busy. She <u>dash</u> from one thing to another.

8. I think she <u>try</u> to do too much between school and her job.

Score: _____   Total Possible: 8

Proofread

Rick's report, entitled "How We Depend on Electricity," has five verbs and subjects that do not agree. Using the proper proofreading mark, delete the verb in each error of agreement. Above it, write the verb form that corrects the agreement problem.

Example: That dog ~~bark~~ barks too much.

We often don't realize how much we depend on electricity until it stop. When

lightning flashes or a powerful wind blow down a power line, we're in trouble!

Want to watch TV or listen to that new CD? Not without electricity. Think you'll

have some dinner? Try it cold. The family member who fix the food will love doing

without a stove. You'd like to read a book? Read while the candle melt!

You feel so thankful when the power come on again. How did people live without it?

Practice

Look at the picture. It shows one way family and friends entertained themselves at night before electricity. Imagine that you will have to live for a period of several weeks or months without electricity. How will you entertain yourself and others? How will you cope with the nighttime darkness? Write a short description of what you would do.

_____

_____

_____

_____

Tips for Your Own Writing: Proofreading ....

Select a piece of your own writing and look for verbs in the present tense. Check for agreement with the subject. Just remember: the verb adds -s or -es when the subject is *he, she, it,* or any singular noun.

 Subjects and verbs that work together make strong sentences.

46 Usage: Subject-Verb Agreement II

Where's the subject? Where's the verb? If you can answer these questions, you're a long way toward understanding this lesson.

························· Did You Know? ·························

There are some special problems of agreement between subjects and verbs. In most cases, the subject comes before the verb. However, sometimes we invert, or reverse the order of, subjects and verbs to make a sentence more interesting.

> Out of the fog **rises** the **castle**.

Sentences that begin with *here, there,* and *where* put the subject after the verb.

> Here **is** the **drawbridge**.
> Where **are** the **gates**?

Sometimes a prepositional phrase comes between the subject and the verb.

> A **knight** with many servants **arrives** at the castle.

A *compound subject* is made of two or more nouns or pronouns. Compound subjects joined by *and* always take a verb that does not end in -*s*. If the verb is irregular, use the form for plural subjects with a compound subject.

> The **knight and** his **squire are** attending the tournament.

Compound subjects joined by *or* or *nor* take a form of the verb that agrees with the subject nearest to the verb.

> Either the queen or **her servants have** the secret key.

Show What You Know

If the subject and verb in each sentence agree, put a C above the underlined verb. If they do not, write the correct present-tense form of the verb above the underlined verb.

Where <u>is</u> evidence of the Ice Age in North America? Many U.S. states and
1

Canadian provinces <u>show</u> such evidence. Objects under a glacial mass <u>forms</u> various
2   3

land features. Moraines and eskers <u>are</u> types of glacial deposits. From glacial ice <u>come</u>
4   5

most of the fresh water on Earth. Glaciers <u>ranges</u> in thickness from 300 to 10,000 feet.
6

Score: _____   Total Possible: 6

Proofread

Following is a report Tara wrote after a field trip with her science class. Find the six errors of subject-verb agreement. Using the proper proofreading mark, delete each incorrect word and write the correction above it.

Example: There ~~is~~ ^{are} five science books on the table.

About twenty thousand years ago, the last glacier of the most recent Ice Age

retreated northward. As a result, many glacial formations dots our fertile farmlands.

Everywhere is low mounds covered with trees. These mounds in each area tells a story.

On some of them grows no crops. Farmers don't always plows the rougher, rockier soil

of the glacial mounds. Glaciers have also left behind kettle lakes. A kettle is a bowl-like

depression. It remains after a huge chunk of glacial ice has melted. Terminal moraines—

long, hilly ridges—also mark the end of glaciers. You can see one if you follow Route 77

westward from Barrytown. But neither kettles nor terminal moraines tells the entire

story of glaciers in the Ice Age. For the whole story, you'll have to study geology.

Practice

Write a paragraph describing the terrain, or land formation, in your area. Is it flat, hilly, or coastal? What kind of vegetation covers the land? Be careful about subject-verb agreement.

_____

_____

_____

_____

_____

Tips for Your Own Writing: Proofreading ....

The next time you write a story or report, try using some compound subjects. If you join the subjects with *and,* use a verb form that does not end in *-s.* If the subjects are joined by *or* or *nor,* use a verb form that agrees with the nearest subject.

 *T*o make verbs and subjects agree, first identify the verbs and the subjects.

47 Usage: Verb Agreement—There/Here

Here *and* there: *how do we find the subjects of sentences?*

.... Did You Know? ....

Sentences that begin with the adverbs *there* or *here* can offer special subject-verb agreement problems. Always use *there is* in the present tense with a singular subject, and *there are* in the present tense with a plural subject.

> **There is** a wonderful **exhibition** at the museum this weekend.
> **There are** always many interesting **exhibitions** at the museum.

Always use *there was* in the past tense with a singular subject and *there were* in the past tense with a plural subject.

> Last year, **there was** a special **show** on dinosaurs.
> **There were** two triceratops **skeletons** in that show.

Always use *here is* with a singular subject and *here are* with a plural subject.

> **Here is** my **Uncle Roger,** the curator of the museum.
> **Here are** the **items** I bought at the museum gift shop.

· ·

Show What You Know

In each blank, write the verb (*is, are, was,* or *were*) that agrees in number with the subject and that is in the proper tense (past or present) for the context of the sentence.

Let's Go to the Museum of Natural History

Here _____ my favorite place in town, the Museum of Natural History. What
         1

do they have? Just about everything—come in and find out. First is the Paleontology

Room. Here _____ skeletons of dinosaurs, life-size and put back together again.
         2

They give me a thrill because once there _____ creatures of this size prowling
                                3

Earth! Let's move on to the Geology Room. There _____ meteorites, or at least
                                       4

the remains of them, in this room. And look! There _____ a photograph of a
                                      5

meteorite that crashed right into someone's living room. Gosh, I'm afraid we can't see

any more today. Last week, there _____ more time to look.
                             6

Score: _____   **Total Possible: 6**

Proofread

Find the five errors of subject-verb agreement in the report on photography. Using the proper proofreading mark, delete each incorrect word and write the correction above it.

Example: Here ~~is~~ ^{are} the answers to our questions.

Some people think that there is nothing more to photography than "point and shoot." But you can do a lot more. In modern cameras, there is settings to control the speed of shooting and the amount of light. In an old-fashioned "box" camera, there was no such controls. You can also set up a darkroom to develop your own photos. Here is a place where no light must enter, or the film will be ruined!

There are more than just technique to think about, though. Photography are an aesthetic, or artistic, activity. When taking photos, group objects thoughtfully. From your perspective, or view, how do the objects appear? Is they bunched tightly together? Is the lighting correct? Photography can be especially rewarding.

Practice

Find a photograph that you especially like—a family photo or one from a magazine, for example. Write what you like about it. Consider composition (how the objects are grouped) and tone (whether it is dramatic or humorous, for example). Begin at least three of the sentences with *there* or *here*.

_____

_____

_____

_____

_____

Tips for Your Own Writing: Proofreading ································

Choose a piece of your own writing. Do any of your sentences begin with *Here* or *There* followed by *is, are, was,* or *were*? Make sure you used *is* and *was* with singular subjects and *are* and *were* with plural subjects.

✏ **H**ere is *a thought:* There are *a lot of things to keep in mind when using* here *and* there *in sentences.*

48 Review: Past Tense Verbs, Subject-Verb Agreement

A. In the blank in each sentence, write the past tense of the verb in parentheses.

1. Jamal's teacher _____ him to perform in the piano recital. (ask)

2. He _____ a piece by Chopin called "Valse Brilliante." (choose)

3. When Jamal walked onto the stage, he _____ very nervous. (feel)

4. He _____ the beginning of his piece, but not the ending. (remember)

5. As Jamal _____ the keys, he felt more confident. (touch)

6. He _____ every single note perfectly. (hit)

7. At the reception, everyone said, "Jamal, you _____ very well." (play)

Score: _____ 　　Total Possible: 7

B. In the blank, write the correct ending (s or es) for each incomplete verb. The completed verb should agree in number with its subject.

Tornadoes are fantastically powerful whirlwinds. A tornado form_____ along a
　　　　　　　　　　　　　　　　　　　　　　　　　　　　　　　　1
front, or narrow zone, between a mass of cool, dry air and a mass of warm, very

humid air. The warm, moist air rise_____ in rapid updrafts. Soon, a column of air
　　　　　　　　　　　　　　　　　2
spin_____. If the updraft is powerful enough, it feed_____ the growing tornado.
　　3　　　　　　　　　　　　　　　　　　　　　　　　4
Air rush_____ up the column.
　　　5

Soon a funnel drop_____ down from the sky. It touch_____ down, raising a
　　　　　　　　　　　　6　　　　　　　　　　　　　　7
black dust cloud. A tornado toss_____ about debris like paper. It sometimes
　　　　　　　　　　　　　　8
pitch_____ automobiles or tractors like softballs. Tornadoes would seem like
　　9
pranksters if they weren't so violent. A twister sometimes levels houses on one side of a

street but miss_____ those on the other side completely. The narrow, whirling
　　　　　　　10
column pass_____ close to some objects without harming them. Thank goodness
　　　　　11
the average tornado live_____ for only a few minutes!
　　　　　　　　　　12

Score: _____ 　　Total Possible: 12

C. In each pair of verbs in parentheses, underline the verb that agrees in number with the subject.

Out of the shadows (step, **steps**) the king's herald. "I declare, according to His
                  1

Majesty's will," he cries, "that from this day forward the queen and her retinue shall be

kept under guard in the palace." Through the crowd (run, **runs**) a low murmur.
                                            2

But where (**is**, are) the key to the secret passage under the palace? Does the
         3

queen have it? No, Prince Renaldo (possess, **possesses**) it. He and Princess Angelina
                             4

(**plot**, plots) to aid the queen.
  5

What is the climax of our story? The queen and her servants (makes, **make**) their
                                           6

escape. Neither the officials of the court nor the king (find, **finds**) a way to stop them.
                                           7

Into the free light and air they (**walk**, walks).
             8

                      Score: _____   **Total Possible: 8**

D. Fill in each blank with *is, are, was,* or *were* so that the subject and the verb agree in tense and number.

Asteroids are rocky chunks that orbit the sun in space. Sometimes an asteroid

comes into Earth's atmosphere and becomes a meteor. Usually, a meteor vaporizes in

the atmosphere. We call the objects that do reach the ground *meteorites.* There

_____ evidence that meteorites have slammed into Earth. They have left very
    1

large craters. In a few cases, there _____ surviving meteorites, too.
                                  2

Meteorites can be very destructive. Scientists believe that there _____ a huge
                                                 3

meteorite above Siberia in 1908. It apparently exploded in the air, flattening and

burning forests. Remember that there _____ once dinosaurs on Earth. Some
                                    4

scientists think that a massive meteorite hit Earth and raised so much dust that it

changed the climate, killing off the dinosaurs. Here _____ something to think
                                            5

about: What would happen if a very large asteroid was predicted to hit Earth very

soon?

                      Score: _____   **Total Possible: 5**

            REVIEW SCORE: _____   **REVIEW TOTAL: 32**

49 Usage: Pronouns—Agreement and Order I

Be a "pro" when using the subject forms of personal pronouns.

.... Did You Know? ....

Personal pronouns have subject forms and object forms, in addition to singular, plural, and possessive forms.

The subject form of a pronoun is used as the subject of the sentence or as a pronoun following a linking verb.

A subject pronoun can be used as the subject of the sentence.

> **He** drew the illustrations in the book.

A subject pronoun can be used after a linking verb. You can decide what form of the pronoun to use by inverting the sentence.

> The author of the book was **she.**/**She** was the author of the book.

Show What You Know

Read the paragraphs. In each set of parentheses, underline the correct subject pronoun.

In 1804–1806, Captains Meriwether Lewis and William Clark led an expedition

across the territory of Louisiana. Today (we, us) know this vast region as the Northern
                                          1
Plains of northwestern U.S.

One woman accompanied the crew—Sacagawea. The courageous daughter of a

Shoshone was (she, her). Because Sacagawea helped with communication, the
                    2
explorers were able to find horses and guides.

The explorers learned much about landforms, wildlife, and Native Americans.

(They, Them) spent their first winter in camp with the Mandan and later met the Nez
3
Percé in the northern Rockies. Finally, in November 1805, the expedition reached the

Pacific Ocean. (It, Its) was an astonishing sight, according to Captain Clark.
             4

Score: _____   **Total Possible: 4**

Proofread

This imaginary newspaper editorial of 1806 speculates that the members of the Lewis and Clark expedition are lost or dead. The writer used four personal pronouns incorrectly. Draw a delete mark through each mistake and write the correction above it.

Example: ~~Us~~ We have received no mail from them.

We fear that the noble expedition of Captains Lewis and Clark has failed. Consider how many conditions were against they. The party was last heard from one year ago, when Corporal Warfington rowed into St. Louis. He was a member of the expedition. Since that time, us have received no word. Yet our ears heard rumors of capture by Spaniards. Some think them suffered an even worse fate. Whatever the truth about the noble explorers, heroes were them all.

Practice

Imagine that you are a member of an exploration party in an unknown territory. Write the body of a letter to someone back home—a family member, friend, reporter, or the President. Tell a story about some challenge you have faced. Use at least four subject pronouns.

_____

_____

_____

_____

_____

_____

Tips for Your Own Writing: Proofreading ....

In a piece of your own writing, check the forms of the pronouns you used. To choose the correct pronoun form, identify how the pronoun functions in each sentence. If a pronoun is used as a subject or after a linking verb, use the subject form of the pronoun.

 The subject of this lesson is subject pronouns as subjects.

50 Usage: Pronouns—Agreement and Order II

Be clear about the uses of object pronouns: as direct objects, indirect objects, and objects of prepositions.

.... **Did You Know?** ....

Personal pronouns have singular and plural subject forms, object forms, and possessive forms.

An object pronoun can be used as a <u>direct object</u> of a verb. Notice that a direct object usually comes after the verb and tells what the verb acted upon.

> Because Anne's cookies are delicious, she is taking **them** to the bake sale.

An object pronoun can be used as an <u>indirect object</u> in a sentence. Notice that the indirect object comes between the verb and the direct object (*cake*). It tells to or for whom the verb acted. A direct object is necessary in a sentence with an indirect object.

> Jim bakes **her** a cake for the birthday party.

An object pronoun can be used as the <u>object of a preposition</u>. Notice that the object of a preposition comes after the preposition *for*.

> Ted and Lisa bake bread for **us**.

Show What You Know

Tell how each underlined personal pronoun is used. Is it a direct object, an indirect object, or the object of a preposition? Write DO, IO, or OP above each underlined personal pronoun.

1. "I'll splatter <u>you</u> with this pie," joked the clown.

2. "Go ahead, entertain <u>us</u>," dared the audience member.

3. "The Great Miranda" performed for <u>them</u>.

4. "Give <u>me</u> the ticket," said the lady at the circus box office.

5. Amazing Amanda the magician sawed <u>him</u> in half.

6. "I think we pleased <u>them</u>," said the master of ceremonies.

7. "We always give <u>them</u> their money's worth."

Score: _____   Total Possible: 7

Proofread

The following music review uses seven personal pronouns incorrectly. Draw a delete mark through each incorrect word and write the correction above it.

Example: Please find a seat for ~~we.~~ us

The City Philharmonic played a dazzling concert last night. The conductor was pleased, and so was I. The audience agreed with he and I. Mellow as ever, the string section soothed and inspired we. The horns blared and bounced with agility. (Give they a hand!) The single brass player blasted his trumpet. (Hats off to he!) But best of all, percussion player Sara Hue punctuated just the right moments. The audience gave she a standing ovation! Between you and I, I think it was one of the orchestra's best concerts ever.

Practice

Write five sentences describing a live performance or movie that you have attended or seen recently. It could be a concert, a sports event, a movie, or a play. Use an object pronoun in each sentence. Try to use an object pronoun as a direct object, as an indirect object, and as the object of a preposition.

_____

_____

_____

_____

_____

Tips for Your Own Writing: Proofreading ....

Reread something that you have written. Identify all of the personal pronouns. Did you use *It's me*? Although that is often used in informal speech, remember that the correct written form is *It is I* because *I* is the subject, not the object. *I* follows a linking verb.

 The object of this lesson is to get you to put object pronouns in the right form.

51 Usage: Double Negatives

One negative is enough! Avoid the double negative.

.... **Did You Know?** ....

No, none, not, nobody, and *nothing* are negative words. Using two such negative words in the same sentence is called a *double negative.* Good writers avoid double negatives.

Incorrect: I do **not** like **nothing** in my lunch box today.
Correct: I do **not** like anything in my lunch box today.

Incorrect: You **can't** eat **no** lunch with us.
Correct: You **can't** eat any lunch with us.

The *n't* in *can't* stands for the negative word *not.* To avoid the double negative, watch for *not* in contractions such as *don't, won't, didn't,* and *isn't.*

The words *barely, hardly,* and *scarcely* are also used as negative words. Avoid using the negative word *not* with these words.

Incorrect: I **couldn't hardly** eat after seeing that movie.
Correct: I could **hardly** eat after seeing that movie.

....

Show What You Know

Correct each double negative that is underlined below. Rewrite the words on the line.

1. Teresa <u>couldn't do nothing</u> with her clay. _____

2. She <u>hadn't barely</u> started sculpting class. _____

3. Todd <u>didn't have no</u> clay on his table. _____

4. He <u>wasn't hardly</u> ready to get his hands dirty. _____

5. The teacher thought he <u>wouldn't never</u> get Todd to try. _____

6. In fact, Todd <u>wouldn't have none</u> of it. _____

Score: _____   **Total Possible: 6**

Proofread

The writer of the following report has overlooked four double negatives. Draw a delete mark through each mistake and write the correction above it.

Example: I don't want ~~none~~. *(any written above)*

A true recycler, the hermit crab doesn't believe in no waste. Because it doesn't

have no protective covering for its soft stomach, it goes looking for one. It can't hardly

wait to find an old shell. A cast-off shell from a shellfish such as a conch will do just

fine. The crab pulls itself into its adopted "home." It uses tail hooks to hold the shell in

place and guards the opening with crusher claws. Once it is inside, nobody won't

bother Mr. or Ms. Hermit Crab!

Practice

Imagine that you are writing a TV ad for a lunch food, such as the one in the picture. Write a description, or write a dialogue between two lunch items, such as a banana and a cookie. Avoid using double negatives.

_____

_____

_____

_____

_____

_____

_____

Tips for Your Own Writing: Proofreading ....

Select a piece of your own writing. Read aloud any sentences that contain negative words. Do you hear more than one negative word in any of these sentences? Watch particularly for contractions that contain the *n't.*

Remember to use only one negative word in a sentence.

Lesson

52 Review: Pronoun Agreement and Double Negatives

A. In the following article, underline the seven subject pronouns.

Maria Mitchell, the daughter of a sea captain in Nantucket, Massachusetts, lived in the 1800s. Maria helped in her father's business. He adjusted navigation instruments for oceangoing ships. They needed to be very accurate instruments. In the meantime, Maria developed an interest in astronomy. She learned how to use a telescope and studied books on astronomy in her free time.

Through careful study and observation, Maria became a very fine astronomer. On October 1, 1847, she noticed a hazy object in the sky. It was an unknown comet. Maria was the first to see it. A famous discoverer was she. Honors came to her, including a medal from the king of Denmark. Later she became professor of astronomy at Vassar College.

Score: _____   Total Possible: 7

B. In each sentence below, identify one object pronoun. If the pronoun is a direct object, draw one line under it. Draw two lines under a pronoun that is an indirect object, and circle a pronoun that is the object of a preposition.

Living things develop defenses against other living things that might eat them. Some plants use poison against their enemies to give them a nasty surprise. If you like the outdoors, poison ivy may be quite familiar to you. Oil from this plant irritates human skin, causing eruptions on it. Eating monkshood, a common garden plant, would probably kill you. But, in fact, poisonous plants can be very useful to us, too. Rotenone, from a tropical plant, weakens harmful insects or kills them. Rotenone breaks down quickly in the environment and doesn't harm it. The garden plant foxglove yields a drug, digitalis. Doctors give it to heart patients.

Score: _____   Total Possible: 9

C. **Underline five sentences with double negatives that you find in this article. Write those sentences correctly on the lines.**

In 1974 a discovery was made near Xi'an (Sian) in China. This wasn't no ordinary find. Buried at the tomb of China's first emperor was a life-size army of 7,500 soldiers and horses made of terra cotta, a type of pottery. Hardly any of them weren't broken.

Archaeologists couldn't hardly believe their good luck. (An archaeologist is a scientist who studies objects from past cultures.) The creators of this "army" didn't want no one to disturb the tomb. Some figures were "booby-trapped." For example, moving a particular object may set off the release of a spear or arrow.

Would you like to see the terra-cotta army? If you think you won't never have the chance, you may be wrong. The Chinese government is allowing some of the figures to be displayed outside of China.

_____

_____

_____

_____

_____

_____

Score: _____   **Total Possible: 5**

REVIEW SCORE: _____   **REVIEW TOTAL: 21**

53 Grammar: Nouns

How could we speak or write without the ability to name things? Nouns are essential.

·························· **Did You Know?** ··························

A <u>noun</u> is a word that tells who or what did the action or was acted upon by the verb in the sentence.

Concrete nouns name things that you can see or touch. They can fit in the blank in this sentence: The _____ stood there.

    house   star   ice   cloth   horse   woman   child

Abstract nouns name intangible ideas or qualities—things that cannot be seen or touched.

    fairness   danger   truth   fear   love   courage   faith

A <u>common noun</u> is the general name for someone or something. A <u>proper noun</u> is the name of a particular person or place. It may consist of more than one word and begin with capital letters, except for small words such as *of*.

Common Nouns	**Proper Nouns**
city	Philadelphia
document	Declaration of Independence
author	Thomas Jefferson

···

Show What You Know

Write *C* or *P* above each underlined noun, identifying it as either a common or a proper noun. Circle any proper noun that is not capitalized.

We expect earthquakes to strike <u>areas</u> along the edges of continental plates. But
1

one of the strongest <u>earthquakes</u> in <u>North America</u> struck along the <u>mississippi river</u> in
2   3   4

1811. This is right in the center of the North American plate. During and after the

quake, one steamboat <u>captain</u> observed that the <u>river</u> reversed its course and ran
5   6

backward. An observer in <u>kentucky</u> reported that "the ground waved like a <u>field</u> of corn
7   8

before the breeze." In northwestern Tennessee, twenty square miles of woodland sank.

We know this place today as <u>Reelfoot Lake</u>.
9

Score: _____   Total Possible: 11

Practice

The paragraph below is missing all of its nouns. First, read the paragraph and then choose the nouns you wish to add in the blanks. Your paragraph may be serious or humorous.

_____ is the worst _____ of the
       1   **2**

_____. This unnecessary and irritating
      3

_____ is produced when _____ is changed
      4   **5**

electronically. The first _____ was made by mixing
                                  6

_____ such as _____ and _____. The
      7   **8**   **9**

_____ is horrible. I think I like _____ better!
      10   **11**

Revise

Read the paragraph below. Above each underlined noun, write another noun that is more specific and interesting.

The average bee <u>group</u> has one important <u>lady</u>, several hundred males, and
                  1   **2**

thousands of young females called workers. By studying these workers, <u>people</u> have
                                                                        3

found that bees are smart, complex, and highly social <u>things</u>.
                                                        4

  Worker bees have many <u>things</u> to do. They clean and protect the <u>home</u>. They also
                          5   **6**

look for <u>juice</u> to make honey.
          7

Tips for Your Own Writing: Revising ....

Review a piece of your writing. Look at the nouns and check to see that you chose the most specific and interesting noun you could in each case. Remember, precise word choice is an important part of effective writing.

 Common nouns or proper nouns?—it's a capital difference.

54 Grammar: Pronouns

Pronouns take over for nouns.

.... **Did You Know?** ....

A <u>pronoun</u> is a word that takes the place of a noun or another pronoun. It keeps language from becoming repetitive.

> **Without Pronouns:** **Heinz** wanted to make **Heinz's** best shot.
> **With Pronouns:**   **Heinz** wanted to make **his** best shot.

Pronouns can be in the first, the second, or the third person.

First person refers to the person(s) speaking.

Subject	Possessive	Object
I, we	my, our	me, us

Second person refers to the person(s) being spoken to.

Subject	Possessive	Object
you	your	you

Third person refers to a person, animal, or thing being spoken of.

Subject	Possessive	Object
he, she	his, her	him, her
it	its	it
they	their	them

The pronouns *it* and *its* refer to animals or things, never to people.

....

Show What You Know

Above each underlined pronoun, write *1*, *2*, or *3* for first, second, or third person.

<u>I</u> think that Wolfgang A. Mozart was one of the greatest composers who ever
1

lived. <u>He</u> wrote an astounding number of great musical works. Opera fans especially
2

love Mozart's operas. One of the best of <u>them</u> is *The Marriage of Figaro.* In this opera,
3

a woman tries to regain <u>her</u> husband's affection. But Mozart's music is what makes this
4

opera special. <u>It</u> is simply sublime! Mozart composed orchestra and piano pieces, too.
5

Have <u>you</u> ever listened to any of <u>his</u> pieces?
6   **7**

Score: _____   Total Possible: 7

Proofread

Mike's story about last night's storm contains five noun repetitions that could be improved by using a pronoun. Two articles will also need to be deleted. Use the proper proofreading mark to delete each repeated noun and the two articles.

Example: Sarah rode ~~Sarah's~~ her bike.

Hiss! Crash! Boom! So began last night's terrible thunderstorm. At about eight o'clock, Dad was finishing up his gardening. Dad came running in the house and cried, "This is going to be a big one. Put the awnings down and fasten the awnings. Awnings are especially prone to wind damage."

We heard three very loud claps of thunder in a row. On the fourth, the oak tree shuddered and split. The oak tree crashed to the ground. At about that time, we smelled ozone, a pungent chemical. Mom knew what this odor was, because Mom's major in college was meteorology, the study of weather.

Practice

Write four descriptive sentences about a person you know well. You can write about a friend, parent, grandparent, or anyone you're close to. Use at least four pronouns to refer to that person. Avoid repeating nouns awkwardly.

_____

_____

_____

_____

_____

Tips for Your Own Writing: Proofreading ....

Pronouns have gender. _Masculine gender_ refers to male people (_he, him, his_). _Feminine gender_ refers to female people (_she, her, hers_). _Neuter gender_ refers to animals or things (_it, its_). Find the pronouns in a piece of your writing. Did you use the appropriate form for each gender?

 **B**e pro-pronoun. Use pronouns where they improve your writing.

55 Grammar: Verbs

Verbs are the threads that tie language together. How could we speak or write without expressing actions or states of being?

························· Did You Know? ·························

A <u>verb</u> tells what the person, place, or thing in a sentence is doing, or it links or connects the subject to the rest of the sentence. A verb might tell about being rather than acting.

Many verbs are *action verbs*.

> Hurricane gusts **whipped** the boat.
> The mast of the ship **crashed** to the deck.

Linking verbs express the existence of something or link the subject with a word that renames or modifies it.

> Here **is** a weather chart. *(expresses a state of being)*
> The storm **becomes** a hurricane. *(links the subject to the renaming word)*

Linking Verbs

am	was	become	look	smell
is	were	feel	remain	sound
are	appear	grow	seem	taste

Some verbs can be used either as action verbs or as linking verbs.

> Rena **feels** the wet grass on her bare feet. *(action verb)*
> After walking in the grass, Rena **feels** good. *(linking verb)*

Show What You Know
Underline the verb in each sentence. Then circle each verb that is a linking verb.

Last year, we visited Uncle Taylor's turkey farm. It is quite modern. The birds dwell in climate-controlled buildings rather than outdoors. The turkeys' claws hardly ever touch the ground. I imagined majestic, colorful, flying birds. But these turkeys appear dull. Only plain, white feathers cover them. Moreover, the turkeys seem quite stupid. Nevertheless, they taste good at the Thanksgiving feast!

Score: _____   Total Possible: 13

Practice

Think about a ride you have enjoyed in an amusement park—a roller coaster, for example. Think of strong action verbs you might use to describe the ride or to express your emotions while on the ride. Write two sentences about the ride, using action verbs.

1. _____

_____

2. _____

_____

Now think of some linking verbs from this lesson that you might use to convey information about the ride. Write two sentences about the ride, using some of these verbs.

1. _____

_____

2. _____

_____

Revise

Read the paragraph below. Above each underlined verb, write another verb that is stronger and more interesting.

The Activity Club at Geller School met in September to <u>get</u> a name for our new
₁

newspaper. Vance Vedder <u>said</u>, "The Activity Club Journal." Sandra Yee <u>said</u>, "The
₂ ₃

News and Doers." The club members <u>talked</u> for two hours. We voted three times, and
₄

each time the vote was 4–4. Then Beth Gonzalez <u>said</u>, "The Geller Gazette." On the
₅

fourth vote, this name <u>was picked</u>.
₆

Tips for Your Own Writing: Revising ....

Select a piece of your own writing. Identify the action verbs that you used. Then, ask yourself, "Are any of these action verbs too vague? Could they be replaced with stronger, clearer action verbs?" Think of other verbs you could use. A thesaurus may help you.

 With effort and practice, you can put more verve in your verbs.

115

56 Grammar: Irregular Verbs

Irregular verbs have forms of their own.

.... Did You Know? ....

Most English verbs are regular. Regular verbs add *-ed* to form the past tense. The past participle is formed in the same way, but it also uses a helping word such as *is*, *was*, *have*, or *had*.

> *Present*—I **walk** a lot.   *Past Tense*—I **walked** yesterday.
> *Past Participle*—I **have walked** every day.

Verbs that do not form the past and past participle by adding *-ed* are irregular verbs.

> *Present*—I **sing** a lot.   *Past Tense*—I **sang** yesterday.
> *Past Participle*—I **have sung** every day.

For a list of more irregular verbs, see page 159 in the *Writer's Handbook.*

Present Tense	Past Tense	Past Participle	Present Tense	Past Tense	Past Participle (+ helping verb)
catch	caught	caught	make	made	made
do	did	done	ring	rang	rung
eat	ate	eaten	run	ran	run
fall	fell	fallen	speak	spoke	spoken
freeze	froze	frozen	take	took	taken
give	gave	given	teach	taught	taught
go	went	gone	throw	threw	thrown
grow	grew	grown	win	won	won

Show What You Know
Write the correct past tense form of the verb in parentheses to complete each sentence.

Beverly Sills _____ up in New York City. From the time she was very young, she
　　　　　　　1 (grow)

wanted to become an opera singer. She _____ her operatic career in 1946. Then she
　　　　　　　　　　　　　　　　　　2 (begin)

joined the New York City Opera in 1955. She _____ one of the greatest operatic
　　　　　　　　　　　　　　　　　　3 (become)

sopranos of the mid-1900s. She _____ fame for her versatile voice and rich tones. Her
　　　　　　　　　　　　4 (win)

superior abilities and warm personality _____ her popular with audiences and musicians.
　　　　　　　　　　　　　　　　　5 (make)

Score: _____　　　　Total Possible: 5

Practice

The paragraph below is missing its verbs. In each blank, write a verb that makes sense in the sentence.

Opera is a play in which the characters _____ their
                                                              1
lines. It is not a drama where the characters _____
                                                              2
their lines. Opera singers must _____ fancy
                                        3
costumes and _____ their roles. They may also
                     4
have to _____ several languages and
                5
_____ to other countries to study.
        6

Revise

Read the paragraph below. Above the underlined words, write verbs that make sense in the story and are in the correct form.

Enrico Caruso <u>got to be</u> a famous opera singer. He first <u>singed</u> at Naples in 1894.
                    1   2
Then he <u>gone</u> to London to perform at Covent Garden. In 1903, he <u>sanged</u> at the
              3   4
Metropolitan Opera in New York City. He had a very powerful voice. His notes <u>rung</u>
                                                                                    5
across the stage and thrilled audiences. He <u>becomed</u> one of the most famous opera
                                                  6
stars in history.

Tips for Your Own Writing: Revising ....

Review a piece of your writing. Check the verb forms. Use these clues to see that you have used the correct forms of the verbs. Find verbs you have used and put each verb into one of these frames.

> Today I _____.   Yesterday I _____.   Tomorrow I will _____.

A dictionary can be your best friend when you need to check the forms of irregular verbs.

57 Grammar: Adjectives

Make your nouns more interesting: modify them with adjectives.

.... **Did You Know?** ....

An <u>adjective</u> is a word that modifies a noun. *Modifies* means "describes" or "gives additional information about something."

Some adjectives tell *what kind.*

> Jamael's sister is a **brilliant** painter.

Some adjectives tell *how many.*

> The band played **many** marches for the crowd.

Some adjectives tell *which one.*

> I liked the **third** song.

Articles (*the, a, an*) are a special type of adjective, also called determiners because they signal that a noun follows.

> **The** tune is **an** old favorite.

Adjectives come before the words they modify or after a linking verb.

> The **shiny** horn blared. The drummer seems **sleepy.**

A <u>proper adjective</u> is formed from a proper noun. It is always capitalized.

> The **Italian** language is used in musical notation.

. . . .

Show What You Know

Underline the adjectives (including articles) in the sentences below. Circle any proper adjectives that should be capitalized.

1. An oceanographer studies many aspects of the seas and oceans.

2. On Earth, the oceans are vast, deep pools of water.

3. But the water in oceans and seas is not drinkable.

4. It contains enormous amounts of common table salt.

5. The Pacific Ocean is the largest ocean on Earth.

6. It has many powerful currents, including the brazil Current.

Score: _____   **Total Possible: 19**

Practice

Think of a place you like to visit—perhaps the seashore, the lake, or the desert. Close your eyes and picture the place, or a part of it. Think of six adjectives to describe it. The adjectives can describe any aspect of your mental picture— sight, sound, smell, or touch. Write the adjectives on the lines.

_____

_____

_____

_____

Now think of three adjectives that describe your _feelings_ about this place. You can use the sentence form "I feel . . ." to express these feelings. Write the sentence on the lines.

_____

_____

_____

Revise

Revise the paragraph below by adding at least seven adjectives to give more details and make the picture clearer and more interesting to the reader. Write the adjectives above the nouns they modify.

The sun shone on the beach and warmed the sand. Waves splashed back and

forth across the cove. Light sparkled on the waves. A boat sailed past in the distance.

With a snort, a scuba diver rose suddenly to the surface by the pier. People played

a game of volleyball at one end of the beach while children made sand castles at the

other end. The sights, sounds, and smells of the beach made it the place to be.

Tips for Your Own Writing: Revising ....

Choose a piece that you have written. Identify the adjectives that you used. Did you use adjectives like _good, bad,_ or _nice_ when you might have used a more descriptive adjective? Replace any adjectives that do not give enough detail.

 _A_djectives help people see the world as a colorful, interesting place.

58 Grammar: Articles

*K*now your articles: the, an, *and* a.

.... Did You Know? ....

<u>Articles</u> **are special adjectives that are used only with nouns. They are also called determiners because they signal that a noun follows.**

The definite article *the* **is used with a noun when the noun refers to a particular thing.**

> **The** Olympic swimmer now speaks at schools.

The indefinite articles *a* **and** *an* **are used with a noun when the noun refers to no particular thing.**

> We heard **a** swimmer speak about careers in sports.
> Next week **an** acrobat will talk to us.

The article *a* **is used before a word that begins with a consonant sound:** *a* **speech.**

The article *an* **is used before a word that begins with a vowel sound:** *an* **audience.**

Show What You Know
Fill in each blank with the appropriate article: *the, an,* **or** *a.*

Jacques Cousteau was _____ important ocean explorer of this century. He
₁

made many contributions to oceanography, _____ science of oceans. Cousteau
₂

developed oxygen tanks for diving. Before divers had these tanks, they had to wear

very heavy, awkward suits. Cousteau's contribution was, therefore, _____ very
₃

important one. Cousteau studied ocean plants and animals that are almost unknown.

He also explored shipwrecks. One of Cousteau's major concerns was pollution. He

opposed _____ French government for dumping nuclear wastes at sea.
₄

It is not _____ exaggeration to say that Jacques Cousteau popularized
₅

oceanography. His TV specials made millions more aware of _____ earth's oceans.
₆

Score: _____   Total Possible: 6

Proofread

Gerry's report on whale music has six mistakes in its use of articles. Use the proper proofreading mark to correct each mistake.

Example: I had ~~a~~ apple for lunch.
an

Whales communicate by a astonishingly rich language. They often use a area of the deep sea called the sound channel to send their sound messages over very long distances. We're not sure what all the whale sounds mean. But whales are known to respond to calls for help from an great distance. Scientists wonder whether the sounds are produced on a hourly or daily schedule of some kind.

In fact, whales seem to produce two distinct groups of sounds. One group includes low-pitched barks, whistles, screams, and moans that humans can hear. Whales also make another group of sounds at an high frequency, or pitch, which humans cannot hear. Whales may use these clicks or squeaks like an kind of radar. Perhaps they locate prey or orient themselves using these sounds.

Practice

Look at the picture. Write three sentences to describe what is happening. Try to use the articles *the* and *a* at least one time each.

1. _____

_____

2. _____

_____

3. _____

_____

Tips for Your Own Writing: Proofreading ....

Choose a piece of your own writing. To check that you used the appropriate article with each noun, read your writing aloud. Listening to the beginning sound of each noun will help you know whether you chose the right article.

 *W*hat an *article! You needed* the *articles* a, an, *and* the *to complete* the *lessons.*

59 Grammar: Adverbs

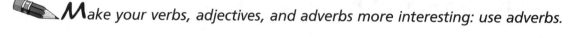

Make your verbs, adjectives, and adverbs more interesting: use adverbs.

.... Did You Know? ....

An <u>adverb</u> is a word that modifies a verb, an adjective, or another adverb. We form many adverbs by adding *-ly* to an adjective. We often change a final *y* to *i* before adding the *-ly*.

> quick + -ly = quickly
> happy + -ly = happily

When adverbs are used with verbs, they tell *how, when, where,* or *to what extent.*

> Brae walked **hurriedly** to the mailbox.
> She slammed the door **afterward.**
> Then she stomped **upstairs.**
> Now Brae relaxed **completely.**

Adverbs that tell *to what extent* can also modify adjectives and other adverbs.

> Arturo's house was **almost** invisible.
> But now the fog is lifting **very** rapidly.

Show What You Know

Underline each adverb in the article. Draw a line to the word that each adverb modifies.

Listen carefully. You can play a violin correctly. First, hold the instrument securely against the neck and under the chin. Take the bow firmly in the free hand. Apply the bow to the strings so that it barely touches them. Then pull the bow evenly. Do this without breaking contact with the strings. When you very nearly reach the end of the arc, reverse the direction of the bow. Now you push it. The sound you hear may be rather scratchy. But remember, learning to play the violin means practicing regularly.

Score: _____   Total Possible: 22

Practice

Write an adverb in each blank in the paragraph. Choose adverbs that tell about the actions of marching bands.

The bass drum _____ announced the start of
1
the parade. The beat of the snare drums signaled the steady, rhythmical pace. The first band played _____ as it
2
marched _____ along the route. Everyone clapped
3
_____ as the trumpets and trombones blared. The whole town _____
4 **5**
cheered as the magnificent cars and floats traveled _____ along the parade route.
6

Revise

Revise the paragraph below by adding at least four adverbs to give more details and make the picture clearer and more interesting to the reader. Insert carets to show where the adverbs should be added.

Example: Beat the drum_{slowly}.

Create your own orchestra. Find some empty pop bottles. Fill them with

water at different levels. To "play" them, blow across their tops. Take a jar with a lid.

Put some dried beans in the jar and close the lid. Shake the jar to make a rhythmic

sound. Find some old metal pots and pans and a clean paintbrush. Invert the pans and

"play" them with the brush, like a snare drum. If you want to get fancy, make your own

set of wind chimes. Use sticks, string, and small pieces of metal for the "chimes." You

can make your own music.

Tips for Your Own Writing: Proofreading ....

Select something from your own writing and find the adverbs. Be sure that you did not use too many adverbs in any one place, as in this sentence: *I read a very, extremely, unbelievably long book.* Like adjectives, adverbs should be used with restraint.

*H*ere is very useful advice: write quite descriptively with adverbs.

60 Grammar: Conjunctions and Interjections

Use conjunctions to connect words or word groups. Use interjections to express emotion.

.... Did You Know? ....

A <u>conjunction</u> is a word that connects words or groups of words.

Coordinating conjunctions such as *and, but,* and *or* connect related words, groups of words, or sentences.

> Meiko **and** Bob go to dance class together.
> The recital was entertaining **but** long.
> Bob danced in the first dance **and** in the finale.
> Meiko forgot the step, **or** her foot slipped.

Correlative conjunctions are conjunctions used in pairs to connect sentence parts.

> **Neither** Tessa **nor** Kato wanted to be first in the lineup.
> Trini had to decide **whether** to dance **or** to study piano.
> We saw **both** Sharon **and** Quinn in the jazz dance.

An <u>interjection</u> is a word or words that express emotion.

> **Wow!** Your performance in the dance recital was stupendous.
> **Oh,** I want to learn how to dance.

Use either an exclamation point or a comma after an interjection. If the emotion being expressed is strong, use the exclamation point.

Show What You Know

Circle each conjunction and underline each interjection in the paragraph below.

Suddenly I heard, "Yipe! It's a big *snake*." The poor snake simply wanted peace and quiet. It neither rattled nor hissed. It quietly uncoiled, and then it slithered away. I wanted to follow the snake, but Terri told me to stay away from it. "Look out!" she said. "It's gone under that rock." Both Dr. Herkimer and I are snake scientists. Oh, and we are both afraid of snakes!

Score: _____   Total Possible: 11

Practice

Look at the picture of a dog show. Write three sentences that describe the scene. Use conjunctions in at least two of the sentences, perhaps to compare and contrast the owners and their dogs. (Name them if you would like.)

1. _____
   _____

2. _____
   _____

3. _____
   _____

Revise

Revise the paragraphs below by adding at least four conjunctions and one interjection to improve the writing. Use proper proofreading marks.

                                    and
Example: We called her. ~~We~~ waited for her.
                       ∧

Susan ran home from school. She was very excited. She raced in the front door.

She looked for her parents. As soon as she saw her father, she yelled, "I won."

"Calm down," said Mr. Campbell. "Tell us what you won."

Susan reported that she had won first place in the science fair. She had gotten a

trophy. She had gotten a medal.

Mrs. Campbell congratulated Susan. She hugged Susan. Mrs. Campbell cried. She

did not cry long. Mr. Campbell smiled a lot. He told Susan they were very proud of her.

Tips for Your Own Writing: Revising ....

Choose a piece of your own writing. Did you use any interjections? If so, did you use them only occasionally? Using too many interjections is like the boy who cried "Wolf!" too often. After a while, the excitement wears off. Save interjections for special occasions.

 Wow! *Conjunctions* and *interjections in the same lesson.*

61 Grammar: Prepositions

✏️ *Use prepositional phrases to modify words in sentences.*

························· **Did You Know?** ··························

A <u>preposition</u> connects a noun or pronoun to the rest of the sentence. The noun or pronoun that follows the preposition is called the <u>object of the preposition</u>.

The object, along with the preposition, its object, and any words that modify the object, make up a *prepositional phrase*. This phrase gives more information about the sentence.

> We glanced ***across*** the treacherous river.

A prepositional phrase modifies a noun, pronoun, verb, adjective, or adverb. In the first sentence, the prepositional phrase *along the beach* is an *adverb phrase* that modifies the verb *walked*. In the second sentence, the prepositional phrase *along the beach* is an *adjective phrase* that modifies the noun *walk*.

> We walked *along the beach.*
> Our walk *along the beach* was enjoyable.

For a list of more prepositions, see page 159 in the *Writer's Handbook.*

Prepositions

about	before	down	of	to
above	behind	for	on	under
across	below	from	over	up
after	beneath	in	since	with
against	beside	like	through	without

Show What You Know

Underline each prepositional phrase. Circle the preposition.

Sweat was running down Matt's face. He couldn't believe that his opponent Marvin would clobber him, even though Marvin *was* champion of the school district. "Fifteen-love. Thirty-love." The scores were announced over the speaker! Matt tried to remember all he'd been taught: grip the end of the racket, but not too tightly. Stay limber and don't stand in one spot. Keep eyes on the ball. Now a serve was coming across the net. Matt crossed his fingers.

Score: _____   Total Possible: 14

Practice

Think of the sights, sounds, feelings, and smells of a storm. It could be a snowstorm, thunderstorm, or hurricane. Write a sentence or poem using as many prepositional phrases as you can.

Example: Rain *from the dark clouds in the sky* pounded *on the roof of the house* and pelted the trees *in the yard* as the lightning flashed *across the sky*.

Possible beginnings:

  Over the trees in the yard

  In the dark of night

_____

_____

_____

_____

_____

Revise

Revise the paragraph below by adding at least four prepositional phrases to provide details about the heat, the drought, or the rainy season. Use proper proofreading marks.

Example: We sat outside.

In the evening,   under the beautiful elm tree

Hot, dry winds sweep across much of southern Asia. The sun bakes the earth, and

crops cannot grow. The people wait for the rainy season. The coming of the rain means

that they can plant crops and produce food.

Tips for Your Own Writing: Revising ....

Choose a piece that you have written recently. Look for places to add prepositional phrases to provide additional information or add interesting details to your sentences. Always try to place each phrase next to the word it modifies.

 Prepositions add details to your writing.

Lesson
62 Review: Parts of Speech

A. Underline the four proper nouns in the article below.

Lucille Ball was one of the most successful comedians of all time. She and her

husband, Desi Arnaz, created an incredibly popular TV show in the 1950s. It featured

their New York apartment and best friend, "Ethel Mertz."

Score: _____   Total Possible: 4

B. Write a pronoun from the list that best completes each sentence.

    you   **her**   **them**   **we**

1. Marla twisted _____ ankle on the ice yesterday.

2. Ben and Rae have won the skating match. Let's congratulate _____.

3. Can _____ join our teams together to put on a bigger skating show?

4. "I know _____ will like skating as much as I do," said the champ to her son.

Score: _____   Total Possible: 4

C. Above each underlined verb, write *A* if it is an action verb and *L* if it is a linking verb.

1. Beavers <u>build</u> lodges in artificial lakes.

2. A lodge <u>is</u> a mound of sticks with an interior chamber.

3. As for the artificial lake, the beaver <u>creates</u> that by damming a stream.

4. It <u>seems</u> strange that a beaver <u>can make</u> such a difference.

Score: _____   Total Possible: 5

D. Underline fourteen adjectives (including articles) in the report below. Circle one proper adjective.

Pluto is the last planet revolving around the sun. It was discovered in 1930 by

American astronomer Clyde Tombaugh. Before this important discovery, astronomers

suspected the existence of a ninth planet. They had noticed that a force seemed to pull

the seventh planet, Uranus, and the eighth planet, Neptune, off their orbits.

Score: _____   Total Possible: 15

128

E. Fill in each blank with the appropriate article: *the*, *an*, or *a*.

1. Find _____ player to pluck the banjo.

2. If you play the harp, then find _____ orchestra to play in.

3. This is _____ guitar that I played in the concert last year.

Score: _____ Total Possible: 3

F. Underline the adverb in each of the three sentences below.

1. Charles Dickens wrote often about children's hardships.

2. Mrs. Havisham trains Estella to treat all men cruelly.

3. Do you know this story well? It is Dickens's *Great Expectations.*

Score: _____ Total Possible: 3

G. Underline eight conjunctions and circle two interjections.

Have you ever experienced a partial or total eclipse of the sun? Oh, my! It's an exciting experience. The moon passes between the sun and Earth. It casts a shadow on Earth. Not only does the sky darken, but also the air chills. Wow, it feels just like nightfall! Both before and after the deepest part of the eclipse, you have to be careful not to look directly at the sun. To do so could injure your eyes. Whether the eclipse is total or partial, a solar eclipse is something to remember.

Score: _____ Total Possible: 10

H. Underline five prepositional phrases below. Above the phrase, write the part of speech that it modifies (noun, verb, adjective).

1. Bread is a staple food for many people.

2. Much of the flour used to make bread comes from wheat.

3. The wheat heads on the stalk tip provide flour's raw material.

4. To harvest wheat, machines beat the heads against a hard surface.

5. The grain is then milled into flour.

Score: _____ Total Possible: 10

REVIEW SCORE: _____ REVIEW TOTAL: 54

63 Grammar: Sentence Types

Use a different sentence type for each different writing purpose: statement, question, request (or command), and exclamation.

.... **Did You Know?** ....

Sentences that make statements, *declarative sentences*, usually end with a period.

> Rudi goes to see a movie once a week**.**

Sentences that ask questions, *interrogative sentences*, end with a question mark.

> What movie did you see this week**?**

Sentences that express strong emotions, *exclamatory sentences* or *exclamations*, end with an exclamation point.

> I can't wait to see that movie**!**

Sentences that express commands, requests, or give instructions, *imperative sentences*, have no subject and end with either a period or an exclamation point. To decide which punctuation mark to use, consider the intensity of the emotion in the sentence. Strong emotions call for the exclamation point.

> Keep your ticket with you at all times**.**
> Be quiet**!**

....

Show What You Know
Write the name of each kind of sentence.

statement	exclamation
question	request

1. This week, our school is having a craft fair. _____

2. A craft is something made by hand from everyday materials. _____

3. Do you want to know what I entered as my craft? _____

4. Go to the auditorium of Oak Grove School between 7:00 and 9:00 P.M. _____

5. Look for the yellow bookcase made of recycled foam packing material. _____

6. I won a blue ribbon for best use of materials! _____

Score: _____   **Total Possible: 6**

Proofread

Read Janna's report below. Check for correct end punctuation of sentences. Use proper proofreading marks to correct the eight errors.

Example: Do you know which road to take.

Have you ever seen a dollhouse in a friend's home. Probably so? Most dollhouses are designed to be open on one side so that people can see inside them. Fine dollhouses are carefully furnished. They may even have real wallpaper and light fixtures. They are amazing?

I can't help wondering whether dollhouses are mainly for kids or for adults? Some of these toys are incredibly fancy. Let me tell you what I mean. A German noble in the 1500s hired someone to build a dollhouse castle! He furnished it with precious metals and miniature tapestries, or woven wall hangings. Was this dollhouse ever used by children as a toy. No, the owner kept it so that he could look at it occasionally.

So, are dollhouses for grown-ups or kids! What do you think.

Practice

Imagine that you are attending the Oak Grove School craft fair. You see an exhibit that you especially like. Write four sentences about it. Make sure that one sentence is a statement, one is a question, one is a command or a request, and one is an exclamation.

1. _____

   _____

2. _____

3. _____

4. _____

Tips for Your Own Writing: Revising ....

Select a piece of your own writing. Check to see whether you used different types of sentences. Using a variety of sentence types can make your writing more interesting and effective.

 State, ask, request, and exclaim!

64 Grammar: Understanding Sentences

Every sentence has a backbone (its subject and verb). Interesting sentences have many details, too.

·························· Did You Know? ··························

The subject of a sentence tells who or what did something (or occasionally, who *is*). The thing that is done (or that simply is) is the verb or the predicate. In the following sentence, *Carla* tells the "who," and *ran* tells the "thing" that Carla did.

Carla ran.

Most sentences are longer and more complex than *Carla ran.* Writers usually hang details on the sentence backbone. This is because they often want to convey more to listeners and readers. Details can give information about people, places, and things. Or they can tell how, when, where, or to what extent something happens.

My new friend Carla ran **fast in the all-state track meet.**

···

Show What You Know

Circle the subject and underline the verb in each question and answer.

1. Why do people think Yosemite National Park is so beautiful? They like the magnificent mountains, deep canyons, and towering waterfalls.

2. Where is Yosemite National Park? The park is located in a wilderness area in California.

3. How many kinds of wildlife live in the park? The park has more than 200 kinds of birds and 60 kinds of other animals.

4. Are there many different plants in the park? Yes, more than 30 kinds of trees and 1,300 kinds of other plants live in the park.

5. What activities can people do in the park? They can go horseback riding, fishing, golfing, hiking, and swimming.

Score: _____   **Total Possible: 21**

Practice

Choose a word or phrase from each column to create a sentence that makes sense. Using this method, make four sentences and write them on the lines.

Subject	Verb	Article/ Adjective	Object	Preposition	Object of Preposition
Marcus	painted	the lovely	canvas	under a	concert hall
You	sang	a sorrowful	melody	into the	acrylic paint
They	found	the shiny	kitten	out of the	board
I	pounded	the scared	nail	with	porch
The teacher	touched	the spinning	story	in the	book

1. _____

_____

2. _____

_____

3. _____

_____

4. _____

_____

Revise

Use information from Show What You Know or an encyclopedia to find additional facts to revise the paragraph below. Use proper proofreading marks.

Example: It is a ^magnificent, spreading^ tree.

Yosemite National Park is in northern California. The scenery is very pretty with

mountains, canyons, and waterfalls. The park has many plants and animals. People visit

the park to participate in many activities.

Tips for Your Own Writing: Revising ....

Select a letter you have written. Try to add details to at least two sentences in your letter. Make sure the details are important and needed.

 If your sentence backbone is solid, you can hang many details on it!

65 Grammar: Combining Sentences I

You can form compound sentences in more than one way.

.... Did You Know? ....

Using compounds to combine short sentences can lead to smoother, less choppy writing.

When sentences have the same subject and verb, you can combine them easily.

> Darryl eats apples.   Darryl eats plums.
> Darryl eats **apples and plums.**

When two sentences have the same subject but different verbs and objects, they can also be combined.

> Heather plays soccer.   Heather writes poetry.
> Heather **plays soccer and writes poetry.**

Sentences with the same verb and object but different subjects can also be combined. Many times the form of the verb will change when it becomes plural.

> Diehl goes to summer camp.   Timothy goes to summer camp.
> **Diehl and Timothy** go to summer camp.

If *I* is one subject in a compound subject, it always comes *last.*

> **Timothy and I** go to summer camp.

Show What You Know
Combine each pair of sentences into one compound sentence.

1. England is in the British Isles. Scotland is in the British Isles.

_____

2. Aunt Tillie visited England. Aunt Tillie visited Scotland.

_____

3. She climbed mountains in Scotland. She visited gardens in England.

_____

4. Tillie sipped tea in the afternoon. Tillie ate scones in the afternoon.

_____

Score: _____   Total Possible: 4

Practice

Make a personal profile. First, list four of your physical characteristics such as hairstyle or color, height, and eye color. Next, list four foods that you like. Finally, list four things that you like to do for fun.

Physical Characteristics

_____   _____

_____   _____

Favorite Foods

_____   _____

_____   _____

Things I Like to Do

_____   _____

_____   _____

Using the information above, write two compound sentences telling about yourself.

1. _____

_____

2. _____

_____

Revise

Revise the paragraph below by rewriting at least two sentences as compound sentences. Use proper proofreading marks.

and dogs
Example: Cats ‸ are mammals. ~~Dogs are mammals too~~.

Alligators belong to the family *Crocodylidae*. Crocodiles belong to that family, too.

They look a lot alike. Some of the crocodiles' bottom teeth show when they close their

mouths. Alligators' teeth are hidden when they close their mouths. Also, crocodiles

have narrow snouts. Alligators have broad snouts.

Tips for Your Own Writing: Revising ....

Choose a piece of your own writing. Look for short, choppy sentences and see whether combining them will improve your writing. Also, look for sentences that are too long. Sometimes a very long sentence should be divided into two shorter sentences.

 Be a joiner! Combine sentences whenever appropriate.

66 Grammar: Combining Sentences II

Do two sentences have some words in common? You may be able to combine the sentences by using an appositive.

· Did You Know? ·

Sometimes we can combine two sentences by taking information from one sentence and attaching it to a closely related noun or a phrase in another sentence. Information that is "attached" in this way is called an *appositive.* If it is at the beginning or end of a sentence, you need only one comma after it or before it.

> A river always has a mouth. A mouth is the place where it flows into a larger body of water.
>
> A river always has a mouth, **the place where it flows into a larger body of water.**

When an appositive adds information but is not necessary to establish the meaning of the sentence, set it off with commas. Delete the appositive and see whether the sentence has the same meaning.

> Our swimming coach teaches summer school. Mrs. Santos is our swimming coach.
>
> Mrs. Santos, **our swimming coach,** teaches summer school.

When an appositive is needed to clarify something, do *not* use commas.

> Rube and Lou played baseball tonight. Rube and Lou are Hornets team members.
>
> Hornets team members **Rube and Lou** played baseball tonight.

Show What You Know

Use an appositive to combine each pair of sentences below.

1. Every country has a capital. A capital is a city where government is run.

_____

2. Rome is full of ancient buildings. Rome is the capital of Italy.

_____

3. A small town is near Rome. The town has many ruins.

_____

Score: _____   Total Possible: 3

Practice

Look at the picture of a large public building. What adjectives does it bring to mind? Write four sentences with appositives about this building or a large public building in your own community (a local museum, for example). Include some descriptive details to help your reader visualize the building.

1. _____

_____

2. _____

_____

3. _____

4. _____

Revise

Revise the paragraph below. Use proper proofreading marks to combine at least two of the sentences by using appositives.

Example: High Street ∧our longest street∧ has a lot of trees. ~~It is our longest street~~.

New York City has more than seven and a half million people. It is the largest

city in the United States. It is one of the largest cities in the world. Only Tokyo, Japan,

is larger. New York is an important center for business, culture, and trade. It is also the

home of the United Nations. The city has banks, stock exchanges, and other financial

institutions. These institutions are located in the famous Wall Street area of the city.

The Statue of Liberty is one of New York's most well-known historic sites. It is visited by

thousands of people every year.

Tips for Your Own Writing: Revising ....

Select and reread a piece of your own writing. Are there any sentences you could combine by using an appositive? Combining information into one sentence will eliminate short, choppy sentences.

When two sentences have a lot in common, they may want to join together.

67 Grammar: Combining Sentences III

Do two sentences have related ideas? Are they of equal importance? If the answer to these questions is yes, you may want to form compound sentences.

.... Did You Know? ....

Similar sentences can be combined when they have closely related ideas of equal importance. We can form such compound sentences by using the coordinating conjunctions *and, but,* or *or.* Place a comma after the first sentence and before the conjunction.

Use *and* to join sentences that have equal importance and similar ideas.

> Mr. Raeford will bake pies. Ms. Tasco will prepare salads.
> Mr. Raeford will bake pies, **and** Ms. Tasco will prepare salads.

Use *but* to join sentences that have equal importance and contrasting ideas.

> We had a picnic on Memorial Day. We stayed indoors on Independence Day.
> We had a picnic on Memorial Day, **but** we stayed indoors on Independence Day.

Use *or* to join sentences that have equal importance and that offer a choice.

> Play games with the children. Talk to the adults.
> Play games with the children, **or** talk to the adults.

Show What You Know

Use *and, but,* or *or* to form a compound sentence from each pair of sentences. Make sure you punctuate the sentences correctly.

1. We make homemade ice cream. Our neighbors enjoy sharing it with us.

_____

2. I like pistachio ice cream. My sister prefers strawberry ice cream.

_____

3. You can have homemade ice cream with us. You can go to the movie with them.

_____

Score: _____   Total Possible: 3

Practice

Think of holiday parties that your family has. Many families have celebrations at Thanksgiving or the Fourth of July. Use one of your family's special holiday celebrations in this writing assignment.

Write three sentences to describe the holiday celebration. Try to use each of the conjunctions *and, but,* and *or* at least one time.

1. _____

   _____

2. _____

   _____

3. _____

   _____

Revise

Revise the paragraph below by combining at least two sentences. Use proper proofreading marks to add the conjunctions *and, but,* and *or.*

Example: I like toppings on my ice cream. My brother doesn't.

(proofreading mark inserting "but" between the two sentences)

   Ice cream is made from milk products, sugar, and flavorings. It is a popular dairy treat. Ice cream is eaten alone. It can also be eaten with cake or pie. It is the main ingredient in milk shakes, sodas, and sundaes. The most popular flavor is vanilla. Chocolate is the next most popular flavor. Ice cream can be found in many parts of the world. Americans eat more ice cream than people in any other country.

Tips for Your Own Writing: Revising ....

Select a piece of your own writing. Did you use the conjunctions *and, but,* and *or* to join sentences that have similar ideas? If the sentences do not have similar ideas, then you should not try to combine them.

When two sentences have a lot in common, they may belong together as one.

68 Grammar: Combining Sentences IV

✏️ *Do two clauses have related ideas? Is one of the clauses more important than the other? This may be a place for a subordinating conjunction.*

.... **Did You Know?** ....

These two clauses can be combined using a subordinate conjunction.

> Granddad fed the livestock. He went to school each day.
> Granddad fed the livestock **before** he went to school each day.

A sentence part that can stand on its own as a complete sentence is a *main clause*. A sentence part that cannot stand on its own is a *subordinate clause*.

If the subordinate clause comes first in the sentence, insert a comma before the main clause.

> Unless you feed them on schedule, the cows won't give milk.

Subordinating Conjunctions

after	how	though	whenever
as	once	unless	where
as if	since	until	while
because	than	when	why

Show What You Know

Draw lines to match main and subordinate clauses and form complex sentences. Add commas where needed.

Although the temperature is above freezing	so that we could dress properly.
No one measured the chilling effect of wind	bundle up in layers.
The Weather Service developed the scale	when it is exposed to cold winds.
Your flesh can freeze very fast	the air feels like it's freezing.
If you expect to be in wind on a cold day	until we had a wind chill scale.

Score: _____   Total Possible: 7

Practice

Look at the picture. On a farm, people have chores to do early in the morning. Think how you would feel if you had to get up early in the morning to do chores. Write four sentences describing how you think it would feel. Use a subordinate clause with a subordinating conjunction in at least one sentence.

1. _____

_____

2. _____

_____

3. _____

4. _____

Revise

Revise at least four sentences in the paragraphs below to include subordinate clauses. Use proper proofreading marks to use subordinating conjunctions such as *after, although, because, even though, while,* and *when.*

                    Because
Example: ˄My mom received her teaching certificate last year. She can teach at my school now.
                                                                       ˄

America lost a great pilot. Amelia Earhart's plane vanished in 1937. Earhart was

making a trip around the world. Her plane went down near the Howland Islands in the

Pacific Ocean. Some people think her plane crashed in the ocean. It ran out of fuel. No

one knows what really happened. No trace of her or her plane has ever been found.

Earhart got her pilot's license in 1922. She began to fly in meets. She became the

first female pilot to fly alone across the Atlantic in 1932. She was the first woman to be

awarded the Distinguished Flying Cross. Her aviation career was full of "firsts." It

was cut short by her disappearance.

Tips for Your Own Writing: Revising ....

Select a report you have written. Look for sentence fragments. A *sentence fragment* is a subordinate clause that has been left to stand on its own. Join it with a main clause.

Use subordinating conjunctions such as after, before, since, until, *and* while *to join sentences.*

69 Grammar: Combining Sentences V

Use relative pronouns such as who, whose, that, *and* which *to introduce dependent sentence parts known as relative clauses.*

.... Did You Know? ....

You can form a complex sentence by combining two short sentences with a relative pronoun.

> Spring rains are good for tulips. Spring rains can begin in March.
> Spring rains, **which** can begin in March, are good for tulips.

In the combined sentence—"Spring rains, . . . are good for tulips"—is the main clause. It can stand alone. The other part of the sentence—"which can begin in March"—is a relative clause that is introduced by the relative pronoun *which*. It cannot stand alone. Some relative pronouns are *who, what, whom, whose, that,* and *which*.

A relative clause can function as an adjective or a noun.

> The girl **who sat next to me** is my new neighbor.
> We found **what we wanted** at the garden center.

Set off a relative clause with commas *only* if it adds information that is not necessary to the sentence. Read the sentence without the clause and see whether the sentence has the same meaning.

Show What You Know

Build a complex sentence using the provided sentence parts. Omit any words in brackets. Write your sentence on the line.

1. [The story] made my skin crawl.   Mr. Gates told a frightening tunnel story.   that

_____

2. I have been in a tunnel on my way to New York.   [The tunnel] cuts through the Smoky Mountains.   which

_____

3. He told you [something] about tunnels.   [It] is not true.   what

_____

Score: _____   Total Possible: 3

Proofread

Read Ferris's report below about hailstorms. Use proper proofreading marks to add four needed commas and to delete three commas that are not needed.

Example: The man⌄who is wearing a red hat⌄is my uncle⌃whom you have met.

A hailstorm is one of the strangest kinds of weather that I can think of. Hailstones, which are lumps of ice fall out of thunderstorm clouds.

One of the worst hailstorms in recent times struck Cheyenne, Wyoming, in August 1985. After the storm, people, who lived there, found six inches of ice on the ground! Their calendars told them it was summer, but the scene looked like winter.

What causes this freakish weather? A thunderstorm piles clouds up very high in the atmosphere. Strong, moist winds rush up to great heights. There, water droplets freeze into tiny ice pellets which get many additional coatings of ice. Finally, the hailstones become so heavy, that they fall to the ground. Hailstones which are usually smaller than a marble can become as large as grapefruits. You wouldn't want one of those to fall on your head!

Practice

Write three sentences about a bridge or a tunnel. Use a relative clause in two of the sentences.

1. _____

_____

2. _____

_____

3. _____

Tips for Your Own Writing: Revising ....

Select a story you have written. Did you begin any relative clauses with *who* or *whom?* Check to see whether you used them correctly.
The woman **who** gave me the coat is my aunt. (subject)
The woman **whom** I visited last summer is my aunt. (object)

 *H*ooray *for all of your relatives—relative pronouns and clauses, that is.*

70 Grammar: Combining Sentences VI

*Words derived from verbs, called **participles**, give us yet another way to combine sentence parts.*

.... **Did You Know?** ....

You can change the verb of one sentence into a participle to combine two sentences as shown.

> Ted's kite soared and dived. Ted's kite was flying in the wind.
> Ted's kite soared and dived, flying in the wind.

You can combine these sentences as shown.

> Val was slowed by the wind. Val made little progress on her bike.
> Slowed by the wind, Val made little progress on her bike.

A *present participle* is a form of a verb that usually ends in *-ing*, and a *past participle* usually ends in *-ed.* They both act like adjectives. Irregular verbs do not follow this pattern for past participles.

Verb	Present Participle	Past Participle
knock	knocking	knocked
find	finding	found
see	seeing	seen

A phrase containing a participle is called a *participial phrase.*

Show What You Know

Choose one word in each column to write four sentences that make sense on the lines below.

Participle	Adverb	Prepositional Phrase	Subject	Verb	Object
Speaking	yesterday	on the platform	Alfredo	recited	my fingers
Racing	often	in our town	the player	made	attention
Seen	slowly	in the street	the kitten	wanted	the salt
Held	tightly	in my hand	the ice cream	froze	a goal
Found	around	on the field	the deer	licked	the poem

1. _____

2. _____

3. _____

4. _____

Score: _____   Total Possible: 4

Proofread

Combine four sentences in the paragraphs below by using proper proofreading marks to change one sentence into a participial phrase and adding it to another sentence.

Seeing
Example: ∧ ~~We saw~~ Jessica on her bike. We waved to her.

The cyclists waited at the starting line. They were ready to go. The starter checked their positions at the line. Then he sounded his horn. That was the starting signal. The cyclists pushed off on their bicycles, beginning the first leg of the Tour de France.

The cyclists were bunched together at first. Then they began to spread out. The faster ones put some distance between themselves and the rest of the pack. They struggled up the hills. They seemed to barely move. But on flat stretches, they whizzed past the spectators. The spectators watched the race from the sides of the road. At last, the finish line was in sight.

Practice

Sometimes things we do, such as riding a bike, seem easy. But at other times, the same activity may seem difficult. Look at the picture. Why is this girl having such a hard time riding her bike? Have you ever had this experience? Write four sentences with participial phrases about riding your bike under difficult conditions.

1. _____

2. _____

3. _____

4. _____

Tips for Your Own Writing: Proofreading ....

Choose something that you have written recently. Look to see whether you used any participial phrases. Make sure you used a comma after a participial phrase that comes at the beginning of a sentence.

Using participial phrases, you can combine sentences to add variety to your writing.

71 Grammar: Combining Sentences VII

When combining sentences, use any and all methods you can. Often, there is more than one good way to combine sentences.

······················· **Did You Know?** ························

A big part of the writer's job is *selection*, that is, deciding which details to include (and which ones to leave out).

There is more than one way to combine the following sentences.

> Mom just planted that rosebush.
> The rosebush was full of blossoms.
> We cut the rose.
> The rose smelled very fragrant.
> The rose had a bright red color.

> We cut the bright red, fragrant rose from Mom's new rosebush, which was full of blossoms.

You could also write:

> Planted recently by Mom, the rosebush yielded a bright red, fragrant rose, which we cut.

Show What You Know

Combine each set of sentences to create a new sentence. Write the new sentence on the line.

1. I recently read a new book.   Elbert Baze wrote it.
   The book is *Dinosaur Music.*   It is an entertaining book.

_____

2. I didn't know that the book signing was scheduled for Tuesday.
   I made other plans with Bert and Ernie.

_____

_____

Score: _____   **Total Possible: 2**

Practice

At a book signing, an author greets people and signs copies of his or her latest book. Think about your favorite author. Imagine that you are going to this author's book signing. Write four sentences that you might say to the author.

1. _____

   _____

2. _____

   _____

3. _____

   _____

4. _____

Revise

Combine sentences in the paragraphs below using any of the methods you have learned. Use proper proofreading marks.

Example: I like to cook. Cooking takes time. My favorite recipe is spaghetti sauce.
(handwritten: If I have time,)

To make this pasta salad, you will need 1/2 lb of vermicelli. Vermicelli are very thin, long Italian noodles. Add 1/2 tsp. of salt to rapidly boiling water. Add the vermicelli to rapidly boiling water. Boil the vermicelli until tender. Drain them in a colander. Rinse them in cold water. Toss the noodles with a little oil. The noodles will stay separated.

Chop up 1/2 cup of black olives. Chop up 1/2 cup of green onions. Cut up 1/4 lb of provolone. Provolone is a mild Italian cheese. Mix the vermicelli, olives, onions, and cheese. Add mayonnaise. Add Italian dressing instead. Use salt, pepper, and garlic. Season the salad. Cover the salad. Refrigerate it for at least two hours.

Tips for Your Own Writing: Revising ....

Look at a piece of your own writing. Did you write many long sentences? Good writers use sentences of different lengths—both short and long—to add variety and interest to their writing.

 Don't be afraid of combining. Put those sentences together!

72 Review: Understanding and Combining Sentences

A. Choose a word or phrase from each column to build a sentence that makes sense. Using this method, make three sentences and write them on the lines.

Subject	Verb	Object	Preposition	Object
Benny	likes	the letters	in	her aunt
We	planted	sunshine	to	the clay pot
Courtney	mailed	a flower	for	the summer

1. _____

2. _____

3. _____

Score: _____   Total Possible: 3

B. Combine the sentences using *and, but,* or *or*. Write the sentences on the lines.

1. Oranges have vitamin C. Grapefruits have vitamin C.

_____

2. Go camping with Gene. Go to the movies with Leslie.

_____

3. We go to the movies frequently. We often see Leslie there.

_____

Score: _____   Total Possible: 3

C. Combine the following sentences, using an appositive. Write the sentence on the line.

Mrs. Tanaka is our librarian.   Mrs. Tanaka helps us with our research papers.

_____

Score: _____   Total Possible: 1

D. In each sentence, underline the subordinate clause and circle the main clause.

1. If you like my model ship, I'll make you one.

2. I think I can build it myself unless the kit is very complicated.

Score: _____   **Total Possible: 4**

E. Build a sentence using the provided sentence parts. Write the sentence on the line.

the green butterfly made a comeback   no one had seen in years   which

_____

Score: _____   **Total Possible: 1**

F. Combine the sentences using a participial phrase.

June was feeling sick.   June lay down and closed her eyes.

_____

Score: _____   **Total Possible: 1**

G. Combine the three sentences. Write the combined sentence on the line.

1. Berne is a new student.   **2.** He has red hair.   **3.** Berne is good at swimming.

_____

Score: _____   **Total Possible: 1**

H. Decide whether each sentence is a statement, question, exclamation, or request. Then write the correct punctuation on the line.

1. What time does Reeva get home from work this evening _____

2. Last night Janice got home at 8:30 _____

3. Don't stay out too late _____

Score: _____   **Total Possible: 3**

REVIEW SCORE: _____   **REVIEW TOTAL: 17**

149

Writer's Handbook

Getting Started with the Writing Process

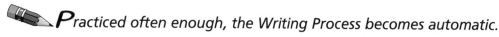 *Practiced often enough, the Writing Process becomes automatic.*

Did You Know?

The writing process can be considered as five parts: **select, connect, draft, revise,** and **proofread.** These parts are constantly flowing into and influencing one another without any clear line between them. Writing does not proceed in nice, neat steps. As the writer, you might get an idea for the conclusion while writing the introduction.

The more you use the writing process, the more it becomes automatic to you. It is like riding a bike. When you first learn to ride, you are a little unsteady and unsure of yourself. With practice, riding a bike becomes more and more automatic. The writing process becomes automatic in the same way.

To begin the writing process, look through your writing folder for topics. You may get topics from television or the newspaper. Then, decide if your purpose will be to explain, describe, or convince your reader before you narrow your general topic. If your topic covers too much ground, pick the part that interests you most. You can select a narrower form of the topic by clustering.

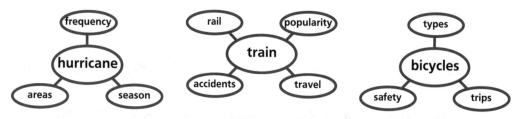

Write your clusters. Add all ideas that come to mind. Choose two or three ideas that interest you the most or that you want to learn more about. Create a new word cluster for each one. Review your new clusters. Select one to write about, and save the others for other projects. Now connect all ideas that go together. Draw lines from one circle to another within your cluster. Draft your ideas into paragraphs. Most likely, this will be the body of your writing. Next, write an introduction or beginning, and add a conclusion or ending. Remember, while you are writing the body of your paper, you might have an idea for an introduction or conclusion. Your writing evolves. Your revision stage can be part of your drafting stage. Read your paper aloud to yourself. Check for spelling and mechanics. Have another student read your work during the revision phase. Proofread your paper, make corrections, and write your final copy.

Tips for Your Own Writing:

- Know whether your purpose is to explain, describe, or convince.
- Select a topic; it may help to cluster ideas you get from reading, observing, or watching television.
- Connect ideas and details within a cluster. If you need to, read about the topic for further details.
- Draft the ideas in your cluster by writing them as sentences and paragraphs.
- Revise with the help of a friend; proofread, revise, and proofread again.

 The more you write, the better you get at it.

Writer's Handbook

Getting Ideas

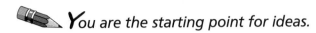 *You are the starting point for ideas.*

Did You Know?

The best source of ideas comes from you. However, you may need a *push* to get you started. Look for ideas and then revert back to what **you** like best or are most interested in. When you write, always consider your resources.

There are many resources to consider when you write; however, your own experiences can bring an outlook to your topic unmatched by any other resource. The key is to choose a topic that you know or would like to know more about. When you know the subject well, you can focus your writing and describe details more distinctly. Brainstorm or cluster special hobbies, talents or skills, travel or other experiences, and people you know. They are good subjects for writing. Experiences, impressions, and perceptions that you have had are the best material for writing. There are lists of topics and ideas in your writing folder that you haven't used.

Imagine a story you would like to write. If you need more information, go to the library or glance through newspapers or magazines. As you preview the information, make a list of topics that interest you. Go through books. Pay attention to the table of contents. Watch information channels on television. The news is a good source of ideas. Again, take notes. Eventually, write down all the ideas and information you gained from previewing the different resources.

Think about your purpose, explore your topic, come up with a narrowed topic, gather material for the details, and decide on who your audience will be and how to appeal to that audience. Develop some sort of method for organizing your information.

Getting ideas involves deciding upon a general topic, and then limiting, or narrowing, that general topic. Then you need to gather details. Go to the library. Brainstorm or cluster by yourself or with others. Make a list of ideas. Group your ideas under related headings. Drop ideas that don't seem to fit in anywhere. Not only do you have ideas, but you now have details that are somewhat organized.

Tips for Your Own Writing:

• Tap your greatest resource by imagining what might happen if . . ., or by thinking about special hobbies, talents or skills, travel or other experiences, and people you know.
• Go to the library and read books, magazines, and newspapers, or watch television for ideas.

Brainstorming and clustering not only help you gather ideas but also help you organize those ideas.

Writer's Handbook

Writing a Paragraph

Writing is a building process. Paragraphs are building blocks just like words and sentences.

Did You Know?

A sentence is a group of words that has a subject and a verb. The verb indicates past, present, or future tense. A paragraph is a group of sentences that belongs together. When you begin a new idea or paragraph, start on a new line and indent the first word several spaces from the left margin like the first word in this paragraph you are reading. A composition is a group of paragraphs about one topic. Sometimes a composition is so short that it is only one paragraph long. No matter how many paragraphs you write, you develop them in the same way unless you are writing dialogue in a story. Remember, all sentences in the paragraph have a close relationship to each other.

First, determine whether your purpose is to entertain, explain, describe, or convince. Second, develop your main idea according to a specific order. Your sentences may be written according to **time, space,** or **order of importance.** Words used to show order include *first, last, second, next, finally, then, tomorrow, before, after, least, smallest,* or *most importantly.*

A paragraph may consist of an introductory sentence that tells the main idea. Supporting sentences add details. The concluding sentence of a composition usually draws together the supporting details and restates the main idea.

Once you know your purpose and order, write smooth-flowing, supporting sentences. They give details, reasons, examples, or likenesses and/or differences.

Details help the reader form a clearer picture. See how the details help you picture Robin's skateboard:

Robin enjoys her new skateboard.

Robin enjoys her shiny red skateboard with the turned-up, pointed front.

Robin taught her puppy tricks by using praise and treats.

Reasons are used when the writer wants to persuade the reader. Sometimes writers show how their topic is like something the reader knows. Vocabulary used to show likenesses includes *also, just as, in the same manner, resembles,* and *similarly.* To develop a paragraph that shows differences, you might include words like *by contrast, on the other hand, unlike, on the contrary,* and *but.*

Tips for Your Own Writing:

- Know your purpose and make your writing fit that purpose.
- Organize sentences or paragraphs by using some type of order.
- Support the topic with details, reasons, or examples.

 Build a paragraph with purpose, order, and details.

Writer's Handbook

4

Staying on Topic

Besides a narrowed topic, knowing your purpose and audience helps you stay on topic.

·· Did You Know? ·····································

If you narrow your subject by clustering, it will not be difficult to stay on topic. Cluster, cluster, cluster! Cluster to find your general topic; cluster to find your narrowed topic; cluster to find the details. This will help your writing be more focused. Once you have a specific subject in mind, decide whether your purpose is to describe, inform, persuade, or entertain. That type of planning helps you stick with your topic. Determining the audience you are writing for will also help you remain on topic.

To stay on topic, think in terms of the whole picture and then parts of that picture. In a one-paragraph composition, the whole picture is the one main idea. The parts of that picture are the sentences that support that one idea. The final sentence completes or ends your piece.

The whole picture of a composition is its subject or main idea. The parts of that picture include the paragraphs that support that one idea. Each paragraph contains reasons, examples, details, or facts. The sentences in the paragraphs are also parts of the bigger picture. Clustering will help you come up with the details for those sentences. Don't forget to eliminate and add details to that cluster. Connect ideas that relate to each other. An introduction and a conclusion will help your subject be even more unified and organized.

One test to determine whether you have stayed on topic is to ask yourself, "What is the main idea of this paragraph?" Read each sentence and ask yourself, "Does this sentence give a reason, example, detail, or fact that directly relates to the main idea of the paragraph?"

Another test to help you stay on topic involves remembering the Ws of writing: *who, what, where, when,* and *why*. Answering those questions will help you identify some very basic information related only to your topic. It will help even more if you add *how* to that list.

Tips for Your Own Writing:··

- Narrow your general subject by clustering.
- Select the purpose and audience for your writing.
- Continue to cluster to support the different areas of your topic with details.
- Ask yourself *who, what, where, when, why* and *how,* and you will identify very basic information that relates only to your subject.
- Ask yourself *why* about your subject until you completely run out of answers.

Getting details by asking who, what, where, when, why *and* how *about your topic helps you stay on topic.*

Lesson 5 Writer's Handbook Proofreading Checklist

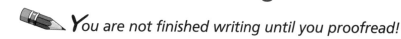 *You are not finished writing until you proofread!*

·············· **Did You Know?** ·····························

Sometimes you think you wrote one thing but actually did not. This makes it difficult for you to find mistakes in your own writing. You read what you meant to say rather than the actual words on the page. It helps to put the writing away overnight. This gives your brain time to forget what you wrote. Later, you will be able to see the words that are actually on the page. It helps to read your work aloud, word for word. Listen to see whether it makes sense. Try to identify missing or extra words. Read your work again, silently. Look carefully for mistakes in punctuation, spelling, and grammar. Find punctuation mistakes by reading the sentences aloud and backwards. Start with the last sentence, then read the next-to-last sentence, and so on. If what you read doesn't sound like a sentence, check the punctuation. The inside back cover of this book lists proofreading marks you can use to mark mistakes.

Proofread for mistakes in spelling, punctuation, capitalization, and verb usage. It is best to check your work for no more than two items at a time. Be sure that your composition is clear, unified, and complete.

The paragraph below shows how to use proofreading marks.

Would I make the team or wo^{ul}d the coach pick someone else?that was the question. I^knew that Ben, Lamar, and Carlos had all ready been chosen Was I next? Just then Jana came and stood in the doorway of the gym. she seemed to ^{be}looking for someone. I hopped she was looking for me, but I didn't want her to see me me fail. What pressure!

Tips for Your Own Writing: ···························

Your proofreading checklist:

I. Mechanics
   A. Spelling
   B. Capitalization
      1. Start all sentences with a capital letter including sentences inside dialogue.
      2. Capitalize specific names of people, places, and things.
   C. Punctuation
      1. Punctuate the end of each sentence properly.
      2. Place commas in compound sentences and in items listed in a series.
      3. Punctuate dialogue or conversation with quotation marks and commas.
II. Usage
   A. Verify your use of commonly mixed words.
   B. Check for correct usage of verbs and plurals.
Read your writing to make sure the meaning is clear, unified, and complete.

 *Proofread with a passion!*

Writer's Handbook

Stories

You can make your story characters seem real through description!

Did You Know?

Every story needs a problem to be met and dealt with or solved, a setting, and interesting characters. It should also have a beginning, a middle, and an end. Actually, the most important part of many stories is the characters. You want readers to care about your characters or people (or sometimes animals). You write about characters in three ways: by what the character says and does; by what other characters say about the character; and by what you, the writer, show us about the character.

Good writers show; they don't tell. See the difference below in telling what a character is like and showing what a character is like.

How a character—	Telling	Showing
Looked:	He was strong.	Muscles bulged under his shirt.
Felt:	He felt sad.	A dark cloud seemed to have fallen over him.
Acted:	She was friendly.	She smiled and waved every time she saw me.
Talked:	She said a car was coming.	She screamed, "Watch out for that car!"

Write so your reader knows what the characters look like, say, do, think, and feel. The best way to do this is to include sensory details that draw upon any of the five senses— sight, sound, smell, touch, and even taste. Help the reader experience the situation just as the character did. Bring your characters to life. "The outside of the spacecraft looked bad" is not as descriptive as "The outside of the spacecraft was scorched and scratched."

The setting of a story is the time (the "when") and place (the "where") of the story. The reader can visualize the setting when you describe it well.

What happens in a story is the plot, or plan. Most likely, the beginning contains a problem of some kind, and the ending has a solution. The solution may be that there is no solution, but at least the character or characters have gained a new insight about the situation. The plot is the heart of the story. Think of an interesting or funny problem, then think of a solution. Don't forget to explain and develop the events or episodes of the story in the proper sequence. That would be the middle of your story. It helps to show the reader a clear connection between the problem, the main character, and the character's feelings.

Tips for Your Own Writing:

- Each story has characters, setting (time and place), and plan, or plot.
- The plan, or plot, of the story has a beginning, a middle, and an end.
- Develop a character by what the character says and does, what other characters say about the character, and/or what you, the writer, tell us about the character.
- Use sensory words and details to describe a character.

Help your reader know the characters and experience what they experience through the use of sensory words and details of sight, sound, smell, touch, and even taste.

Writer's Handbook

7 Expository Writing–Planning a Report

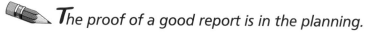 *The proof of a good report is in the planning.*

.... Did You Know? ....

Expository reports give information about a subject using description, facts, or examples. Reports inform and explain. In a report that informs, the writer gives information about a topic. In a report that explains, the writer explains how to do something. Once you have chosen a narrowed topic and decided whether you need to inform or explain, make a K-W-L chart.

K- What I **K**now	W- What I **W**ant to Know	L- What I Have **L**earned

First, list all the things you know about your topic in the **K** column. Next, list all the questions you have about your topic under the **W** column. Then, research the topic. List the most important things you learned about your topic in the **L** column.

Take notes regarding the subject. If you want, you may use note cards. Put one fact or detail on a card with a note as to the source of the information. Add as much information as necessary in case you need to find the source again.

Review all your note cards once again. Choose the fact or detail that you find most interesting, and use that as your main idea. Go through your note cards again, and choose the facts and details that support your main idea. Eliminate unnecessary notes.

Sort cards into three or four categories. Those categories will be the main points of your report. If your teacher requires an outline, these main points may be used as the main headings of your outline. Write each main point on a different piece of paper with one main point at the top of each piece. Each main point should support your main topic. Arrange the note cards in some sort of logical order. Next, write under each main point all the notes from the cards that support the main idea on the top of the paper. Write each note in the proper order. Work with one paper and one stack of note cards at a time. In the next lesson, you will, one at a time, draft or shape the details and facts from each piece of paper into paragraphs. You have done most of the difficult work in the planning stage of your report.

Tips for Your Own Writing:...

- Choose a topic and narrow it according to Lessons 1 and 2.
- Gather facts and details by reading and taking notes about your topic.
- Choose the most interesting fact as your main point.
- Arrange notes in a logical order to support your main idea.
- Draft details and facts into paragraphs.

Narrowing and organizing your topic is an immense help when writing an expository report.

Writer's Handbook
Expository Writing–Writing a Report

After you finish your research and organize your notes, it is time to write your first draft.

·············· Did You Know? ··············

In Lesson 7, you were asked to organize your notes in some logical order and then to write them on one of three or four pieces of paper with one main idea at the top of each piece. Next, look at the notes on that paper and decide how to organize the information. Here are three possible choices:

1. **Time order:** Use this approach if you are writing about something that happened over time, such as a war, a famous person's life, the life cycle of an animal, or changes in climate. You will describe the events in the order they happened.

2. **Order of importance:** This is a good approach if you are writing about the causes of something (such as allergies), the uses of something (such as gold), or a scientist's inventions. Start with the most important item and go to the least important items.

3. **Problem-cause-solution:** This approach is helpful for topics such as ways to avoid skin cancer, better ways to distribute the world's food, ways to save energy, or ways to solve another problem. Describe the problem, explain the cause, and end with the solution.

Work with one piece of paper at a time. That is, work with one main idea at a time. Organize the notes in the order of your choice, and draft sentences and paragraphs with the examples, facts, or details from those notes. After writing all the paragraphs, draft an introduction and a conclusion. Remember, this is merely a draft; it can be revised at any time. Go through your paper to determine whether any part of it needs more development. If so, add more details, facts, or examples in the margins. You may decide to use carets (∧) where you want to insert new information and write it at the bottom of the page. Delete parts that do not support or relate to the main idea or the main points. Add charts or illustrations if needed. Use your proofreading list from Lesson 5 to proofread your paper, and ask someone to review your paper. Make revisions again before writing your final copy. Proofread one more time, and your report is finished.

Tips for Your Own Writing:·····················

- Decide whether to organize your report by **time, importance, problem-cause-solution,** or some other type of order, and arrange your notes accordingly.
- Keep in mind the main idea listed at the top of each paper, and draft sentences and paragraph(s) using the examples, facts, or details from your notes.
- Draft an introduction and conclusion for your report.
- Revise the paper by deleting or adding information.
- Proofread, revise, write your final copy, and proofread again.

Choose a way to organize your report before you write your first draft.

9

Writer's Handbook

Writing a Persuasive Composition

To effectively persuade, first determine what you believe about an issue and who you are trying to persuade.

Did You Know?

When you write a composition, you are putting together a written message. The message in a **persuasive** composition is that you want to *coax* or talk someone into believing or acting a certain way. Write a letter to that person asking them to let you do something. Your letter is a form of persuasive writing.

In a persuasive composition, first decide **what** you want to talk someone into doing or believing. Narrow your topic as you have learned to do in Lessons 1, 2, and 4. Next, think **who** your audience or readers will be. Will your composition be read only by your peers or by adults?

Gather evidence to support your belief, or gather evidence and then formulate an opinion. Evidence includes **facts and information.** A **fact** can be proved and checked. On the other hand, an **opinion** is a belief or feeling. It cannot be proved or checked.

Fact: Northville city government plans to tear down the old school.
(If you check with city officials, they will tell you that they do plan to tear down the school.)

Opinion: The old school is very beautiful, and it should be preserved. (That is your opinion as a writer. Not everyone would agree with you.)

You need to learn about your subject to make a convincing argument. Go to the library and read, interview people, or write for information to gather evidence. Determine *why* you believe what you do about your subject. Make note of your source if necessary. Sometimes noting your source strengthens your argument. It backs up your opinion with the opinions of authorities.

Organize your notes or ideas in a specific order. Write a conclusion and include a general statement that can be logically drawn from the information you have collected. Your conclusion needs to be supported by the evidence you have gathered.

Now draft the remainder of the composition. The introduction needs to present your position with a strong statement about your stand on the issue. The body of the composition simply supports your position with clear reasons, facts, and examples as to *why* you believe as you do.

You have completed your first draft. Revise and edit your paper. Ask someone to help you edit it. Revise as many times as necessary. Proofread your final copy.

Tips for Your Own Writing:

- Decide **what** you want someone else to believe or do, and **who** you want to convince.
- Gather evidence and learn more about your topic.
- Ideas are organized as to how they support your position.
- The introduction presents your position with a strong statement on the issue.
- The conclusion makes a general statement that is supported by the evidence.

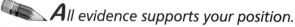 *All evidence supports your position.*

Writer's Handbook
Word Lists

....

VERBS: Forms of some irregular verbs.

PRESENT Today I...	PAST Yesterday I...	PAST PARTICIPLE I have...
★be	★was/were	★been
become/becomes	became	become
begin/begins	began	begun
burn/burns	burned/burnt	burned/burnt
burst	burst	burst
dive/dives	dived/dove	dived
drink/drinks	drank	drunk
forget/forgets	forgot	forgotten/forgot
lay/lays	laid	laid
lead/leads	led	led
lend/lends	lent	lent
lie (recline)/lies	lay	lain
lose/loses	lost	lost
rise/rises	rose	risen
see/sees	saw	seen
shake/shakes	shook	shaken
strike/strikes	struck	struck/stricken
swim/swims	swam	swum

★conjugation of *to be*:	**Singular** I **am** you **are** he, she, *or* it **is**	**Plural** we **are** you **are** they **are**

VIVID VERBS

absorb	ebb	inspect	praise	sandbag	smack
bolt	glance	laud	rattle	scream	swoop
decline	glare	peek	rip	screech	zoom

ADJECTIVES

beaming	dark	featherbrained	inviting	quizzical
beefy	deceitful	glossy	lustrous	sinister
bulky	enchanting	immense	magnificent	vast
curious	engrossing	intriguing	moldy	wicked

PREPOSITIONS: Below is a partial list of some common prepositions.

aboard	considering	from between	in place of	outside
alongside	despite	from under	inside	over to
away from	down from	in addition to	instead of	regarding
behind	except for	in behalf of	on account of	underneath
besides	from among	in front of	on behalf of	within

Writer's Handbook

Postal State and Possession Abbreviations

Use these abbreviations on envelopes to be read by postal workers. In other writing, spell out the names of the states.

States

Alabama	AL
Alaska	AK
Arizona	AZ
Arkansas	AR
California	CA
Colorado	CO
Connecticut	CT
Delaware	DE
Florida	FL
Georgia	GA
Hawaii	HI
Idaho	ID
Illinois	IL
Indiana	IN
Iowa	IA
Kansas	KS
Kentucky	KY
Louisiana	LA
Maine	ME
Maryland	MD
Massachusetts	MA
Michigan	MI
Minnesota	MN
Mississippi	MS
Missouri	MO
Montana	MT
Nebraska	NE
Nevada	NV
New Hampshire	NH
New Jersey	NJ
New Mexico	NM
New York	NY
North Carolina	NC
North Dakota	ND
Ohio	OH
Oklahoma	OK
Oregon	OR
Pennsylvania	PA
Rhode Island	RI
South Carolina	SC
South Dakota	SD
Tennessee	TN
Texas	TX
Utah	UT
Vermont	VT
Virginia	VA
Washington	WA
West Virginia	WV
Wisconsin	WI
Wyoming	WY
District of Columbia	DC

U.S. Possessions

American Samoa	AS
Guam	GU
Puerto Rico	PR
Virgin Islands	VI

SPECTRUM

Language Arts

Grade 6
Answer Key

Lesson 1

Lesson 1 — Capitalization: Sentences, Titles, Days, Months, People

To capitalize or not to capitalize? Writers need to know how to answer this question about the words they write.

.... Did You Know? ....

The first word of a sentence is capitalized.

Please sign your name on the line at the bottom.

The names of people and pets are capitalized. So are people's initials and titles.

David Jacobson   Buck   Mr. Alfonso Garcia, Jr.

Words used to name relatives are capitalized *only* when the words are used as names or as part of names. They are not capitalized when preceded by a possessive pronoun, such as *my, your,* or *his*.

Will **D**ad pick up **M**other at the train station?
I like staying with my grandmother.

The names of days, months, and holidays are capitalized, but the names of seasons are not.

On **M**onday, **M**arch 12, Sasha will interview the mayor.
Our family always has a picnic on Independence **D**ay.

The pronoun *I* is capitalized.

Michael and **I** went to the video store.

Show What You Know
Circle the twenty-three letters that should be capitalized.

(G)alileo was an Italian astronomer and physicist. (H)e was born in Italy on (F)ebruary 15, 1564. (I)n 1609 (G)alileo built his first telescope. (I) heard about (G)alileo when (I) went to a planetarium with my father. (T)he guide also talked about the (E)dwin (H) (H)ubble Space Telescope, which was released on (S)unday, (A)pril 15, 1990. (H)e spoke of the mission that made repairs on the telescope in 1993. (C)ol. (R)ichard (O) (C)ovey and (D) (K) (N)an (D)avis were part of the crew that repaired the telescope.

Score: _____   Total Possible: 23

6

Proofread
Read the newspaper article. The writer left out 32 capital letters. Use the proper proofreading mark to show which letters should be capitalized.

Example: tuesday, april 5

Pet Party a Huge Success

On saturday, october 21, mr. and mrs. Howard c. jahn, jr., hosted an unusual event at their home to benefit a local animal shelter. they invited their friends to a costume party and competition—for their pets! Dozens of animals came to the party dressed as everything from donald duck to sherlock holmes. the Jahns' dog dodger, outfitted as count dracula, greeted the guests. First prize went to dr. caroline t. Sturgis's cockatoo claude for his Batman costume. "claude is very honored—i think," said Dr. sturgis. The jahns' nephew, mr. sidney K. abert, accompanied by his cat delilah, said, "This is the best party that uncle Howard and aunt Stella have had since New year's eve."

Practice
Imagine that you have just met this girl and her dog. Write a short paragraph describing the meeting.

Review the paragraph to be sure your child has:

• capitalized all names.

• capitalized the pronoun *I*.

• capitalized the first word of every sentence.

• written a paragraph that makes sense and relates to the topic.

Tips for Your Own Writing: Proofreading ....
Choose something you have written recently. Check your writing, asking yourself this question: Did I capitalize the first word in every sentence, all names, and the pronoun *I*?

Was the answer to the question "Yes"? Capital!

7

Lesson 2

Lesson 2 — Capitalization: Places, Documents, Groups

Check the capitals—Declaration of Independence (document) for Americans (people) in Washington's White House (places).

.... Did You Know? ....

The names of specific places and things—cities, states, countries, divisions of the world, regions of the United States, streets, parks, and buildings—begin with a capital letter.

He flew from **B**oston, **M**assachusetts, to **P**aris, **F**rance.
The **W**hite **H**ouse is located at 1600 **P**ennsylvania **A**venue.

The names of historic documents begin with a capital letter.

The **M**agna **C**arta was written in 1215.

The names of races, nationalities, religions, and languages begin with a capital letter.

Many **C**ubans speak **S**panish and **E**nglish.

Show What You Know
Read the paragraph. On the lines, write the names that should have capital letters. Be sure to capitalize the words when you write them.

José Ubico was born in el salvador, a small country in central america. Ten years ago, he came to the united states, fleeing from the war in his homeland. José settled in los angeles where other salvadorans lived. José, who spoke spanish, learned english as well. One summer he went to washington, d. c., to see its many historic sights. His favorites were the jefferson memorial and the national archives museum where he saw copies of the constitution and the bill of rights.

1. El Salvador
2. Central America
3. United States
4. Los Angeles
5. Salvadorans
6. Spanish
7. English
8. Washington, D. C.
9. Jefferson Memorial
10. National Archives Museum
11. Constitution
12. Bill of Rights

Score: _____   Total Possible: 12

8

Proofread
Here is part of an essay about a world-famous building. The writer forgot to capitalize fifteen words. Use the proper proofreading mark to show which letters should be capitalized.

Example: south america

Every year, people from all over the world—americans, Japanese, british, chinese—come to see the taj mahal. It was built on the jumna River in agra, india, by Shah Jahan, the mogul emperor of India (1592–1666). The domed, white marble building is both an islamic monument and a tomb for the emperor's beloved queen, Mumtaz Mahal.

During his reign, Shah Jahan expanded india's territory in the far east. He also made islam the state religion and placed the country's capital in Delhi. But today he is remembered for constructing one of the world's most beautiful buildings—the Taj mahal.

Practice
Look at or imagine a map of your state. Choose a place that you think is interesting, unusual, or fun. Write a short paragraph telling about the place. Explain why a visitor to your state should plan to see this place.

Review the paragraph to be sure your child has:

• written about a place located in your state.

• given reasons why someone should visit the place.

• capitalized the names of specific places and things.

Tips for Your Own Writing: Proofreading ....
Choose a piece of your own writing and give it to a partner to proofread while you proofread your partner's paper. Look for the names of places and things. Check to see whether your partner capitalized the names. Use proofreading marks to show what should be changed.

Remember ... a name always wears a cap! A capital letter, that is.

9

Lesson 3

Lesson 3 Capitalization: Titles

Just as names of people are capitalized, names or titles of books and other materials are also capitalized.

.... Did You Know? ....

The first, last, and key words in the title of a book, magazine, movie, play, story, report, poem, painting, or song are capitalized.

The articles *a*, *an*, and *the*; the conjunctions *and*, *or*, *nor*, and *but*; and short prepositions such as *at*, *in*, and *of* are not capitalized unless they are the first or last words of the title. Notice that the titles of books, magazines, movies, and plays are italicized. When handwritten, these titles are underlined.

> Jayne's favorite book is *A Wrinkle in Time*.
> My mother likes to read the magazine *The New Yorker*.
> Last night we watched the movie *Close Encounters of the Third Kind*.
> A local theater group put on the play *A Raisin in the Sun*.
> Henry read aloud the story "The Fox and the Crow."
> The title of my report is "Lincoln as a Country Lawyer."
> Tanya memorized the poem "Stopping by Woods on a Snowy Evening."
> The painting "House by the Railroad" is by Edward Hopper.
> The entire chorus joined in the song "Oh, What a Beautiful Morning!"

....

Show What You Know
Circle each word that should begin with a capital letter.

the kids world almanac of baseball
sarah plain and tall
under a telephone pole
raiders of the lost ark
nothing gold can stay

the little house on the prairie
tales and legends of india
ramona and the three wise persons
born on the fourth of july
song of the open road

Score: _____ Total Possible: 35

10

Proofread
Here is part of an article about how to write a report. The writer did not properly capitalize the nine titles in the article. Use the proper proofreading mark to show which letters should be capitalized.

Example: "the fall of the house of usher"

where to find information

After seeing the painting "a woman in Black at the opera," you have decided to write your report on the artist Mary Cassatt and call it "an american artist in Paris." You have some general information about Cassatt from encyclopedias, such as *world book* or *Encyclopaedia britannica*. Now, where else should you look? Read any books about the artist, such as *an american impressionist* or *mary cassatt*. Check the indexes of magazines, such as *art and history* and *American artists*, that might have articles about her.

Practice
What is your favorite book or movie? Write a short summary of the book or movie and then explain why you like it. Give your paragraph a title. Remember to underline the title of the book or movie in the summary.

Review the paragraph to be sure your child has:

• written about a book or movie.

• summarized the book or movie.

• offered reasons why he or she liked the book or movie.

• written a title for the paragraph.

• capitalized the title of the book or movie correctly.

• capitalized the title of the paragraph correctly.

• underlined the title of the book or movie.

Tips for Your Own Writing: Proofreading
Look at several pieces of your own writing. Do they have titles? Did you use any titles within the copy? Check to see whether you capitalized the titles correctly.

Titles name books or other materials. Capitalize the key words in their names.

11

Lesson 4

Lesson 4 Capitalization: Direct Quotations

The first word of what I say is always capitalized. But if what I say is in parts, then it's a case of sometimes a capital and sometimes no capital.

.... Did You Know? ....

A direct quotation shows a person's words. A writer puts quotation marks before and after the quotation. The first word in the quotation is always capitalized.

> "This award is a great honor," said Ms. Tannoy.
> She exclaimed, "No one was more surprised than I was."

In a divided quotation, words such as *she said*, called speaker's tags, are in the middle of the quotation. The first word in the first part of the quotation is always capitalized. But the first word in the second part is capitalized *only* if it begins a new sentence.

> "This award is a great honor," said Ms. Tannoy. "Thank you for giving it to me."
> "This award," said Ms. Tannoy, "is a great honor."

....

Show What You Know
Read the sentences. Circle the twelve words that should begin with a capital letter.

Cara asked, "so what are we going to do our group report on?"

"i think," said Wayne, "we should do our report on the Squealing Wheels."

"oh no," groaned Ahmed, "not that awful rock group again!"

"the Wheels are great," Wayne insisted. "they've had three number-one hits."

"let's vote," Cara interrupted. "all those for the Squealing Wheels? All those against? Okay, no Wheels. Any other suggestions?"

"if we want to do a music topic," Rachel offered, "how about focusing on a particular trend, like the return to acoustic recordings?"

"that's a good idea," said Cara. "what do you guys think?"

"it's okay, with me," said Ahmed, "if it's okay, with Wayne."

Wayne grumbled, "yeah, all right. But I still say the Wheels are the best."

Score: _____ Total Possible: 12

12

Proofread
Here are some famous quotations. They are missing six capital letters. Use the proper proofreading mark to show which letters should be capitalized.

Example: Eleanor Roosevelt said, "no one can make you feel inferior without your consent."

1. "and so, my fellow Americans," said John F. Kennedy, "ask not what your country can do for you; ask what you can do for your country."

2. Gertrude Stein said, "a rose is a rose is a rose."

3. "what's in a name?" asked Romeo. "that which we call a rose by any other name would smell as sweet."

4. "always do right," said Mark Twain. "This will gratify some people and astonish the rest."

5. "in spite of everything, I still believe," Anne Frank said, "that people are really good at heart."

Practice
Work with a partner. Think of three questions to ask each other. Write your partner's answers as direct quotations. Try writing one of the answers as a divided quotation. When both of you are finished, check each other's writing for correct capitalization.

Review the answers to be sure your child has:

• written each answer as a direct quotation.

• written one answer as a divided direct quotation.

• used capital letters in quotations correctly.

Tips for Your Own Writing: Proofreading
The next time you write a story, make sure to write a conversation for two or more of your characters. Capitalize the first word in each quotation and the first word in the second part of a divided quotation when it begins a new sentence.

What do sentences and quotations have in common? Their first words are always capped.

13

Lesson 5

Lesson

5 Capitalization: Friendly and Business Letters

The first words in certain parts of letters, such as greetings and closings, need capital letters.

.... **Did You Know?** ....

There are two kinds of letters: friendly letters and business letters. Each kind of letter has its own form, but both letters have a greeting and a closing. The first word in a greeting is capitalized. So are any names or titles used in the greeting. Only the first word in a closing is capitalized.

Friendly Letter	Business Letter

Friendly Letter

1296 Meadow Drive
Glenview, IL 60025
August 17, 2000

Dear **T**eresa,
 I have been home for a week, but it seems much longer! I really miss you and Rico. I had such a good time staying at your ranch.

 Your friend,
 Carolina

Business Letter

1296 Meadow Drive
Glenview, IL 60025
December 2, 2000

Appleby, Incorporated
1348 Forest Avenue
Houston, TX 77069

Dear **S**ir or **M**adam:
 I am returning the sweater you sent. I ordered a Large and received a Small. Please send me the correct size.

 Sincerely yours,
 Carolina Ramirez
 Carolina Ramirez

Show What You Know

Circle each word that should begin with a capital letter.

1. (dear) (aunt) (catherine)
2. (your) patient cousin,
3. (hope) to hear from you soon,
4. (dear) (mr.) (oglethorpe)
5. (sincerely)
6. (dear) (customer) (service) (department)
7. (yours) truly,

Score: _____   Total Possible: 14

14

Proofread

Here are two short friendly letters. There are five missing capital letters in each. Use the proper proofreading mark to show which letters should be capitalized.

Example: My aunt kathy will arrive in may.

129 Wickam Way
Hillville, NJ 08505
April 28, 2000

dear uncle fred,
 mom told me that you fell down the back steps and sprained your ankle. I'm sending you several of my favorite books to help pass the time.

 your nephew,
 Wilson

4490 Main Street
Weston, IA 50201
may 4, 2000

dear wilson,
 The books arrived, and i have already read one. Thank you for thinking of me. A sprained ankle is painful and boring!

 love,
 Uncle Fred

Practice

Think of a school or community problem. Write a letter to the editor of your local paper explaining the problem and your solutions to the problem. Write a draft of the body of your letter on the lines below. Then, using the business form, write the entire letter on a separate sheet of paper.

Review the letter to be sure your child has:

• written a letter to the editor.

• described a problem.

• offered solutions to the problem.

• used the business form for the letter.

• capitalized the appropriate words in the greeting and closing.

Tips for Your Own Writing: Proofreading ....

Look at a letter or note you have written recently. Check to see that you capitalized the appropriate words in the greeting and closing.

A phone call is nice, but a letter is better!

15

Lesson 6

Lesson

6 Review: Capitalization

A. Use the proper proofreading mark to fix thirty missing capital letters.

 last saturday, which was august 23, my brother bill married suzanne. it's about time, too, because everyone has been working on that wedding since valentine's day! my sister jenny was the maid of honor, and i was an usher. it was hot, crowded, and uncomfortable. when rev. benson finally introduced mr. and mrs. william j. krupski, i wanted to cheer. of course, mom was crying, but then so were dad, aunt shirley, uncle dave, and lots of other people. maybe they were just glad it was over, as i was!

Score: _____   Total Possible: 30

B. Use the proper proofreading mark to show fifteen words (names of places, buildings, groups, religions) that should begin with capital letters.

 In northwest cambodia, not far from its border with thailand, lies the ruined city of angkor. From about 880 to about 1225, angkor was the capital of the mighty Khmer Empire. The city has several temple complexes, all larger than the egyptian pyramids, that were built to honor hindu gods. The greatest of these temples is angkor wat. Its vast stone walls are covered with scenes from hindu mythology. Angkor was abandoned about 1434, and the capital was moved to phnom penh. Rediscovered by french missionaries in the 1860s and now regarded as one of southeast asia's great masterpieces, Angkor has begun to attract many tourists from the west.

Score: _____   Total Possible: 15

C. Write the titles from the title and paragraph below in the blanks on the following page, adding capital letters where they are needed. If the title is in italics, also underline it.

 that versatile writer: edgar allan poe

 Edgar Allan Poe wrote his first book *tamerlane and other poems* in 1827 when he was 18. He soon began writing fiction. Five of his stories were published in a newspaper, the *philadelphia saturday courier*, and a sixth story won a $50 prize. Poe then became editor of a magazine, the *southern literary messenger*. His story "the murders in the rue morgue" is considered to be the first classic detective story. Some of his poems, such as "the raven," are still well-known today.

16

---

1. That Versatile Writer: Edgar Allan Poe
2. Tamerlane and Other Poems
3. Philadelphia Saturday Courier
4. Southern Literary Messenger
5. "The Murders in the Rue Morgue"
6. "The Raven"

Score: _____   Total Possible: 6

D. Use the proper proofreading mark to add five capital letters where needed.

"senator Brock," the reporter asked, "do you know Hiram M. Douglas?"

"no, I do not," said Senator Brock. "the name is unknown to me."

"but look at this picture," insisted the reporter. "isn't that you and Douglas?"

Score: _____   Total Possible: 5

E. Use the proper proofreading mark under five lowercase letters that should be capitalized.

1422 Bristol Road
Columbus, OH 43221
may 22, 2000

dear kaitlin,
 thank you for the birthday present. It was very clever of you to remember how much I liked Tina Weems's CD *Sweet Weems* and to give me a copy of my own. Isn't Tina supposed to have a new CD next month?

 your friend,
 Tyesha

Score: _____   Total Possible: 5

REVIEW SCORE: _____   REVIEW TOTAL: 61

17

Lesson 7

Lesson 7 — Punctuation: Sentences, Abbreviations, and Initials

Periods can be used to end a sentence, but they also let you know that a word is an abbreviation. That little dot is a valuable mark.

.... Did You Know? ....

A period is used at the end of a sentence that makes a statement.

Football is a popular sport.

A period is used after abbreviations for titles, the months of the year, and the days of the week.

Doctor—Dr.   Mister—Mr.   Senator—Sen.
October—Oct.   January—Jan.   December—Dec.
Friday—Fri.   Wednesday—Wed.   Monday—Mon.

A period is used after initials in names.

Susan Brownell Anthony—Susan **B.** Anthony
Booker Taliaferro Washington—Booker **T.** Washington

Show What You Know

Read the paragraph below. First, add periods at ends of sentences where needed. Then, change each bold word to an initial or abbreviation by adding a period and drawing a line through the unnecessary letters. Circle each period.

Early on **Saturday**, the first of **November**, Joseph **Andrew** Simon got into his car. Mr. Simon is a teacher at Lyndon **Baines** Johnson High School. Every **Monday** and **Wednesday** in September and October, he taught exercise classes for some heart patients of Dr. **Pablo** Gonzalez These classes were held at Dwight **David** Eisenhower Elementary School The classes were so popular that other programs hired him. Every **Tuesday** and **Thursday** morning, he worked at Gerald **Rudolph** Ford University **Professor** Althea **Jane** Perkins sponsored the program. **Senator** Gutierrez and **Reverend** Tanaka participated in that class Now each Saturday in November and **December**, Mr. Simon will be coaching a wheelchair basketball team in the James **Francis** Thorpe fieldhouse.

Score: _____   Total Possible: 23

18

Proofread

Read these notes for a report. Use proper proofreading marks to add nine missing periods.

Example: Dr. Bashir

Margaret H. Thatcher was born on Oct. 13, 1925. Mr. and Mrs. Alfred Roberts were her parents. The family lived in Grantham, Lincolnshire, England. After graduating, Margaret became a tax attorney and eventually was elected to Parliament in 1959. Becoming a member of Parliament is similar to being a senator in the United States government. Margaret Thatcher became the first woman leader of Britain's Conservative Party on Feb. 11, 1975. Four years later on May 3, 1979, she was elected Prime Minister. She resigned that post in Nov. of 1990.

Practice

Write notes to summarize the events of the school week. Write your notes in complete sentences, and use abbreviations when possible.

1. _____   Review the notes to be sure your child has:
   • put a period at the end of each sentence.
2. _____   • put a period after each initial.
   • put a period after each abbreviation.
3. _____
4. _____   • written notes that make sense and relate to the topic.
5. _____

Tips for Your Own Writing: Proofreading ....

Look for lists, notes, and other informal writing you have done. Check your writing to make sure you put a period at the end of sentences that are statements, and after initials, abbreviations, and each title.

Remember . . . periods put an end to statements and abbreviations.

19

Lesson 8

Lesson 8 — Punctuation: Other Abbreviations

Don't be fooled—there are some abbreviations that do not use periods!

.... Did You Know? ....

Two-letter postal abbreviations for state names do not have periods. See page 160 for a complete list.

Tennessee—TN   California—CA
Idaho—ID   New York—NY

Abbreviations for metric measurements do not have periods.

meter—m   kilogram—kg   milliliter—mL
liter—L   gram—g   kilometer—km

Initials for the names of organizations or companies do not use periods.

American Broadcasting Companies—ABC
Boy Scouts of America—BSA

Some terms that are made up of more than one word are known by their initials. These do not use periods.

videocassette recorder—VCR
gross national product—GNP

Show What You Know

Write the abbreviations or initials for the following items.

1. Indiana _IN_
2. milligram _mg_
3. Texas _TX_
4. centimeter _cm_
5. Illinois _IL_
6. Nevada _NV_
7. Maine _ME_
8. Washington _WA_
9. kiloliter _kl_
10. Florida _FL_

11. National Basketball Association _NBA_
12. recreational vehicle _RV_
13. American Heart Association _AHA_
14. World Health Organization _WHO_
15. Eastern Standard Time _EST_
16. Environmental Protection Agency _EPA_
17. decimeter _dm_
18. most valuable player _MVP_
19. North Dakota _ND_
20. Unidentified Flying Object _UFO_

Score: _____   Total Possible: 20

20

Proofread

Proofread this part of a report and change the bold words to abbreviations. Write the abbreviations on the lines below the report.

Hurricanes sweep the Gulf of Mexico during the summer months. The whirling storms can measure 200 to 300 **miles** (320 to 480 **kilometers**) in diameter. The eye of a hurricane travels at a speed of 10 to 15 **miles per hour**, or 16 to 24 kilometers per hour. The cloud forms may rise 10,000 **feet** (3048 **meters**) high and cover thousands of miles. One of the costliest hurricanes to strike the United States was Hurricane Andrew, which hit the Bahamas and headed **northwest** to **Florida** and **Louisiana** in 1992.

1. _mi._   5. _m_
2. _km_   6. _NW_
3. _mph_   7. _FL_
4. _ft._   8. _LA_

Practice

Find out about a storm in your state or imagine one that could hit. Write some notes using abbreviations. Your notes should be in complete sentences.

Review the notes to be sure your child has:
• put a period at the end of each sentence.
• used abbreviations in their notes.
• used the correct punctuation for each abbreviation.
• written notes that make sense and relate to the topic.

Tips for Your Own Writing: Proofreading ....

Look at some of your math papers or science reports to find examples of measurements. Check to see that you wrote the metric and customary measurement abbreviations correctly.

Abbreviations save time and space when you are taking notes or making lists.

21

Lesson 9

Lesson 9 Punctuation: End Marks

"What does this say this is confusing" Can you read those sentences? Punctuation marks will make them clear! "What does this say? This is confusing."

.... **Did You Know?** ....

A period is used at the end of a sentence that makes a statement.

Machines help us with many daily tasks.

A period is used at the end of a sentence that gives an order or makes a request.

Turn on the dishwasher.

A question mark is used at the end of a sentence that asks a question.

How many machines do you use each day?

An exclamation point is used at the end of a statement, order, or request that expresses strong feeling.

That machine is awesome!
Pull that plug right now!

....

Show What You Know

Put the correct punctuation mark at the end of each sentence. Circle any periods you add so they will be easier to see.

Do you think robots will replace the workforce? I doubt it! However, many of tomorrow's jobs will be performed by robots. Think about the advantages this will bring for humans. They can do work that is dangerous for people to do. Noise, heat, smoke, and dust do not bother them. Neither does the freezing cold of outer space. A built-in computer controls a robot's actions so it can be programmed to do many difficult jobs.

The word *robot* comes from the Czech word *robota*, which means "drudgery." What does *drudgery* mean? It's work that is repetitive and tiresome. Robots don't care what the task is. They can work twenty-four hours a day at a steady pace. Best of all, they never make mistakes. How super! Robots never get bored and they never complain. They are truly special.

Score: _____ Total Possible: 17

22

Proofread

Use proofreading marks to add twelve end punctuation marks where they are needed.

Example: I love to swim.

Hiking is one of the most enjoyable forms of exercise. Walking is a form of hiking. Almost anyone can do it. All you really need is comfortable clothing and very comfortable walking shoes. Shoes are probably the most important hiking tool. You will be on your feet a lot, so take care of them! Get properly fitting shoes to avoid blisters and sore feet. It's also wise to check the weather report before you start. You can then select the correct type of clothing.

Find a special place to walk. It can be on a sidewalk in a park, a trail in the forest, or a path in the country. What can be better than walking along in a wooded area? Nothing on earth! As you walk, the sights and sounds of nature are all around you. You hear the leaves rustling. Are you listening to the birds? What beautiful sounds!

Practice

There are many kinds of exercise. What is your favorite? Write a paragraph about your favorite exercise that will convince your friends it is a great activity.

Review the paragraph to be sure your child has:

• written about a kind of exercise.

• given reasons to support the statement that the activity is great.

• put the correct punctuation mark at the end of each sentence.

Tips for Your Own Writing: Proofreading

Select a story you have recently written. Check to see if you put periods after sentences that are statements, orders, or requests, question marks after questions, and exclamation points after sentences that express strong feelings.

Punctuation is the key to others understanding what you write. Use the right marks when you write!

23

Lesson 10

Lesson 10 Punctuation: Sentences

Sentences that run into each other need end punctuation. Use end punctuation marks to separate them.

.... **Did You Know?** ....

Two or more sentences written as though they were one sentence are hard to read. Correct use of end punctuation and capital letters will help you write better sentences.

Incorrect punctuation: Sundials, water clocks, and hourglasses were the earliest timekeepers they were made from natural materials in the A.D. 1000s, mechanical clocks were invented in China.

Correct punctuation: Sundials, water clocks, and hourglasses were the earliest timekeepers. They were made from natural materials. In the A.D. 1000s, mechanical clocks were invented in China.

A comma cannot be used as an end mark. Two sentences separated by only a comma are incorrectly punctuated.

Incorrect punctuation: Sundials tell time by measuring the angle of the shadow cast by the sun, hourglasses do not.

Correct punctuation: Sundials tell time by measuring the angle of the shadow cast by the sun. Hourglasses do not.

....

Show What You Know

Add periods where they are needed to correct the punctuation in this paragraph. Then circle the words that should be capitalized.

Early European mechanical clocks were huge. The gears of the mechanical clocks often occupied whole rooms. They had no dials or hands but marked the time by ringing a bell. These clocks, like other early clocks, were inaccurate. By 1400, the mechanical timekeeper had become a part of everyday life. Almost every town had an enormous "town clock."

Score: _____ Total Possible: 10

24

Proofread

The paragraph below has four places where the punctuation is incorrect. Correct the sentences by using proper proofreading marks to add four end punctuation marks and four capital letters.

Example: Seals are interesting animals. They are found in many parts of the world.

Harbor seals spend most of their time on floating ice chunks or land. Bearded seals enjoy spending their time in the same way. Harbor seals weigh between 100 and 150 pounds. They are usually about five feet in length. The weight of the larger bearded seals can be up to 1,500 pounds. They can grow to be twelve feet long. Harbor seals like to play in groups. Bearded seals are happy spending time alone. Seals have generally poor hearing, but their sight is good. Bearded seals have big, brushlike whiskers. Harbor seals have small, delicate ones.

Practice

Choose a pair of the animals in the picture and write a paragraph comparing them. How are they alike? How are they different? When you are finished, reread your paragraph to check for sentences that are missing end marks.

Review the paragraph to be sure your child has:

• explained how animals are alike and different.

• put a punctuation mark at the end of each sentence.

• avoided sentences that run on and on.

• used correct capitalization.

Tips for Your Own Writing: Proofreading

The next time you write a report, check for sentences that need end marks. Read the sentences aloud to listen for mistakes in end punctuation.

Punctuation marks will help mark "the end" of sentences.

25

Lesson 11

Lesson
11 Punctuation: Sentence Fragments

"When I got on the bus." Is this a sentence? Add the missing parts to make a complete sentence.

·························· **Did You Know?** ··························

A sentence fragment is a group of words that is not a sentence. A *fragment* is a part of a sentence.

Fragment: Until it got dark.
Sentence: We played baseball until it got dark.

Fragment: After we ate dinner.
Sentence: After we ate dinner, we did our homework.

Show What You Know

Rewrite the paragraph to eliminate the sentence fragments. You can do this by adding the fragment to the beginning or end of the sentence it should be part of.

Itaipú, the most powerful electricity-producing dam in the world, is in Brazil. Paraguay and Brazil built the dam on the Paraná River. Which is in an area of dense tropical vegetation. The dam is 633 feet high and 5 1/2 miles long. After the dam was completed in 1991. The total cost of building it was determined to be $18 billion. The dam contains enough building materials to build a city for four million people. Because the water running over the dam sounds like music. It is called Itaipú, which means "singing dam" in Portuguese.

Itaipú, the most powerful electricity-producing dam in the world, is in Brazil. Paraguay and Brazil built the dam on the Paraná River, which is in an area of dense tropical vegetation. The dam is 633 feet high and 5 1/2 miles long. After the dam was completed in 1991, the total cost of building it was determined to be $18 billion. The dam contains enough building materials to build a city for four million people. Because the water running over the dam sounds like music, it is called *Itaipú*, which means "singing dam" in Portuguese.

Score: _____ Total Possible: 3

26

Proofread

Eliminate the three sentence fragments by adding the fragments to the beginning or end of a sentence.

George Washington Carver helped save farm industry in the South by showing farmers how to rotate crops. Which means to plant different crops from year to year. Through his bulletins and speeches. Carver taught farmers many things. He spent many years researching peanuts. Which was one of his great achievements.

1. George Washington Carver helped save farm industry in the South by showing farmers how to rotate crops, which means to plant different crops from year to year.

2. Through his bulletins and speeches, Carver taught farmers many things.

3. He spent many years researching peanuts, which was one of his great achievements.

Practice

Write a paragraph that tells what you believe to be the most exciting summer Olympic sport to watch. Give reasons for your choice. Be sure to use complete sentences.

Review the paragraph to be sure your child has:

• written a paragraph that makes sense and relates to the topic.

• avoided sentence fragments.

• put a punctuation mark at the end of each sentence.

• used correct capitalization.

Tips for Your Own Writing: Proofreading ···············

Choose a favorite piece of your writing. Reading your work aloud can help you find sentence fragments. Some writers find it helps to "hear" problem sentence fragments if they read their papers "backwards," starting with the last sentence first.

Remember to make sentences "whole"—no parts or fragments allowed.

27

··

Lesson 12

Lesson
12 Review: Punctuation

A. Read these notes. Use the proper proofreading mark to add ten missing periods after sentences, abbreviations, and initials.

In an address to Congress in 1961, Pres. Kennedy called for a commitment to land a man on the moon before the end of the 1960s. *Apollo 8* was launched on Dec. 21, 1968. Astronauts James A. Lovell, William Anders, and Frank Borman were on board. The spacecraft reached the moon on Tues. the 24th and proceeded to make ten orbits around the moon. Splashdown occurred early on Fri. the 27th of Dec.

Score: _____ Total Possible: 10

B. Write an abbreviation for each bold term.

In math class today we used formulas to change measurement systems. We changed **miles** (mi. / 1) to **kilometers** (km / 2) and **feet** (ft. / 3) to **meters** (m / 4). Then we used the map scale to measure the distance of the Oregon Trail from Independence, **Missouri** (MO / 5), to Fort Walla Walla, **Washington** (WA / 6). Finally, we calculated the travel time on the trail for a wagon and a **recreational vehicle** (RV / 7). We discovered that the **miles per hour** (mph / 8) were very different!

Score: _____ Total Possible: 8

C. Use the proper proofreading marks to add seven missing end punctuation marks to these directions.

Have you ever made homemade clay? These directions will help you create a small quantity of clay. Take one cup of warm water, one cup of salt, and two cups of cooking flour. Mix the ingredients together. Squeeze the wet flour until it is smooth and does not stick to your fingers. It's ready for modeling! You can create any type of sculpture you wish. You may also want to add food coloring to various batches to make colorful figures of clay. Have fun!

Score: _____ Total Possible: 7

28

D. The paragraph below has three incorrect sentences. Correct the sentences using proper proofreading marks to add three end punctuation marks and three capital letters.

For many years, people in the United States used streetcars to travel in cities. At first, streetcars were called horsecars because they were pulled by horses. Later, streetcars were powered by steam in the 1800s. People began trying to use electric power, but making electricity was considered to be too expensive. In 1888 a machine was invented that made electricity inexpensively. In that same year, the first electric-powered streetcars were put into use. They quickly replaced the steam-powered streetcar. With the invention of the gas engine, electric streetcars were soon replaced by buses and cars. By 1930 the streetcar had begun to disappear from city streets. Interest in streetcars revived in the 1970s. Streetcars use less energy per person and create less pollution than automobiles.

Score: _____ Total Possible: 6

E. Find and circle five sentence fragments. Then rewrite the paragraph by adding each fragment to the end of a sentence.

Garrett A. Morgan invented the gas mask. Morgan had to prove that his mask would work. Before people would use it. He showed a man going into a small tent. That was filled with smoke. The man stayed in the tent. For about twenty minutes. Next, the man went into a small room filled with poison gas. He stayed for fifteen minutes and was fine. When he came out. In 1916 Morgan used his gas mask to rescue more than twenty workers. Who were trapped in a smoke-filled tunnel in Cleveland.

Garrett A. Morgan invented the gas mask. Morgan had to prove that his mask would work before people would use it. He showed a man going into a small tent that was filled with smoke. The man stayed in the tent for about twenty minutes. Next the man went into a small room filled with poison gas. He stayed for fifteen minutes and was fine when he came out. In 1916 Morgan used his gas mask to rescue more than twenty workers who were trapped in a smoke-filled tunnel in Cleveland.

Score: _____ Total Possible: 5

REVIEW SCORE: _____ REVIEW TOTAL: 36

29

Lesson 13

13 Punctuation: Commas I

Commas are the road signs writers use to separate things so they are easier to read.

···················· **Did You Know?** ····················

Commas are used to separate three or more items in a series. Put a comma after each item except for the last one.

Rolls, bagels, scones, and muffins are displayed in the bakery.
Customers can see, smell, and admire the different kinds of bread.
I bought carrot muffins, rye rolls, blueberry scones, and onion bagels.

Commas are used after introductory words such as *yes, no,* and *well*.

Yes, that bakery makes the best sourdough bread in the city.
Well, you have to get there early before the bread is gone.

An appositive follows a noun and gives more information about the noun. In the examples below, the appositives are in bold type. Commas are used to set off appositives from the rest of a sentence.

Mr. Schultz, **the bakery owner,** is very proud of his breads.
My favorite is pumpernickel, **a sour rye bread.**

Commas are used in direct address. Commas separate the name of the person spoken to from the rest of the sentence.

Do you have any wheat bread, Mr. Schultz?
Jerry, I put a loaf aside just for you.
You know, Mr. Schultz, you are a wonderful man!

···

Show What You Know
Read the paragraph. Add fourteen commas where they are needed.

Dogs come in all sizes, shapes, and colors. The American Kennel Club, the official dog breeding organization, recognizes 130 breeds in seven categories. For example, sporting dogs include pointers, setters, and retrievers. Collies, sheepdogs, and corgis are considered herding dogs. Ben, my boxer, is classified as a working dog. But to me, Ben is a companion. When I say, "Ben, come," he always comes. Well, maybe he doesn't *always* come. But he certainly comes when I say, "Dinner, Ben." Yes, *dinner* is definitely a word he knows!

Score: _____   Total Possible: 14

30

Proofread
Add eleven commas to this conversation where they are needed. Use the proper proofreading mark to show where each comma should be placed.

Example: Well, are you ready to begin?

"Lionel, I've got the telescope, two blankets, and some hot chocolate. Let's go outside and look at the moon, the stars, and the planets."

"Well, I don't know, Lucy. Will there be any snakes, spiders, or bats out there?"

"No, I don't think so, Lionel. Annie Callahan, my next-door neighbor, goes out star-gazing every night. So does Harry Thoreaux, your dentist. Last night he saw a meteor. Wouldn't you like to see a meteor, Lionel?"

"Yes, Lucy, I would. But only if I don't have to see any rats, roaches, or worms!"

"Then I suggest you look up, Lionel, rather than down!"

Practice
Write a paragraph in which you describe your favorite foods to a friend. In the first sentence, list at least three different foods. Then describe them. Use your friend's name in at least one sentence.

Review the sentences to be sure your child has:

* written sentences about his or her favorite foods.

* listed at least three foods and described them.

* addressed at least one of the sentences to a friend.

* used commas correctly with items in a series.

* used commas correctly in direct address.

Tips for Your Own Writing: Proofreading ····················
Choose a piece of your own writing and ask a partner to proofread it, checking for commas between items in a series and with introductory words, appositives, and direct address.

Commas separate things to make your writing as clear as a bell.

31

···

Lesson 14

14 Punctuation: Commas and Sentences

Use the correct road signs (commas with words) to combine short sentences into a larger one.

···················· **Did You Know?** ····················

Sometimes two or more sentences are written as though they were one sentence without space or punctuation between them.

An anteater has powerful front claws it uses its claws to tear open ant nests.

One way to correct the punctuation is to put an appropriate punctuation mark at the end of the first sentence and capitalize the first word of the second sentence.

An anteater has powerful front claws. It uses its claws to tear open ant nests.

Another way to correct the punctuation is to put a comma at the end of the first sentence and add an appropriate conjunction, such as *and, but,* or *or,* at the beginning of the second one.

An anteater has powerful front claws, **and** it uses its claws to tear open ant nests.

···

Show What You Know
Read the following paragraph. Add commas and periods where they are needed. Underline the conjunctions, and circle any words that should be capitalized.

Last summer I visited my grandparents. They live near Corpus Christi, Texas. I saw many new and interesting things, but one of the most unusual things I saw was an armadillo. One night my grandfather took me into the backyard, and he pointed to an animal in the bushes by the garage. The animal had a pointed snout and rabbitlike ears, but strangest of all, it looked as if it were covered in armor. It was an armadillo and it was looking for insects and frogs to eat. Its name means "the little armored one" in Spanish. Its armor helps protect it from enemies. It can pull in its feet and nose, or it can roll into a ball. I watched the armadillo for a long time, but it didn't roll into a ball.

Score: _____   Total Possible: 16

32

Proofread
Correct the eight sentences by adding a comma and a conjunction to each sentence. Use the proper proofreading mark to show where each comma and the conjunction should be placed.

Example: Summer vacations can be boring or fun, but mine was a lot of fun.

An aardvark is an odd-looking animal, and it is also called an ant bear. *Aardvark* comes from the Afrikaans language, and it means "earth pig." You might have to look very closely, but an aardvark does look a little like a pig. However, it has a long, sticky tongue, and it also has large, rabbitlike ears. An aardvark cannot see very well, but it has good hearing. It has long, sharp claws, and it uses them to burrow dens and open ant and termite nests. Maybe aardvarks are shy, or maybe they do not want to get sunburned. You can look for them during the day, but they come out only at night.

Practice
Look up information about an animal whose name begins with an *a*. Write a paragraph about the animal. What does it look like? Where does it live? What does it eat? Try to use commas and conjunctions to combine some of your sentences.

Review the paragraph to be sure your child has:

* written a paragraph about an animal whose name begins with an *a*.

* included information he or she found about the animal.

* used commas and conjunctions correctly to combine sentences.

Tips for Your Own Writing: Proofreading
Look at a story that you have written. Check to see if you have sentences that need separating. Use end punctuation or commas and conjunctions to correct the punctuation. Remember, commas alone cannot be used to combine sentences.

Your thoughts may run together, but don't let your sentences do that!

33

Lesson 15

Lesson
15 Punctuation: Commas After Phrases and Clauses

Sentences are easier to read and understand when commas are used to set off phrases and clauses at the beginning of the sentences.

.... **Did You Know?** ....

A comma is used after a long prepositional phrase at the beginning of a sentence. A comma is not necessary if the prepositional phrase is very short. A prepositional phrase is a group of words that begins with a preposition such as *at, in, on,* and *of.*

On a beautiful August morning, Mark went climbing.
At noon he reached the mountain peak.
In 1998 Mark climbed his highest peak.

A comma is used after a subordinate clause at the beginning of a sentence. A subordinate clause is a group of words that begins with a subordinate conjunction such as *after, although, before, if, unless, when,* and *while.* Even though the clause has a subject and a verb, it cannot stand alone as a sentence.

After he got to the top, Mark sat down to rest.
While he was resting, he admired the view.

....

Show What You Know
Add seven commas where they are needed in this paragraph.

After La Salle explored the area, the French claimed the land in 1682 and called it Louisiana. After the French and Indian wars in the 1700s, France had to give Louisiana to Spain. In 1800 Spain had to give Louisiana back to France. Although Napoleon I wanted an American empire, he wanted money more. In 1803 he decided to sell Louisiana. For about $15 million, the United States could buy the land. When President Thomas Jefferson heard about the offer, he was delighted. Before Napoleon could change his mind, Jefferson bought the land. With one bold, decisive stroke, the United States doubled in size.

Score: _____   Total Possible: 7

34

Proofread
Read this paragraph and add four commas that are needed. Use the proper proofreading mark to show where each comma should be added.

Example: After grapes have been dried, they're called raisins.

If you want something good to eat, have some raisins. For a long, long time, I didn't like raisins. But one day there wasn't anything else to eat, so I popped a few raisins in my mouth. As I chewed, I realized, hey, these are good! Now I eat them all the time. At lunch I have a box for dessert. After a long day at school, I have a box as a snack. When I get the urge to munch, I go for the raisins. Without a doubt, I am now a raisin raver.

Practice
Describe what is happening in these pictures. Write your description on the lines below. Try to begin some of your sentences with subordinate conjunctions or prepositions.

Review the description to be sure your child has:
• described the given sequence of pictures.
• begun some sentences with subordinate conjunctions.
• used commas after long introductory prepositional phrases.
• used commas after introductory subordinate clauses.

Tips for Your Own Writing: Proofreading ....
The next time you write a report, check to see if you used any long phrases or clauses to introduce sentences and used commas to set off those phrases and clauses from the rest of their sentences.

Think of commas as places to pause briefly.

35

Lesson 16

Lesson
16 Punctuation: Commas II

Commas are used to make sentences as clear and easy to read and understand as possible.

.... **Did You Know?** ....

A comma may not be required in a sentence, but it may be needed to avoid confusing the reader. Remember, the purpose of all punctuation marks is to help a reader easily read and understand what is written.

I didn't know whether to wait for Henry was very late.
I didn't know whether to wait, for Henry was very late.

When he called Henry apologized to me.
When he called, Henry apologized to me.

Henry brought his raincoat and his umbrella was in his briefcase.
Henry brought his raincoat, and his umbrella was in his briefcase.

....

Show What You Know
Read the paragraph below. Add nine commas where they are needed to avoid confusion.

Because the director was new, students were reluctant to get involved in the jazz band. But when the director called, James was eager to try out for first trumpet. However, before he could answer, James had to ask Elliot's advice. To James, Elliot is the expert on music. To be successful, groups must play music that appeals to many people. Soon after they played, the jazz band was declared a success. It got good reviews from everyone, but the *Chronicle* critic was particularly kind. Whether amateur or professional, musicians like to be applauded and appreciated. When the jazz band finished its concert series, the musicians were sorry it was over.

Score: _____   Total Possible: 9

36

Proofread
To avoid confusion, add a comma to each bold sentence in the paragraph below. Use the proper proofreading mark to show where each comma should be added.

Example: When the Wright brothers began, flying was still a dream.

Orville and Wilbur Wright became interested in airplanes in 1898. **They began by testing kites, and gliders were the second step in their program.** They flew their gliders from a beach near Kitty Hawk, North Carolina. **By the time they had finished, their glider tests numbered more than 700.** The men had to solve many problems. **For example, because engines were heavy, planes could not get off the ground.** The Wrights designed and built a small, lightweight engine for their plane. On December 17, 1903, Orville was the pilot of the first successful airplane flight. **When he landed, the plane was already part of history.**

Practice
Can you think of sentences in which the lack of a comma can cause a misreading? Read the examples below. Then, write at least one sentence of your own, once with and once without a comma.

Examples: After cleaning up my sister took a nap.
After cleaning up, my sister took a nap.

Review the sentences to be sure your child has:
• understood what was meant by "misreading."
• written his or her sentences both with and without the commas.

Tips for Your Own Writing: Proofreading ....
Exchange one of your papers with a partner. Proofread each other's writing to see whether punctuation marks, especially commas, were used in ways that will help a reader easily understand the writing.

Clear up confusion! Use commas!

37

Lesson 17

Lesson 17 Punctuation: Semicolons and Colons

Semicolons and colons look a lot alike. Semicolons separate sentences. Colons come before lists, after the greeting in a business letter, and in numbers used to tell time.

.... **Did You Know?** ....

A semicolon (;) can be used when combining two related sentences.

I rushed to the shelf; the book was already gone.

A semicolon also can be placed before a conjunction such as *besides, however, nevertheless, moreover,* and *therefore,* when combining two related sentences. A comma should be placed after those conjunctions. When using a conjunction such as *and, but,* or *or,* place a comma, not a semicolon, before the conjunction.

The book is very popular; **therefore,** it is hard to find.
I rushed to the shelf, **but** the book was already gone.

A colon (:) is used before a list of items. Usually, the colon follows a noun or pronoun. Do not use a colon after a verb or a preposition that introduces a list.

I looked for these books: a mystery, a biography, and an almanac.
The library has books, magazines, CDs, and audiocassettes.

A colon is also used between the numbers for hours and minutes in time.

The library opens at 9:00 A.M. and closes at 5:30 P.M.

A colon is used after the greeting in a business letter.

Dear Ms. Sloan:

....

Show What You Know
Read the paragraph. Add semicolons and colons where they are needed.

At 9:00 P.M. I watched a program about Pompeii. Pompeii was a Roman city in southern Italy; it was located near a volcano, Mt. Vesuvius. The people thought Vesuvius was extinct; however, they were wrong. On August 24, A.D. 79, Vesuvius proved it was active; it erupted suddenly and violently. Thick layers of ash and rock buried these towns: Herculaneum, Stabiae, and Pompeii. In 1748 Pompeii was excavated. These public buildings were found in the city center: temple, council chamber, assembly hall, courthouse, and market.

Score: _____ Total Possible: 6

38

Proofread
Two semicolons and three colons are missing in the paragraph below. Use proper proofreading marks to show where each semicolon or colon should be placed.

Example: Caroline's alarm didn't go off at 7:00 A.M. It was the beginning of a bad day.

Caroline sat fuming on the school bus; it was stuck in traffic on the highway. She tried to stay calm; however, she was afraid she would be late for school. The deadline to sign up for the ski trip was this morning at 9:15. It was now 8:45. Mentally, Caroline made a list of things she could do: cry, scream, walk, or laugh. She tried to breathe deeply; she tried to focus on a happy thought. No happy thoughts came to mind; nevertheless, she did feel a little better. It was now 9:05. There was nothing she could do; all the spots for the ski trip would be filled by the time she got to school. Caroline wrote the following notes: return new ski hat, take up bowling, and sign up for special school activities earlier next time!

Practice
Imagine that you are having a party. Using complete sentences, write an invitation in which you tell your guests the kind of party, the date, the time, the place, and any other information you think they should know. Use colons and semicolons.

Review the invitation to be sure your child has:

• included all necessary information about the party.

• used colons correctly in time expressions.

• used semicolons correctly between related sentences.

Tips for Your Own Writing: Revising
As you write your next report, think about the structure of your sentences. Are there any related sentences that you could combine using either a semicolon, or a semicolon and a conjunction? Are there any lists that you could rewrite using a colon?

Despite its name, a semicolon is not just half a colon. It's half a colon plus a comma!

39

Lesson 18

Lesson 18 Review: Commas, Colons, Semicolons

A. Add twelve commas that are needed in the paragraph below. Use the proper proofreading mark to show where each comma should be placed.

Hey, I'm home, Mom! Wow, I'm out of breath! I ran all the way because I didn't want to miss *Beanie and Frank,* my favorite TV show. Tonight Beanie is finally going to tell Frank, Chloe, and Spike her big secret. Sure, I can set the table now. The show doesn't start for ten minutes. Mom, will you please get Joey, Donna, and the dog out of here? No, take the dog with you, Joey! Donna, that little whiner, really gets on my nerves. Okay, I'm finished. Mom, if I can just watch this show, the one I've been waiting to see, all by myself, I promise I'll wash, dry, and put away the dishes after dinner without being asked. Thanks, Mom.

Score: _____ Total Possible: 12

B. Correct the punctuation by either making two separate sentences or combining them with a comma and a conjunction (and, but, or). Write the sentences on the lines.

Sample answers are given.

1. Other people may prefer roses or orchids I like sunflowers best.
   Other people may prefer roses or orchids, but I like sunflowers best.

2. Sunflowers turn their heads to face the sun they also look like little suns.
   Sunflowers turn their heads to face the sun. They also look like little suns.

3. They have large heads of yellow flowers the heads contain many small black seeds.
   They have large heads of yellow flowers. The heads contain many small black seeds.

4. Sunflowers grow in people's gardens they are grown as a crop.
   Sunflowers grow in people's gardens, or they are grown as a crop.

5. The seeds are processed for vegetable oil they are used as bird food.
   The seeds are processed for vegetable oil, and they are used as bird food.

6. Birds may like to eat sunflower seeds so do people.
   Birds may like to eat sunflower seeds, but so do people.

Score: _____ Total Possible: 6

40

C. Add two commas where needed in this paragraph. Use the proper proofreading mark to show where each comma should be added.

In the mid-nineteenth century, the main overland route to the Northwest was the Oregon Trail. From Independence, Missouri, people walked 2,000 miles to reach the Williamette Valley in Oregon. In 1836 a group of missionary families made the long trip on the trail. When people back East read the reports of the trip, many of them decided to go to Oregon, too. By 1846 more than 6,000 people had used the Oregon Trail. After gold was discovered in California in 1848, fewer people made the trek to Oregon. Soon the trail was all but forgotten.

Score: _____ Total Possible: 2

D. Add five commas where they are needed to make the sentences less confusing to read. Use the proper proofreading mark to show where each comma should be added.

When the storm hit, Maya was working at home. She waited patiently for the storm would soon be over. Maya held her dog and her cat hid under the bed. By the time the storm had finished, the power lines were down. Inside, the house was dark but safe.

Score: _____ Total Possible: 5

E. Add either one semicolon or one colon to each sentence in the paragraph below. Use proper proofreading marks to show where they should be added.

Every day at 6:15 A.M., the alarm clock goes off and Jenny gets out of bed. She always does the same thing: wash face, brush teeth, get dressed, and eat breakfast. Jenny always eats a bowl of cornflakes; she always drinks a glass of milk. Jenny laughs about her routine; however, she has no intention of changing it.

Score: _____ Total Possible: 4

REVIEW SCORE: _____ REVIEW TOTAL: 29

41

Lesson 19

Lesson 19 Punctuation: Quotation Marks and Dialogue

Quotation marks signal that someone is talking. Use them to find out who said what!

.... Did You Know? ....

Dialogue, only a speaker's actual words, is set off from the rest of a sentence by a comma and quotation marks. A speaker's tag, such as *Ana Maria said,* is not enclosed in quotation marks.

"Oh, look! They have posted roles for the play," Ana Maria said.

If the speaker's tag is placed before the dialogue, a comma is placed after the last word of the tag to separate it from the dialogue.

Ana Maria said happily, "I'm going to be Dorothy."

When the speaker's tag interrupts dialogue, quotation marks are placed around each part of the quotation. The interrupting speaker's tag is separated from the quoted words by commas.

"Yes, he is," continued Ana Maria, "and Theo's the Cowardly Lion."

Show What You Know

Rewrite the four sentences below. Enclose the dialogue within quotation marks. Separate with commas the speaker's tag from the dialogue.

1. Ana Maria asked Are you coming to the dress rehearsal after school, Jason?

   Ana Maria asked, "Are you coming to the dress rehearsal after school, Jason?"

2. Yes replied Jason but I will be late.

   "Yes," replied Jason, "but I will be late."

3. I left my costume at home he continued and I have to pick it up.

   "I left my costume at home," he continued, "and I have to pick it up."

4. I think we are going to be great Jason concluded as he ran toward home.

   "I think we are going to be great," Jason concluded as he ran toward home.

Score: _____   Total Possible: 4

42

Proofread

Read the play review below. Use proper proofreading marks to add the missing quotation marks and commas. Ten commas or quotation marks need to be added.

Example: I wonder how everyone liked the play said Ana Maria.

The sixth-grade class of Elm Place School performed in a production of *The Wiz.*

The following comments were made by parents attending the play:

"I really enjoyed the play," said Mrs. Fiore.

Mr. Moreno agreed, saying, "Yes, the kids did a terrific job."

"You're right," said Mr. Goldberg, "and the best performer was my son, Jason."

"Oh, no," said Mr. Moreno, "the best performer was my daughter, who played Dorothy."

"I disagree," said Mrs. Fiore. "The best performer was my son, Aaron, who played the Scarecrow."

The parents laughed. They agreed that all the performers were wonderful.

Practice

Write a short dialogue that you may have had with a friend about an event in your town. Begin a new paragraph each time the speaker changes.

Review the dialogue to be sure your child has:

• enclosed all dialogue within quotation marks.

• not enclosed the speaker's tag within the quotation marks.

• used commas to separate the speaker's tag from the dialogue.

• positioned the commas correctly.

• written a conversation that makes sense and relates to the topic.

Tips for Your Own Writing: Proofreading ....

Choose a story you have written that contains dialogue. Exchange papers with a partner. Check your partner's writing for opening and closing quotation marks, commas that separate the speaker's tag from the dialogue, and new paragraphs each time the speaker changes.

The reporter asked, "May I quote you?"
"Sure," I replied, "if you enclose my comments in quotation marks."

43

Lesson 20

Lesson 20 Punctuation: Dialogue—Commas and End Marks

Commas and periods always go within closing quotation marks. No questions asked. Exclamation points and question marks are open to question, aren't they?

.... Did You Know? ....

Commas and periods are *always* placed inside closing quotation marks.

"Until 1996," the sports fan said, "the Los Angeles Lakers held the record for the most team wins in a single season."

Question marks and exclamation points are placed inside the closing quotation marks if they are part of the quotation.

Her friend asked, "How many games did the Lakers win in one season?"

Question marks and exclamation points are placed outside the closing quotation marks if they are *not* part of the quotation.

How exciting to hear, "The Bulls broke the Lakers' record"!

Show What You Know

Add a total of twenty-nine quotation marks, commas, and end punctuation where they are needed in the sentences.

How excited Jan was when she heard the sportscaster say, "Last night the Chicago Bulls broke the team record for games won in a single season"!

"The Bulls broke the record," she shouted as she ran into my room.

I asked calmly, "What record did they break?"

Jan asked, "How could you not know? Don't you pay attention to sports?"

"No," I replied. "I don't pay much attention to sports."

How could I have known that Jan was about to give me a crash course in sports trivia when she said, "Come over here and sit down"?

"The Chicago Bulls just won seventy games for this season," Jan explained, "and that's the most games ever won in a single season by an NBA team."

Score: _____   Total Possible: 29

44

Proofread

Read this conversation between two sportscasters. Use proper proofreading marks to add eleven missing quotation marks, commas, and end punctuation marks.

Example: I told my family, "There is absolutely no sport as exciting as basketball!"

Bart said, "Listen to the crowd shouting!" The Chicago Bulls had just won their seventy-second game of the 1995–1996 season. "Who would have believed that we would be sitting here tonight announcing that the Chicago Bulls have established a new record for the most games won in a single season?"

"Yes," said Bob. "it wasn't too long ago that people were asking whether the Bulls could break the record."

"Now that the Bulls have won their seventy-second game," said Bart, "people are asking me whether the Bulls' record can be broken."

Bob replied, "Only time will tell."

Practice

Think about an exciting sports event you have participated in or seen. Write a dialogue between you and a friend in which you talk about the event. Remember to start a new paragraph each time the speaker changes.

Review the account to be sure your child has:

• enclosed all dialogue within quotation marks.

• not enclosed the speaker's tag within the quotation marks.

• positioned the commas and periods within the quotation marks.

• placed question marks and exclamation points appropriately.

• written a dialogue that makes sense and relates to the topic.

Tips for Your Own Writing: Proofreading ....

The next time you write a story, include some dialogue. Make sure you place all periods and commas within closing quotation marks, and question marks and exclamation points outside quotation marks in quoted material.

In or out—"Watch your quotation marks and end punctuation!"

45

Lesson 21

Lesson 21 Punctuation: Direct and Indirect Quotations

Adam said, "Take it directly from me. This is a direct quotation." He then added *that an indirect quotation restates something that was said.*

.... **Did You Know?** ....

A <u>direct quotation</u> is the exact words someone said or wrote. A direct quotation is enclosed within quotation marks.

Abraham Lincoln said, **"A house divided against itself cannot stand."**

An <u>indirect quotation</u> is a restatement or rephrasing of something said or written. An indirect quotation is *not* enclosed in quotation marks.

Abraham Lincoln said that **a house in which there is no unity cannot withstand pressure from outside forces.**

An indirect quotation is often introduced by the word *that*, and a comma is not used to separate the speaker's tag from the indirect quotation.

Abraham Lincoln said **that** a house in which there is no unity cannot withstand pressure from outside forces.

....

Show What You Know

Decide whether each sentence includes a direct or an indirect quotation. If a sentence includes a direct quotation, add quotation marks where they are needed. If a sentence is an indirect quotation, write *indirect* on the line.

1. In one speech, Abraham Lincoln commented, "The ballot is stronger than the bullet." _____

2. Lincoln said in a campaign speech that no one would ever consider him a person who would become a President. __indirect__

3. "What is conservatism?" is a question Lincoln once asked. _____

4. Discouraged by news during the Civil War, Lincoln noted in 1861, "If McClellan is not using the army, I should like to borrow it for a while."

5. Lincoln stated that persons must stand firm in their important basic beliefs. __indirect__

6. In a letter to the editor, Lincoln noted that he supported giving the privileges of government to all those who helped bear the burdens of being involved in government. __indirect__

Score: _____   Total Possible: 9

46

Proofread

Read the article about Lincoln. It contains eight errors in punctuation involving direct and indirect quotations. Use proper proofreading marks to correct the errors.

Example: Mrs. Rainbucket said, "How about grabbing an umbrella?" Mr. Hailstorm said that we could expect wet weather.

Abraham Lincoln attended school less than a year but actually wrote his own math book. He said, "There were some schools, so called, but no qualification was ever required of a teacher, beyond readin', writin', and cipherin', to the Rule of Three."

One book that made a lasting impression on Abe was *Life of Washington*. Of this book he said, "I recollect thinking then, boy even though I was, that there must have been something more than common that those men struggled for."

Lincoln became a lawyer simply by reading law books to familiarize himself with the law. He said that if someone is resolutely determined to make a lawyer of himself, the thing is more than half done already.

Practice

Imagine that you are a reporter who interviewed Abraham Lincoln during the Civil War. Write an article, using direct and indirect quotations.

Review the article to be sure your child has:

- enclosed only direct quotations within quotation marks, not the speaker's tag.
- positioned the end punctuation correctly within or outside the quotation marks.
- not used a comma or quotation marks with indirect quotations.
- written an article that makes sense and relates to the topic.

Tips for Your Own Writing: Proofreading ....

See if you can find a piece of your own writing that includes direct and indirect quotations. Make sure the speaker's tags are separated from direct quotations with commas, both opening and closing quotation marks are used, quotation marks with indirect quotations were avoided, and indirect quotations were introduced by the word *that*.

Knowing who said what and what was said puts a reader in the know!

47

....

Lesson 22

Lesson 22 Punctuation: Titles

If you use quotation marks, you won't go wrong When writing the name of a poem, story, report, or song. But for names of newspapers, magazines, books, and movies it's wrong. Use underlining to mark them bold, dark, and strong.

.... **Did You Know?** ....

The titles of short written works, such as reports or articles, short stories, songs, and poems, are enclosed in quotation marks.

"Secrets of the Maya" (magazine article)
"The Celebrated Jumping Frog of Calaveras County" (short story)
"America the Beautiful" (song)
"Southbound on the Freeway" (poem)

The titles of long works, such as books, magazines, newspapers, plays, and movies, are underlined. In printed materials, the names appear in italic type.

<u>Missing May</u>, or in printed type *Missing May* (book)
<u>Time for Kids</u>, or in printed type *Time for Kids* (magazine)
<u>Miami Herald</u>, or in printed type *Miami Herald* (newspaper)
<u>Oklahoma!</u>, or in printed type *Oklahoma!* (play)
<u>The Lion King</u>, or in printed type *The Lion King* (movie)

Show What You Know

Add quotation marks or underlining to the titles in these sentences.

1. In 1932 Pearl Buck won a Pulitzer Prize for her book <u>The Good Earth</u>.

2. "The Muddy Puddle" is a nonsense poem by Dennis Lee.

3. On April 18, 1995, the last issue of the newspaper <u>Houston Post</u> was published.

4. Langston Hughes is best remembered for his poetry including "Mother to Son."

5. "My Favorite Things" is a song from the play <u>The Sound of Music</u>.

6. Did you see the article "There's a Sense of Urgency about Amphibian Census" in the <u>Chicago Tribune</u>?

Score: _____   Total Possible: 12

48

Proofread

Read this article about children's literature. The writer used quotation marks and underlining incorrectly for six titles. Use proper proofreading marks to correct them.

Example: "Winnie the Pooh" is my favorite book, and "I Remember" is my favorite poem.

Literature has long entertained children. Children have been amused by poems such as "Whistling" from Jack Prelutsky's book "Rainy Rainy Saturday." They have cheered for Wilbur the Pig as they read <u>Charlotte's Web</u>, by E. B. White. Mr. White was not only a children's author but also the founder of the magazine "The New Yorker."

Children have even delighted in movies based on literature. In 1939 L. Frank Baum's book <u>The Wonderful Wizard of Oz</u> was made into the movie "The Wizard of Oz." In the movie, Dorothy sang the song "Somewhere Over the Rainbow." The movie Aladdin was based on the short fairy tale "Aladdin and the Wonderful Lamp." In 1996 Roald Dahl's book "James and the Giant Peach" was adapted into a movie. Literature will always be a rich source of entertainment for children, both young and old.

Practice

Imagine you are a reviewer of books for very young children. Write a paragraph naming two books, stories, or poems that you like and tell why you like them.

Review the article to be sure your child has:

- enclosed the titles of poems and stories in quotation marks.
- underlined the titles of books.
- written a paragraph that makes sense and relates to the topic.

Tips for Your Own Writing: Proofreading ....

Select a piece of your own writing that includes titles. Check your writing to make sure that you have underlined titles of books and movies or placed the titles of poems and stories in quotation marks.

Titles of books, magazines, newspapers, and movies = <u>underlining</u>. Titles of stories, poems, reports, and songs = "quotation marks."

49

Lesson 23

Lesson 23 Punctuation: Friendly and Business Letters

Are you sending a friendly or a business letter? The only major differences are that business letters have an inside address, and the greeting is followed by a colon.

.... Did You Know? ....

A friendly letter and a business letter both have distinct parts. The only difference in punctuation is following the greeting. A comma is used in a friendly letter and a colon in a business letter.

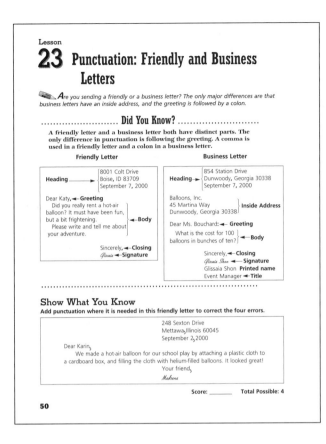

Friendly Letter

Heading ⟶ 8001 Colt Drive
Boise, ID 83709
September 7, 2000

Dear Katy, ◄ Greeting
Did you really rent a hot-air balloon? It must have been fun, but a bit frightening.
Please write and tell me about your adventure. ◄ Body

Sincerely, ◄ Closing
Glissia ◄ Signature

Business Letter

Heading ► 854 Station Drive
Dunwoody, Georgia 30338
September 7, 2000

Balloons, Inc.
45 Martina Way
Dunwoody, Georgia 30338 ◄ Inside Address

Dear Ms. Bouchard: ◄ Greeting
What is the cost for 100 balloons in bunches of ten? ◄ Body

Sincerely, ◄ Closing
Glissia Shon ◄ Signature
Glissaia Shon ◄ Printed name
Event Manager ◄ Title

Show What You Know

Add punctuation where it is needed in this friendly letter to correct the four errors.

248 Sexton Drive
Mettawa, Illinois 60045
September 2, 2000

Dear Karin,
We made a hot-air balloon for our school play by attaching a plastic cloth to a cardboard box, and filling the cloth with helium-filled balloons. It looked great!
Your friend,
Madrona

Score: _____ Total Possible: 4

50

Proofread

Correct the punctuation in this business letter. Use proper proofreading marks to correct the five errors.

Example: Sea Isle City, FL 34746

513 Elm Wood Place
Kansas City, Missouri 64112
August 23, 2000

Country Music Association
One Music Circle South
Nashville, Tennessee 37203

Dear Music Director:

Our band, Country Nights, has played together for more than eight years. We have recently written and performed a new song that we think you will like. The song "Days into Nights" is recorded on the enclosed tape. Please let us know if you are interested in this song and others we have written.

Sincerely,
Mitch Fellfield
Mitch Fellfield
Manager, Country Nights Band

Practice

Think about a musical group that you would like to see perform. Write the body of a business letter to the group asking if they will be performing somewhere near you. Ask about prices, dates, and locations of the upcoming performances. On another sheet of paper, write your letter adding all the necessary parts. Review the letter to be sure your child has: • included a heading and inside address. • used a colon after the greeting. • used correct punctuation.

Tips for Your Own Writing: Proofreading ....

Choose a letter you have recently written. Check the letter to make sure it has the correct parts and is correctly punctuated.

Greetings to friends, use a comma in a letter. Greetings in business letters: use a colon.

51

Lesson 24

Lesson 24 Review: Punctuation

A. Use proper proofreading marks to add commas and quotation marks to each sentence. You will need to make sixteen corrections.

1. Homer wrote, "Your heart is always harder than a stone."
2. "Absence," Sextus Propertius wrote, "makes the heart grow fonder."
3. In *Othello*, Shakespeare wrote, "My heart is turned to stone."
4. "And what my heart taught me," wrote poet Robert Browning, "I taught the world."
5. "But it is wisdom to believe the heart," wrote George Santayana in one of his poems.

Score: _____ Total Possible: 16

B. Read the conversation below. Use proper proofreading marks to add end punctuation and quotation marks where they are needed. You will need to make nineteen corrections.

How did Vice-President Harry Truman feel when he heard Mrs. Franklin D. Roosevelt say, "Harry, the President is dead"?

He gave a clue, when he said to the press, "I felt like the moon, the stars, and all the planets had fallen on me."

"Harry Truman," our teacher said, "took over the presidency during World War II after President Roosevelt died from a stroke."

She then asked us, "How did Truman indicate that he knew the job of being President would be difficult?"

"His comments to the press," Mai answered, "showed that it would be difficult to replace Roosevelt."

Score: _____ Total Possible: 19

52

C. Use proper proofreading marks to add quotation marks to all direct quotations below. You will need to make sixteen corrections.

1. My younger brother asked, "How many planets are there?"
2. I told him that there were nine planets, and Earth was one of them.
3. Then he asked me if Earth was the largest planet.
4. "No," I told him, "Jupiter is the largest planet, and Earth is very small in comparison."
5. He continued to question me, asking, "Is Earth the smallest planet?"
6. I explained that Pluto was the smallest planet.
7. "But Earth is the best planet," he said.
8. "Yes, it is," I agreed, "because only on Earth can plants and animals live."
9. Then he told me that Earth was the best planet because I lived here.
10. I laughed and said, "No, Earth is the best because we both live here."

Score: _____ Total Possible: 16

D. Use proper proofreading marks to correct the nine errors in the paragraph below. Be sure to underline the names of books, plays, movies, newspapers, or magazines. Enclose the names of poems, articles, stories, or songs in quotation marks.

My partners and I are preparing a presentation about the Mississippi River. Jessica is reading a passage from Mark Twain's book Life on the Mississippi. Matt and Carlos are singing the song "Ol' Man River" from the play Show Boat. Sonia is reading part of the article "The Great Flood of 1993" that appeared in the October 1993 issue of National Geographic World. I am providing background information and closing the presentation with a poem that my partners and I wrote. It is called "The River of History."

Score: _____ Total Possible: 9

REVIEW SCORE: _____ REVIEW TOTAL: 60

53

Lesson 25

Lesson 25 Usage: Verbs—Froze, Shook, Rang

Verbs, or action words, come in different forms. Which form do you use?

.... **Did You Know?** ....

A <u>verb</u> is an action or being word in a sentence. It tells what happens or what is. The form that you use depends upon the action that is being described. For example, the <u>past</u> form of a verb describes a past action. It usually consists of one word. The <u>past participle</u> form consists of the past form that is used with a helping verb such as *have, has, had, was,* or *were.*

Look at the present, past, and past participle forms of each of the troublesome verbs below. Then read the sentences that follow. They show correct usage for each form of these verbs.

Present	Past	Past Participle
Today they **freeze**.	Yesterday they **froze**.	They **have frozen**.
Today they **shake**.	Yesterday they **shook**.	They **have shaken**.
Today they **ring**.	Yesterday they **rang**.	They **have rung**.

We **froze** peach ice cream on the Fourth of July.
Dad **had frozen** the hamburger meat that he cooked on the grill.

We **shook** the whole way home after seeing the action movie.
The city residents **had been shaken** by the disasters that occurred.

Tina **rang** the dinner bell for the members of the camp.
She **has rung** that bell every evening for twenty years.

Show What You Know
Underline the correct form of each verb in parentheses.

Carlos was worried. He was sure he had (froze, <u>frozen</u>) the ice cream dessert long enough. But would it be ready for the club members thirty minutes from now? Carlos took the pan out of the freezer and (<u>shook</u>, shaken) it lightly. Well, no ripples disturbed the surface—a good sign! Just then the phone (<u>rang</u>, rung): Dana was sick and couldn't come. After the phone had (rang, <u>rung</u>) four more times, the meeting was off. Too many members were sick or busy. "I (<u>froze</u>, frozen) that dessert for nothing," said Carlos. "But this has not (shook, <u>shaken</u>) my confidence. I know I made a tasty treat!"

Score: _____ Total Possible: 6

54

Proofread
The following TV editorial uses the verb pairs *froze/frozen, shook/shaken,* and *rang/rung*. Each verb form is used incorrectly once. Using the proper proofreading marks, delete each incorrect word and write the correction above it.

Example: The people were ~~shook~~ by the accident.

The people of this county have ~~froze~~ through one of our worst winters, and earthquakes have ~~shook~~ our homes. We cannot blame nature on politicians. But we can blame them for failing us. In a recent session, the state legislature ~~frozen~~ funds for earthquake relief. This act ~~shook~~ our faith in the government.

Just one week ago, we ~~rung~~ in a new year. Let us resolve to shake up the government. Politicians, take notice: we have ~~rang~~ the alarm!

Practice
You may notice that the verbs in this lesson describe sensory actions. Write a strong sensory sentence for each verb in each pair. Use the same topic within each pair, but vary the sentences enough to make them interesting.

froze/frozen

Review the sentences to be sure your child has:

• written a sentence for each lesson verb.

shook/shaken

• written strong, evocative sensory sentences.

• written sentence pairs that are on the same topic.

rang/rung

• written sentences that make sense and are mechanically correct.

Tips for Your Own Writing: Proofreading ....
Choose a piece of your own writing. See whether you find any of the three verb pairs from this lesson and if you used the correct form of each verb.

Froze, shook, and rang can stand by themselves, but frozen, shaken, and rung need a little help.

55

Lesson 26

Lesson 26 Usage: Verbs—Swam, Tore, Took

Some verbs don't conform to the patterns we expect. Swam, swum? Tore, torn? Took, taken? How do you know which is right?

.... **Did You Know?** ....

The <u>past</u> form of a verb describes a past action. It usually consists of one word. The <u>past participle</u> form consists of the past form that is used with a helping verb such as *have, has, had, was,* or *were.*

Look at the present, past, and past participle forms of each of the troublesome verbs below. Then read the sentences that follow. They show correct usage for each form of these verbs.

Present	Past	Past Participle
Today they **swim**.	Yesterday they **swam**.	They **have swum**.
Today they **tear**.	Yesterday they **tore**.	They **have torn**.
Today they **take**.	Yesterday they **took**.	They **have taken**.

The bluefish **swam** together in a vast school off the coast.
They **have swum** along this coast for hundreds of years.

"You **tore** the jacket!" gasped the actress.
The curtain **was torn** from the stage in the scuffle that followed.

"I think you **took** more than your share," complained the hungry camper.
But she **had taken** exactly what was her due.

Show What You Know
Write the word that best completes each sentence.

The bluefin tuna ___tore___ at its unfortunate prey. Then it ___swam___
  1(tore, torn)   2(swam, swum)
swiftly toward another victim. That helpless fish had ___torn___ one of its fins badly. A
                   3(tore, torn)
sea bass had ___taken___ a large shrimp for its dinner. The shrimp had ___swum___
     4(took, taken)   5(swam, swum)
by lazily and carelessly. The hunter of the sea was no longer hungry, so it
___took___ no more victims.
6(took, taken)

Score: _____ Total Possible: 6

56

Proofread
The following radio script uses the verb pairs *swam/swum, tore/torn,* and *took/taken*. Using the proper proofreading marks, delete four incorrect words and write the correction above each one.

Example: We ~~swum~~ for an hour.

NARRATOR: Here comes our hero, Pam Pekinese. Pam has swum across the lagoon in record time. (*Sound effect for swimming.*)

PAM: I have ~~swam~~ my last mission! It's true that I'm the world's greatest swimming Pekinese, but I have ~~took~~ all I can take! See? Those playful dolphins ~~torn~~ two of my favorite hair ribbons. Yap, yip.

MEL MYNAH: You didn't expect any dolphins you swam by to pass up a chance to tease you? They did the same thing when you ~~swum~~ by them last week.

NARRATOR: Tune in next week for "Strange Animals Do Strange Things."

Practice
Write a brief description of a giant squid attacking a boat at sea. Use all the verb pairs presented in this lesson. Choose other words carefully to give the story a strong sense of action.

Review the description to be sure your child has:

• used all of the verbs from this lesson.

• used action-packed verbs and colorful, descriptive adjectives and adverbs.

• written sentences that relate to the topic and are mechanically correct.

Tips for Your Own Writing: Proofreading ....
Choose a sample of your own writing. Look for *took/taken, swam/swum,* and *tore/torn*. Check to see that you used a helping verb with *taken, swum,* and *torn*.

If you swam through this lesson without hitting a snag, you have swum well!

57

174   Answer Key

Lesson 27

Lesson 27 — Usage: Verbs—Wrote, Stole, Began

✏️ *Troublesome verbs refuse to conform. You have to learn them one by one—or two by two!*

.... **Did You Know?** ....

The <u>past</u> form of a verb describes a past action. It usually consists of one word. The <u>past participle</u> form consists of the past form that is used with a helping verb such as *have, has, had, was,* or *were.*

Look at the present, past, and past participle forms of each of the troublesome verbs below. Then read the sentences that follow. They show correct usage for each form of these verbs.

Present	Past	Past Participle
Today they **write**.	Yesterday they **wrote**.	They **have written**.
Today they **steal**.	Yesterday they **stole**.	They **have stolen**.
Today they **begin**.	Yesterday they **began**.	They **have begun**.

"Where is the poem that I **wrote?**" bellowed Milton.
The weary poet **had written** many stanzas last night.

Someone **stole** Hannah's gym shoes.
My favorite sneakers **were stolen** from the gym, also.

The mourning dove **began** its sorrowful song.
The birds **had begun** their chorus at 4:30 in the morning!

Show What You Know
Read the paragraph. Underline the correct form of each verb in parentheses.

In an ancient land called Sumer, scholars (<u>wrote</u>, written) on clay tablets with a
stylus. The stylus was a tool that made wedge-shaped marks in wet clay. Young
students (<u>began</u>, begun) their education by learning to write with this tool. Why did the
Sumerians develop this type of writing? One reason was that they had (began, <u>begun</u>)
to record laws. Writing down a code of laws allows a society to apply laws equally. For
example, Sumerian judges could punish any powerful person who (<u>stole</u>, stolen) goods
the same as anyone else who had (stole, <u>stolen</u>). Soon, people found easier ways to
write. Keepers of records have not (wrote, <u>written</u>) on clay tablets for centuries!

Score: _____   Total Possible: 6

58

Proofread
The following interview uses the verb pairs *wrote/written, stole/stolen,* and *began/begun.* Each verb form is used incorrectly once. Using the proper proofreading mark, delete each incorrect word and write the correction above it.

Example: We ~~begun~~ *began* our day early.

INTERVIEWER: Tell us what you have ~~wrote~~ *written* lately, Pete.

PETE PORTER: Well, Zara, I have been writing an epic poem about the dawn of the computer age. Some critics might claim that I ~~stolen~~ *stole* the idea from Beryl Brinkley, but that's not true.

INTERVIEWER: Critic Natalie Naster claimed that you had ~~stole~~ *stolen* the rhymes. But enough of that. You ~~written~~ *wrote* ten short poems last year, didn't you?

PETE PORTER: Right. But now I have ~~began~~ *begun* to create epic poetry!

INTERVIEWER: Fascinating. When you ~~begun~~ *began* your career, we had no idea you'd write epic poetry. We look forward to your new poem.

Practice
Imagine the dispute between poets Pete Porter and Beryl Brinkley. Write a short letter that one of these poets might write to the other one. Include the verbs presented in this lesson.

Review the letter to be sure your child has:

• used at least three of the verbs from this lesson.

• used language that conveys some of the emotional content of a dispute.

• written sentences that relate to the topic and are mechanically correct.

Tips for Your Own Writing: Proofreading ....
Choose a story you have written. See whether you find any of the three verb pairs from this lesson. Make sure you used a helping verb when necessary.

✏️ *"Wrote/written, stole/stolen, began/begun—Learning verbs in pairs can be lots of fun!"*

59

Lesson 28

Lesson 28 — Usage: Verbs—Blew, Sank, Fell

✏️ *Studying past forms of verbs in pairs gives us clues to solving verb mysteries. Elementary, my dear Watson!*

.... **Did You Know?** ....

The <u>past</u> form of a verb describes a past action. It usually consists of one word. The <u>past participle</u> form consists of the past form that is used with a helping verb such as *have, has, had, was,* or *were.*

Look at the present, past, and past participle forms of each of the troublesome verbs below. Then read the sentences that follow. They show correct usage for each form of these verbs.

Present	Past	Past Participle
Today they **blow**.	Yesterday they **blew**.	They **have blown**.
Today they **sink**.	Yesterday they **sank**.	They **have sunk**.
Today they **fall**.	Yesterday they **fell**.	They **have fallen**.

The wind **blew**, slapping rain across the deck.
Fiercer gales **had blown** before.

One storm last fall **sank** a freighter ten miles off the coast.
But no ship of mine **has** ever **sunk**.

In a shocking crash, the main mast **fell** to the deck!
It **had fallen** so suddenly, no one could sound a warning.

Show What You Know
In each pair of sentences, draw a line to match each sentence with the verb form that it should use.

The BBW Story (Big Bad Wolf)

1. The BBW had a reputation to keep up: he ____ houses down. — blown
   This wouldn't be the first straw hut he had ____ away. — blew

2. But when the pigs heard him, their hearts had ____ to their toes. — sank
   Before hiding, they ____ their valuables into the well. — sunk

3. What was the outcome? The house had ____—no big deal. — fallen
   "We really ____ for that huff-and-puff story," said Pig Junior. — fell

Score: _____   Total Possible: 6

60

Proofread
The following is an imaginary diary entry by a sailor in the 1700s. The writer used the verb pairs *blew/blown, sank/sunk,* and *fell/fallen* incorrectly six times. Using the proper proofreading mark, delete each incorrect word and write the correction above it.

Example: The sun ~~sunk~~ *sank* below the horizon.

At about 9:00 A.M., a gust of wind ~~blown~~ *blew* suddenly, shaking the ship to its keel. Just then the second mate fell to the deck. Others had ~~fell~~ *fallen*, too, so great was the jolt. The tempest blew, and then it had ~~blew~~ *blown* some more. Another dreadful gust hit. "Have we ~~sank~~ *sunk* for good?" cried the first mate. "The enemy never ~~sunk~~ *sank* this scow," shouted Captain Cruz, "nor will Mother Nature now!" When the wind had ~~fell~~ *fallen*, we knew that the ship had not sunk.

Practice
Imagine that you are at sea on a boat like the one in the picture. Suddenly, an intense storm blows up. Describe the experience, using strong action verbs and vivid descriptive words. Also, use the three pairs of verbs presented in this lesson.

Review the paragraph to be sure your child has:

• used at least three of the verbs from this lesson.

• used other strong action verbs and vivid adjectives.

• written sentences that relate to the topic and are mechanically correct.

Tips for Your Own Writing: Proofreading ....
Review a report you have written. Look for the words *blew/blown, sank/sunk,* and *fell/fallen.* Check the sentences to see that you have used a helping verb with *blown, sunk,* and *fallen.*

✏️ *You neither sank nor fell in this lesson, nor have you sunk or fallen! If you blew your own horn, then you have blown it for good reason.*

61

Lesson 29

Lesson
29 Usage: Verbs—Lie/Lay, Rise/Raise

Many writers have trouble with these tricky verb pairs. See whether you can beat the averages!

.... **Did You Know?** ....

The following word pairs have related meanings that invite confusion. Read on to learn how to use them correctly.

Lie means "to be at rest or recline." *Lay* means "to put or to place (something)."

> Beth just wanted to **lie** on the beach for a whole week.
> You should **lay** your beach towel on the sand away from the surf.

Rise means "to move in an upward direction." *Raise* means "to lift (something)" or "to move something higher."

> The moon should **rise** in the early evening, according to the script.
> Jenny tugged on the rope to **raise** the cutout moon in the theater set.

Show What You Know
Correctly fill in each blank with one of these words: *lie, lay, rise, raise.*

A Night in Camp

I am happy as I ___lie___ on the air mattress, gazing at the brilliant, starry sky. I
feel I could grab the low, oval moon and ___lay___ it here beside me. Instead, I
___lie___ very still. No noise disturbs the quiet. No breeze rustles the leaves above.
Nearby, I see smoke ___rise___ lazily from the dying campfire. It curls and twists up to
the leafy ceiling of tree limbs. Hypnotized, I watch it ___rise___ higher and then
disappear. When I ___raise___ my head a little, I see that the embers have at last died
out. I want to wake up before dawn so that I can see the sun ___rise___. All is well in
camp. This is the life!

Score: _____ Total Possible: 7

62

Proofread
The following bread recipe uses the verbs *lie/lay* and *rise/raise* incorrectly four times. Using the proper proofreading mark, delete each incorrect word and write the correct word above it.

Example: Does the cookbook ~~lay~~ *lie* on the table?

Della's Old-Fashioned Bread

1. Mix the yeast, sugar, and warm water in a small bowl. Put the bowl in a warm place for the yeast to ~~raise~~ *rise*.

2. In a separate bowl, mix the flour and salt. ~~Lie~~ *Lay* this bowl aside for now.

3. After ten minutes, mix everything together in a large bowl. Make a ball of dough.

4. If the dough will ~~lay~~ *lie* in your hand without sticking, it is just right. If not, add flour.

5. Put the dough on your board. ~~Rise~~ *Raise* your hand and push your palm into the dough. Raise your hand and repeat the action. (This action is called "kneading" the dough.)

Practice
Look at the drawing. What time of year does it suggest? Write a brief story or description in response to this picture. Use the verb pairs *lie/lay* and *rise/raise.*

Review the story or description to be sure your child
has:

• used the verbs *lie, lay, rise,* and *raise.*

• chosen words to convey the feelings he or she remembers
from having experienced such a fall evening.

• written sentences that make sense and are mechanically correct.

Tips for Your Own Writing: Proofreading
Choose a piece of your own writing. Look for the verbs *lie* and *lay.* Check to see that *lie* is used when you mean "to be at rest" and *lay* when you mean "to put or place." Look for other troublesome word pairs such as *rise* and *raise.*

Don't lie down on the job, don't lay your troubles down, and don't raise your voice. Just rise to the occasion! Get it?

63

Lesson 30

Lesson
30 Usage: Verbs—Can/May, Let/Leave, Teach/Learn, Bring/Take

With some confusing verb pairs, we just have to learn and remember the difference. It's hard work, but the payoff is appropriate usage!

.... **Did You Know?** ....

The following word pairs have related meanings that invite confusion.

Can means "to be able to (do something)." *May* means "to be allowed or permitted to (do something)."

> Incorrect: "**Can** I be excused?" asked Carmen.
> Correct: "**May** I be excused?" asked Carmen.

Let means "to allow." *Leave* means "to depart" or "to permit something to remain where it is."

> Incorrect: "**Leave** me go!" begged the caged animal's eyes.
> Correct: "**Let** me go!" begged the caged animal's eyes.

Teach means "to explain" or "to help (someone) understand." *Learn* means "to gain knowledge."

> Incorrect: Please **learn** me how to tie a square knot.
> Correct: Please **teach** me how to tie a square knot.

Bring means "to fetch" or "to carry toward (oneself, something, or someone)." *Take* means "to carry in a direction away from (oneself, something, or someone)."

> Incorrect: **Bring** your mom to that countryside restaurant.
> Correct: **Take** your mom to that countryside restaurant.

Show What You Know
Underline the correct form of each verb in parentheses.

1. (Can, May) I speak six languages? Yes, (can, <u>may</u>) I show you now?

2. (Leave, <u>Let</u>) me just say this before I have to (<u>leave</u>, let).

3. Teachers want to (<u>teach</u>, learn) their pupils. Pupils want to (teach, <u>learn</u>) from them.

4. (Bring, <u>Take</u>) your lunch, but (take, <u>bring</u>) me the extra money.

Score: _____ Total Possible: 8

64

Proofread
The following report contains the verbs presented in this lesson. In six places, those verbs are used incorrectly. Using the proper proofreading mark, delete each incorrect word and write the correction above it.

Example: ~~Leave~~ *Let* us do the work.

The Chinese write their language in a different way than people write their
languages in the West. They do not use an alphabet, if you ~~may~~ *can* imagine that. Instead,
the Chinese learn a unique character for every word. There are about fifty thousand
characters in all. Imagine having to learn all those characters or having to ~~learn~~ *teach* them to
someone else. In fact, educated Chinese can read thousands of characters. This
knowledge will ~~leave~~ *let* them read a newspaper easily.
~~Can~~ *May* I tell you one more thing? I am studying Chinese, and I will ~~bring~~ *take* you to my
class if you'd like. Just be sure to ~~take~~ *bring* an open mind with you.

Practice
Write one sentence for four of the verbs introduced in this lesson. Then use a dictionary to find definitions for these verbs that are different from the ones presented here. Write a sentence for each different definition you find.

Review the sentences to be sure your child has:

• written a sentence for four of the eight verbs *can, may, let,
leave, teach, learn, bring,* and *take.*

• located different definitions of the words (*can:* to put up by the
canning process; *may:* to admit possibility; *let:* to rent; *leave:* to bequeath; *teach:* to instruct
in school; *learn:* to become aware of, and so on).

Tips for Your Own Writing: Proofreading
The next time you write a story or report, be aware of how you can use *can* and *may.* Remember, *can* means "to be able to" and *may* means "to be allowed to."

May I congratulate you on this lesson? You can now ace these difficult verbs!

65

Lesson 31

Lesson 31 — Review: Verbs (page 66)

A. The following is a fictional account of an expedition to the South Pole. Underline the correct form of each verb in parentheses.

The expedition consisted of Woods, Danner, and Abaji, the captain. On December 1, the crew (<u>began</u>, begun) its trek inland across the ice shelf. The first mishap occurred that very day. One of the dogs lost its footing and (<u>fell</u>, fallen) into the icy water. [2] Though it (<u>swam</u>, swum) to safety, the dog (<u>shook</u>, shaken) all over and was badly [3] [4] chilled. That night, the wind (<u>blew</u>, blown) with a terrible force. Earlier, it had [5] (blew, <u>blown</u>) down one of the tents in camp. The crew soon learned that a gust had [6] (tore, <u>torn</u>) this tent beyond repair. The very next day, they watched helplessly as one [7] of the supply sleds (<u>sank</u>, sunk) into a crevasse. Weighted down with food, it had [8] (sank, <u>sunk</u>) with terrifying speed. Hungry and engulfed by bitter cold, the party [9] (<u>fell</u>, fallen) into despair. [10] Three days later, all but one had (froze, <u>frozen</u>) to death. This was Captain Abaji, [11] who (<u>wrote</u>, written) in his diary every day. His last entry was "We have (fell, <u>fallen</u>). [12] [13] Here I have (wrote, <u>written</u>) the truth: we perished with courage." [14]

Score: _____ Total Possible: 14

B. Decide whether the underlined word in each sentence is used correctly. If it is, put a C above the word. If it is not, write the correct word above the underlined word.

C   took
Brett had <u>stolen</u> a candy bar from his sister Ann's lunch box. He <u>taken</u> it without [1] [2] tore thinking about his action. As he <u>torn</u> off the wrapper, he realized what he'd done. [3] Though the candy looked tasty, Brett <u>began</u> to feel very ashamed. He <u>wrote</u> a note of [4] C [5] frozen apology to put in Ann's lunch box with the candy bar. Just then, Ann came into the kitchen. Brett was <u>froze</u> in his tracks. [6]

Score: _____ Total Possible: 6

66

C. In each blank, write a verb from the list. Some verbs may be used more than once. Some may not be used at all. (page 67)

| raise | rise | take | bring | let | leave | can | may | lie | lay |

Clyde's Bad Break in Show Biz

MS. DÍAZ: Please _____bring_____ something to school for your demonstration speech. 1

LOU: _____May_____ I bring my pet snake Clyde? It will _____lie_____ quietly in one 2   3 place and not bother a soul. We'll only have to worry if we see it _____raise_____ its tail. 4

MS. DÍAZ: But _____can_____ your snake bite? 5

LOU: Maybe. But I'll tell Clyde: "You _____may_____ not bite!" 6

MS. DÍAZ: Thanks, but I cannot _____let_____ Clyde come to school. You will have to 7 _____leave_____ your talented snake at home. 8

Score: _____ Total Possible: 8

D. Write the verb in the parentheses that correctly completes each sentence.

1. (rang, rung) The year is 1905. The school bell has just _____rung_____. The teacher _____rang_____ that bell by hand at the same time yesterday.

2. (teach, learn) The one-room schoolhouse is full of youngsters eager to _____learn_____. The school has one teacher. She will _____teach_____ students of all ages.

3. (lie, lay) The students sit down and _____lay_____ their hands together on their desks. No one will slouch or _____lie_____ down in this schoolroom!

4. (rise, raise) To ask a question, students must _____raise_____ their hands. The teacher says, "Yes, Maude (or Clarence), you may _____rise_____."

5. (bring, take) There is no lunchroom. Students _____bring_____ cold food from home to school. They _____take_____ the leftovers home after the closing bell rings.

Score: _____ Total Possible: 10

REVIEW SCORE: _____ REVIEW TOTAL: 38

67

Lesson 32

Lesson 32 — Usage: Adjectives (page 68)

Writing—and life—would be dull without comparisons. We have rules in English for how to compare using adjectives.

.... **Did You Know?** ....

Adjectives—words that modify nouns or pronouns—use different forms when used to make comparisons. The <u>comparative</u> form of an adjective is used to compare two things.

This fish is **larger** than that one.   Sara is **more talkative** than Li.

The <u>superlative</u> form of an adjective is used to compare more than two things.

The Siberian tiger is the **largest** member of the cat family. The **most talkative** person I've ever known is Kareem.

Did you notice two of the adjectives end with -er or -est and the other two adjectives use more or most? Short adjectives usually add -er or -est. Longer adjectives usually add more or most.

Most adjectives are regular: they follow the above patterns in forming their comparatives and superlatives. But a few adjectives are irregular: they form their comparatives and superlatives in different ways.

Regular Adjectives	Comparative Adjectives	Superlative Adjectives
good	better	best
bad	worse	worst

The only way to learn these irregular forms is to memorize them.

....

Show What You Know
Rewrite each adjective in bold type. Write it in the blank in either the comparative or superlative form.

1. On the tennis court, Mei is a **powerful** opponent. Is she ____more powerful____ than Jo?

2. But Jo has a **strong** backhand. It may be ____stronger____ than Mei's.

3. They are both **good** players. But which one is the ____better____ player?

4. Their match was a **long** one. It was the ____longest____ match in the tournament.

5. It was also **exciting**. It was the ____most exciting____ match I saw all week.

Score: _____ Total Possible: 5

68

Proofread
In the following report, underline the five adjectives that are used in their comparative or superlative form. For each of the four forms used incorrectly, use the proper proofreading mark to delete it and write the correction above it. (page 69)

slower **Example:** A car moves ~~more slow~~ than a train.

The pyramid is a basic form in geometry. Human beings have built pyramids as tombs or places of worship throughout history. Of all the pyramids in the world, the tallest ~~taller~~ one is King Khufu's Great Pyramid in Egypt. It rises more than 450 feet (137 most beautiful meters). Some people consider this the ~~beautifulest~~ as well as the <u>largest</u> pyramid.

Native Americans also built many pyramids. American pyramids had a stair-stepped most complete side and a flat top. The ~~completest~~ one today is the Temple of Inscriptions at Palenque, shorter Mexico. Though quite beautiful, this structure is much ~~more short~~ than Egypt's Great Pyramid.

Practice
Write a story using at least five comparative or superlative adjectives.

Review the story to be sure your child has:

• used at least five adjectives in comparative and superlative forms.

• used expressive action verbs and colorful modifiers in addition to the required adjectives.

• written a story that makes sense and is mechanically correct.

Tips for Your Own Writing: Proofreading ....
The next time you write a description in a story, be sure you use -er or more with adjectives when comparing two things, and -est or most with adjectives when comparing more than two things.

When comparing two, use two letters (-er); when comparing three or more, use three letters (-est).

69

Answer Key **177**

Lesson 33

Lesson
33 Usage: Adverbs

Add spice to your writing with adverbs—especially adverbs of comparison.

.... **Did You Know?** ....

Adverbs—words that modify verbs, adjectives, or other adverbs—use different forms when used to make comparisons. The <u>comparative</u> form of an adverb is used to compare two actions.

Deb arrived **later** than Heather.
Bill shuffled his test papers **more noisily** than Tyrone.

The <u>superlative</u> form of an adverb is used to compare more than two actions.

Jewel climbed the **highest** of all.
Of all the students, Ernesto worked the **most rapidly**.

Short adverbs add *-er* or *-est*.

Most adverbs that end in *-ly* form their comparatives and superlatives using *more* and *most*. A few that do not end in *-ly* also use *more* and *most*.

I eat olives **more often** than Mom, but Dad eats them the **most often**.

Most adverbs are *regular*: they follow the above patterns in forming their comparatives and superlatives. A few adverbs are *irregular*.

Regular: The Badgers played **badly** in the play-offs.
Comparative: The Tigers played **worse** than the Bears.
Superlative: Of all the teams, the Lions played the **worst**.

....

Show What You Know

Rewrite the adverb in the bold type. Write it in the blank in either the comparative or superlative form.

1. Our hockey team skated **badly**. We skated ___worse___ than we usually do.

2. The coach arrived at the rink **late**. The goalie arrived ___latest___ of all.

3. Carl missed the goal **frequently**. He also shot ___more frequently___ than others.

4. Our fans cheered **noisily**. Of all the schools' fans, we cheered the ___most noisily___.

Score: _____   Total Possible: 4

70

Proofread

In the following school newspaper article, underline the eight adverbs that are used in the comparative or superlative form. For the four forms used incorrectly, use the proper proofreading mark to delete the word and write the correction above it.

Example: That race is ~~more easy~~ than this one. *(easier)*

The Science Club sponsored a Turtle Derby last Thursday. Three candidates—Ralph, Ed, and Trixie—lined up at the starting gate. At the pop of a balloon, they were off! Trixie moved slowly to start. But Ralph moved <u>more slowly</u> than Trixie. Ed moved the <u>more slowly</u> *(most slowly)* of the three. (It was clear that Trixie took the race <u>seriouser</u> *(more seriously)* than Ralph.)

When interviewed, a spectator, Perry Plum, said: "Trixie started badly, but Ed started <u>worse</u> than she did. Ralph started the <u>baddest</u> *(worst)* of the three." Not everyone agreed. Tilly Towson said, "I rate Trixie pretty high, Ed <u>higher</u> than Trixie, and Ralph the <u>highest</u> of all!"

So who won? The turtle who tried <u>most hard</u> *(hardest)*—Trixie, of course.

Practice

Look at the picture. Write a description of the skier's run down the ski slope. Use at least two adverbs in their comparative or superlative form.

Review the description to be sure your child has:

• used at least two adverbs in comparative and superlative forms.

• captured the feeling of elation that one experiences when engaged in a challenging (sometimes even dangerous) physical activity.

• used the adverbs appropriately (they should convey feelings similar to those described previously).

Tips for Your Own Writing: Revising ....

Choose a piece of your own writing. Exchange it with a partner to find the adverbs. Then, look for places to use adverbs that compare. Revise your writing.

What have you done superbly? Then think of something you did more superbly, and finally, something you did the most superbly of all!

71

···

Lesson 34

Lesson
34 Usage: Adjective/Adverb

Here is some advice: Don't mix up your adjectives and adverbs.

.... **Did You Know?** ....

Some adjectives and adverbs look and sound nearly alike. Often, the only difference is that the adverb has the ending *-ly* added.

My head sank into the **soft** pillow.
I padded **softly** down the hall to avoid waking my mom.

An adjective modifies or describes a noun or a pronoun. It also tells which one, what kind, or how many. An adjective fits into both blanks in this sentence: The _____ dog was very _____.

An adverb modifies or describes a verb, an adjective, or another adverb. It also tells when, how, where, or to what extent. Most adverbs end in *-ly* and can be moved to several places in a sentence.

In English, there are many of these similar adjective/adverb pairs. Here are a few more examples: *quiet/quietly, deep/deeply, sad/sadly, bright/brightly, dark/darkly.*

....

Show What You Know

Write the word that completes each sentence.

1. In May 1980, Mount Saint Helens in Washington exploded ___loudly___. (loud, loudly)

2. Previously ___quiet___, this volcano had not erupted in 123 years. (quiet, quietly)

3. It raised a very ___dark___ mushroom cloud like a bomb blast. (dark, darkly)

4. Hot ash spread ___rapidly___ outward from the blast. (rapid, rapidly)

5. In nearby areas, it piled up ___deeply___, almost like snow. (deep, deeply)

6. ___Soft___ and featherlight, the ash created a breathing hazard. (Soft, Softly)

7. We must ___sadly___ report the deaths of many wild animals. (sad, sadly)

8. A ___late___ count revealed that 60 people died. (late, lately)

Score: _____   Total Possible: 8

72

Proofread

Read Tim's report about his recent visit to a wetlands area. Pay careful attention to his use of adjectives and adverbs. For each of the six that have been used incorrectly, use the proper proofreading mark to delete the word and write the correction above it.

Example: I walked across the street ~~quick~~. *(quickly)*

Last month, I spent a ~~busy~~ *(busy)* week with my cousin Daneale in Peachtree City. We had an ~~easily~~ *(easy)* time finding things to do. Peachtree City has lakes, wetlands, bicycle paths, and recreational areas. You could walk into some wetlands on strongly constructed walkways. You started in bright light, but this changed to shady and then to ~~dimly~~ *(dim)* light as the canopy of leaves thickened. The air smelled of cypress trees and wet earth. It was a time for ~~quiet~~ *(quiet)* observation. At the end of the walk, Daneale and I saw a water moccasin. At least, that's what we think it was, but we didn't look too ~~close~~ *(closely)*. To be honest, I was a bit scared. I squeezed Daneale's hand ~~tight~~ *(tightly)*.

Practice

Write a sentence for the adjective and the adverb in each of the following word pairs. Express the same idea in both sentences. Here is an example:

weak: I felt weak after running five miles.
weakly: I weakly lifted the weights after my run.

close: _____

closely: Review the sentences to be sure your child has:

prompt: • used each adjective/adverb pair correctly.

promptly: • expressed the same or nearly the same idea in both sentences.

sad: • written sentences that make sense and are mechanically correct.

sadly: _____

Tips for Your Own Writing: Proofreading ....

Look at a story you have written. Circle the adjectives and underline the adverbs. Then, check the adjectives, using this sentence: The _____ (noun) is very _____.

A strong effort will be strongly rewarded.

73

178   Answer Key

Lesson 35

Lesson 35 Usage: Good/Well, Bad/Badly

✏️ *Good and well are as tangled as a plate of spaghetti! Read on to untangle them. (Thank goodness bad and badly are pretty straightforward.)*

.... **Did You Know?** ....

Good and *bad* are adjectives. Use them to modify nouns or pronouns. Sometimes they follow the verb. *Well* and *badly* are adverbs. Use them to modify verbs, adjectives, or other adverbs.

> I helped Raoul choose a **good** book.
> I feel **good** about the food we collected for homeless people.
> Mrs. Choy told me that Raoul read **well** in class.
> We had a **bad** thunderstorm last night.
> The weather forecaster predicted **badly**.

The word *well* is a special problem. It usually functions as an adverb, but it can be an adjective when it is used to mean "healthy." Usually, the adjective *well* follows a linking verb such as *am*.

> **Adverb:** Marita sang **well** at her concert last night.
> **Adjective:** "I am **well**," replied Ms. Slocum.

Remember that *good* is *always* used as an adjective. Also, remember that "feeling good" describes a state of mind, while "feeling well" describes someone's health.

....

Show What You Know
Underline the correct word in each word pair in parentheses.

Weightlessness is a potential health problem in space travel. Muscles can weaken (bad, <u>badly</u>) if astronauts fail to exercise enough. Another (<u>bad</u>, badly) effect is that the heart may get larger. On the other hand, some astronauts say that weightlessness makes them feel (<u>good</u>, badly). It brings on a mood of contentment. Scientists have found ways to help people cope with weightlessness. So, if you should meet an astronaut, ask, "How are you? Are you (good, <u>well</u>) today?" Maybe she or he will answer, "I'm fine. I have coped (good, <u>well</u>) with weightlessness."

Score: _____ Total Possible: 5

74

Proofread
Bonita Bower's campaign speech has been published. It has five errors in it. Using the proper proofreading mark, delete each incorrect word and write the correction above it.

Example: The runner ran ~~good~~ [well] in the race.

Good evening. I'm running for mayor. During the last election, I was defeated ~~bad~~ [badly]. But since then, I have talked to many people from all walks of life. And I feel ~~well~~ [good] about that. I've learned that we must all take an interest in city government.

I support conservation. As mayor, I will educate my staff to use supplies wisely. If we do ~~good~~ [well] at this, I will not request an increase in office budgets for two years.

I also want to improve public transportation. Service isn't always very ~~well~~ [good]. People who work far from home and don't drive are getting a ~~badly~~ [bad] deal.

Please vote for me, Bonita Bower, next Tuesday. I promise to do a good job!

Practice
Look at the picture. Have you ever thought about how difficult it must be to perform simple, daily tasks in space? Use your imagination to think of a way that this young astronaut could solve his problem. Use the word pairs introduced in this lesson.

Review the paragraph to be sure your child has:

• used *good/well* and *bad/badly* correctly.

• chosen action verbs and modifiers carefully.

• created imaginative solutions to the problem posed in the art.

• written sentences that make sense and are mechanically correct.

Tips for Your Own Writing: Proofreading ....
Choose a piece of your own writing. Look for the words *good, well, bad,* and *badly*. Make sure that you used *good* and *bad* to describe nouns and pronouns, and *badly* to describe verbs, adjectives, and other adverbs. Pay particular attention to the word *well*.

✏️ *Did you do well in this lesson? Then you should feel good about it!*

75

Lesson 36

Lesson 36 Usage: Accept/Except, Loose/Lose, Than/Then

✏️ *Words that sound alike or are spelled similarly can trap you. Don't get caught!*

.... **Did You Know?** ....

Because the following word pairs are similar in spelling and pronunciation, writers tend to confuse them. Be careful to use each word in the appropriate context.

Accept means "to take or receive (something)" or "to consent to (something)." *Except* means "other than."

> I'd like to **accept** your invitation to address your computer club.
> Any day of the week **except** Monday is all right with me.

Loose means "not fastened" or "not tight." *Lose* means "to be unable to find" or "to fail to keep."

> The chain has come **loose** from my bicycle's back wheel.
> The wheel wobbled and I started to **lose** my balance.

Than introduces the second part of a comparison. *Then* means "at that time" or "afterward."

> New Jersey has a larger land area **than** Connecticut.
> We went to Connecticut, and **then** we went to New Jersey.

....

Show What You Know
Underline the word in parentheses that correctly completes each sentence in the paragraphs below.

"I (<u>accept</u>, except) the challenge," responded the game-show contestant. "Just this one try, and (than, <u>then</u>) I'll stop."

The host read the question: "What nations have more land (<u>than</u>, then) the U.S.? Uh-oh. I think Rachel's microphone came (<u>loose</u>, lose). Let's try again. Rachel? (Buzzer.) The correct answer is Russia, (than, <u>then</u>) Canada, (than, <u>then</u>) China. So sorry, Rachel, but you (loose, <u>lose</u>). You won't get any prizes, (accept, <u>except</u>) the play-at-home game."

Score: _____ Total Possible: 8

76

Proofread
The following story contains words presented in this lesson. Five of them are used incorrectly. Using the proper proofreading mark, delete each incorrect word and write the correction above it.

Example: I ~~except~~ [accept] your invitation.

One day, Lucy's pet parakeet flew away. After two weeks of looking for it, Lucy's mom told her that she'd have to ~~except~~ [accept] her loss. "It is painful to ~~loose~~ [lose] a pet like Teresa," said Lucy sadly. "I should never have let her loose from her cage."

~~Than~~ [Then] one day Lucy was visiting her cousin Dee in a nearby town. They heard a "tap, tap, tap" on the kitchen window. Dee exclaimed, "I believe it's Teresa!"

Dee's mom said, "This is the wildest pet story I've ever heard."

"~~Accept~~ [Except] for Juan's snake story," suggested Dee. "Juan claimed that when his pet snake got ~~lose~~ [loose], it came out of the wall in his neighbor's apartment!"

Practice
Write sentences for each of the word pairs presented in this lesson. Use your imagination to create interesting sentences.

Review the sentences to be sure that your child has:

• written a sentence for each lesson word.

• used each lesson word correctly in the sentence.

• written imaginative sentences that make sense and are mechanically correct.

Tips for Your Own Writing: Proofreading ....
Scan a piece of your writing looking for the words in this lesson. Use *then* for "next"—*than* for "compare"; *accept* for "receive"—*except* for "not"; *loose* for "not tight"—*lose* for "no win."

✏️ *Accept the fact that English words are sometimes tricky to spell (except when you know all the spellings)!*

77

Answer Key **179**

Lesson 37

Lesson

37 Usage: Principle/Principal, There/They're/Their, Its/It's

✎ *Homophones are words that sound alike but have different spellings and meanings. The words in this lesson are homophones.*

.... Did You Know? ....

Because the following words sound the same and look alike, writers tend to confuse them. Context is the best clue as to which word to use in a sentence.

Principle means "a basic rule or belief." *Principal* means "most important" or "main." It also means "the chief or main person."

This science experiment demonstrates the **principle** of inertia.
Mrs. Monetti's **principal** objection was the noise.
Mrs. Monetti is the **principal** of our school.

There means "at that place." *They're* is a contraction for "they are." *Their* means "belonging to them."

The people in Lake Landis really like it **there**.
They're having a wonderful festival in July.
Have you seen **their** brochure for the festival?

Its is the possessive form of *it*. *It's* is a contraction for "it is."

The bird fluffed up **its** feathers.
You know **it's** going to be a cold day.

Show What You Know

Underline the word in parentheses that correctly completes each sentence in the paragraph below.

Today I'll demonstrate the (principle, **principal**) of osmosis. (Its, **It's**) the
¹ ²
(principle, **principal**) lesson that we'll cover this week. Osmosis is the movement of one
³
solution to another when (**they're**, their) separated by a membrane. A plant absorbs
⁴
most of (**its**, it's) water by the process of osmosis. Would the lab groups please pick up
⁵
(there, **their**) notebooks and follow me? If you will gather around Table 2, you will see
⁶
that a demonstration is set up (**there**, their).
⁷

Score: _____ Total Possible: 7

78

Proofread

In Talia's report, use the proper proofreading mark to delete each of the six incorrect words and write the correction above it.

                       their
Example: They forgot their books.

                                                    principal
Dragonflies are among the most beautiful insects. Because their ~~principle~~ food is

  they're   their
insects, ~~their~~ helpful, too. They can eat their own weight in insects in a half hour.

                                       its
It's hard to believe, but a dragonfly lives almost it's entire life in a wingless form

called a nymph. The beautiful, gauzy-winged flier that we know represents only a few

weeks to a few months of this insect's life. Dragonflies live for several years.

                                 There
No insect can fly as fast as a dragonfly. ~~They're~~ are reports of these fliers darting

as fast as a car on the highway—60 mph! No wonder they can catch so many insects.

Some extinct ancestors of today's dragonfly were huge. They had wingspans of
                        It's
almost three feet. ~~Its~~ hard to imagine that!

Practice

Look at the picture. How would you react to seeing a giant dragonfly? Write a description of this dragonfly as if you were seeing it in real life. Try to use the words introduced in this lesson.

Review the description to be sure that your child has:

• used rich vocabulary (adjectives, adverbs, verbs)
  to describe what he or she sees.

• written a strong description of his or her emotional response to the scene.

• written sentences that make sense and are mechanically correct.

Tips for Your Own Writing: Proofreading ....

Search for any of these troublesome words—*principal/principle, there/they're/their, its/it's*—in a piece of your own writing. Determine whether you have used the words correctly.

✎ *Don't forget the apostrophe! It's a small mark, but its presence can make all the difference.*

79

....

Lesson 38

Lesson

38 Review: Adjectives, Adverbs

A. In the following movie review, underline the correct form of the adjective in each set of parentheses.

For a *really* (**good**, best) film, see *Danada Square* by director George Chan. It is a
¹
(**more sentimental**, sentimentaler) movie than Chan's previous film, *Run Home! Danada*
²
Square tells the story of a young Asian-American woman who starts a business in a

shopping center. She encounters many difficulties, including prejudice. But the

(baddest, **worst**) part of all her troubles is conflict with the landlord of her store. Of
³
course, this (**bad**, worst) person is the villain of the movie. Of Chan's four films, I think
⁴
that this is the (goodest, **best**) one.
⁵
On the other hand, *Damage in Kuala Lumpur* is the (baddest, **worst**) movie I've
⁶
seen in years. It's a disaster movie about three high-rise towers in that Asian capital.

The (taller, **tallest**) of the three, called the "Black Tower," has a bomb scare. Then the
⁷
"Green Tower," which is (**taller**, tallest) than the "White Tower," catches fire. So it goes.
⁸
Stay away from this movie and save your money!

Score: _____ Total Possible: 8

B. In each sentence in the paragraph below, underline the correct form of the adverb in parentheses.

Ziggy Zales hit (**low**, more low) in yesterday's opening match. He hits the
¹
(most low, **lowest**) of any tennis player that I can recall. Laura Farfone delivers the
²
(most fast, **fastest**) serve of any tennis player. Her serve is definitely (fast, **faster**) than
³ ⁴
that of champion Maria Rivera. Some people think tennis moves (**more quickly**,
⁵
quicklier) than baseball. Laura slept (**badly**, bad) before the tennis match. But Ziggy
⁶
slept (more badly, **worse**) than Laura.
⁷

Score: _____ Total Possible: 7

80

C. Choose the word from the parentheses that correctly completes each sentence and write it in the blank.

1. The defense attorneys were certain that their case was very ___strong___. (strong, strongly)

2. "I ___strongly___ object!" exclaimed the lawyer. (strong, strongly)

3. The main witness for the defense related a ___sad___ story. (sad, sadly)

4. She ___sadly___ wiped her tears away, which was a nice touch. (sad, sadly)

5. The attorney wants a ___prompt___ conclusion to this trial. (prompt, promptly)

6. "The court will reconvene ___promptly___ at ten o'clock," said Judge Wu. (prompt, promptly)

Score: _____ Total Possible: 6

D. Read Marla's report on "Weird Planets." There are twelve errors. Using the proper proofreading mark, delete each incorrect word and write the correction above it.

                             principal
The more we know about the ~~principle~~ planets in our solar system, the more
                                              they're
normal our planet Earth seems. Earth has eight planet cousins, and their really weird!

Consider Mercury, the planet closest to the sun. A day on Mercury is 88 Earth days
                                        badly
long. One side of Mercury faces the sun for 88 days in a row, getting ~~bad~~ burned at
                                      lose   It's
800°F. The opposite, shady side must ~~loose~~ heat for those 88 days. ~~Its~~ frigid!
                             except
Saturn is beautiful, ~~accept~~ it is deadly. It has the largest and most visible rings,
                its   there
which circle it's middle like a belt. You wouldn't want to vacation ~~their~~. Saturn's winds
                                                    than
blow at speeds of 1,000 mph. That's about five times faster ~~then~~ a severe tornado's

winds.
                                              principle
But the weirdest planet is Uranus. This planet violates the ~~principal~~ by which the

other planets rotate like tops. Instead, Uranus spins oddly on its side. (If I were Uranus, I
              well   accept
wouldn't feel very ~~good~~ after eons of this motion.) Uranus should ~~except~~ the "weirdest"

planet" award!

Score: _____ Total Possible: 12

REVIEW SCORE: _____ REVIEW TOTAL: 33

81

Lesson 39

Lesson 39 Usage: Plural Nouns

One, two, three—how many? Two or more means "use the plural."

.... Did You Know? ....

A singular noun names one person, place, thing, or idea. A plural noun names two or more persons, places, things, or ideas.

Plural nouns are formed in the following ways:

- most nouns, add -*s*.
  girl**s**   friend**s**
- nouns ending in *s, sh, ch,* or *x*, add -*es*.
  boxe**s**   churche**s**
- nouns ending in *y* preceded by a consonant, change *y* to *i* and add -*es*.
  bod**y**—bod**ies**
- nouns ending in *y* preceded by a vowel, add just -*s*.
  toy—toy**s**   boy—boy**s**
- some nouns ending in *o*, add -*s*. Some ending in *o* preceded by a consonant, add -*es*.
  radio**s**   echo**es**

- many nouns ending in *f* or *fe*, change the *f* to *v* and add -*es* or -*s*. Some nouns ending in *f*, add only -*s*.
  calf—cal**ves**
  knife—kni**ves**
  chief—chief**s**
- a few nouns, make *no* change between the singular and plural.
  sheep   moose
- a few nouns form the plural irregularly.
  goose—geese
  child—children

Show What You Know
Write the plurals of the underlined words on the lines.

1. the echo of two banjo — echoes, banjos
2. recipe: ten ripe cherry and two tomato — cherries, tomatoes
3. some essay challenge your belief — essays, beliefs
4. the report "Wolf and Fox" — Wolves, Foxes
5. a new play, "Do Sheep Have Tooth?" — Sheep, Teeth

Score: _____   Total Possible: 10

82

Proofread
Read Dino's story. He has formed seven plurals incorrectly. Using the proper proofreading mark, delete each incorrect plural and write the correct word above it.

Example: I read three ~~story~~ today.   *stories*

My ~~friendes~~ and I wanted to have a computer club. We're crazy about ~~computeres~~.   *friends*   *computers*

We started inviting everyone we thought would like to join. We decided not to have a

president because we don't like the idea of having bosses. Instead, we have two

~~chieves~~: a chief program chairperson and a chief refreshment chair. They will have no   *chiefs*

~~vetos~~ over club ~~decisiones~~.   *vetoes*   *decisions*

Thinking up a clever name wasn't easy. In the end, we chose "~~Torpedos~~." Why?   *Torpedoes*

Because sometimes ~~torpedos~~ come after you, figuratively speaking, when you carelessly   *torpedoes*

key in a mistake!

Practice
Write a brief story about an afternoon "lineup" on the radio. Include plural nouns in your writing.

Review the story to be sure that your child has:

- used the plural word forms correctly.
- included a variety of topics.
- written sentences that make sense and are mechanically correct.

Tips for Your Own Writing: Proofreading ....
If a plural form you want to use in your writing is not shown in this lesson, look the noun up in the dictionary. Most dictionaries list irregular plurals. Otherwise, add *s* or -*es* to the noun.

Adding -s is a good bet for forming a plural, but it won't always be right.

83

....

Lesson 40

Lesson 40 Usage: Possessive Nouns

It's mine! It's mine! Possessive nouns show ownership.

.... Did You Know? ....

A possessive noun shows ownership of a noun that follows. Remember: a noun is a word that names a person, place, thing, or idea.

The following rules show how to form the possessive of nouns:

If the noun is singular, add an apostrophe and *s*.

> I'm going to my sister**'s** new office.
> Cass**'s** job is public relations director of the national fair.

If the noun is plural and ends in *s*, add an apostrophe only.

> This national fair is the cities**'** showcase.

If the noun is plural and does not end in *s*, add an apostrophe and *s*.

> The fair has a children**'s** pavilion.

Show What You Know
On the line, write the correct possessive form of each underlined noun.

1. birds adaptations for flight — birds'
2. a bird wing — bird's
3. an ostrich story — ostrich's
4. an ibis story — ibis's
5. owls quiet hunting flights — owls'
6. mice chances when a hawk is near — mice's

Score: _____   Total Possible: 6

84

Proofread
Read Marianne's report. Using the proper proofreading mark, delete each of the five incorrect possessive nouns and write the correction above it.

Example: What is your ~~cousins~~ name?   *cousin's*

In ancient Greece, many myths were told and later written down. One such myth

is about Icarus, who was ~~Daedalus~~ son. Daedalus was a marvelous builder and   *Daedalus's*

inventor. But he had been imprisoned in a maze for a crime. Daedalus saw a way to

escape. He made wings for himself out of ~~birds~~ feathers and some wax. Using the   *birds'*

wings, Daedalus was able to fly out of the maze.

Icarus was so excited by the ~~wings~~ power and the thrill of flying that he ignored   *wings'*

his father's warning. He used his ~~father~~ wings and flew higher and higher. He got too   *father's*

close to the ~~suns~~ burning rays and melted the wax that held together his wings. He fell   *sun's*

to his death.

Practice
Look at the picture. Imagine that you are the rabbit and that you are being hunted by the owl. What emotions would you feel? What strategies would you devise to outwit this bird of prey? Write a paragraph of the rabbit's thoughts below. Use some possessive nouns in your paragraph.

Review the paragraph to be sure that your child has:

- used possessive nouns correctly as he or she expressed his or her emotions.
- created colorful summaries written from the rabbit's point of view.
- written sentences that make sense and are mechanically correct.

Tips for Your Own Writing: Proofreading ....
Choose something you have written recently. Check any possessive nouns you used to make sure you have used apostrophes correctly.

You've done another day's work. Or is it two days' work?

85

Lesson 41

Lesson 41 Usage: Plural/Possessive

With plurals and possessives, you don't always hear the difference, but you can see it.

·············· Did You Know? ··············

A **plural noun** names two or more things, persons, places, or ideas.
A **possessive noun** shows ownership of a noun that follows.

Sometimes we have difficulty deciding whether a noun is plural, possessive, or both. The following guidelines will help you:
Some plural possessive nouns end in an apostrophe only.

houses' colors   cities' population

Irregular plurals form the possessive by adding **'s**.

women's club   mice's hole   sheep's wool

All singular possessive nouns end in **'s**. Remember that a singular noun names one thing, person, place, or idea. Every singular noun forms the possessive by adding **'s**, regardless of the noun's ending.

girl's dress   school's playground

To distinguish singular possessives from plural possessives ending in **'s**, you must know the irregular plurals for words, such as *mice* or *children*.

Show What You Know

Is the underlined word a singular possessive, a plural possessive, or a plural? Write *SP*, *PP*, or *P* on the line.

1. We found Mr. Jackson's golf ball in our backyard. — SP
2. "It bounced and skidded through several neighbors' yards." — PP
3. "I will be playing in the men's tournament next week!" — PP
4. "Although I've golfed for three years, this is my first tournament." — P
5. Mr. Jackson hit the ball, and it bounced off Mrs. Karas's house. — SP
6. Perhaps they should warn the spectators at the tournament! — P

Score: _____   Total Possible: 6

86

Proofread

Read Matthew's report about the saber-toothed cat. It contains six errors in plural and possessive nouns. Using the proper proofreading mark, delete each incorrect word and write the correction above it.

Example: That ~~house~~ house's shutters should be painted.

About twelve thousand ~~year's~~ years ago, the last of the saber-toothed cats died. You may know this ~~creatures~~ creature's name as *saber-toothed tiger*, but it wasn't actually a tiger. The ~~cat~~ cat's name comes from the long, sharp front teeth that it possessed. A saber is a kind of sword.

It is many scientists' belief that the saber-toothed cat used its ~~teeth~~ teeth's razor-sharp edges to prey upon thick-skinned animals such as mastodons. A mastodon was a hairy animal similar to an elephant. It, too, is now extinct.

Today we know much about the saber-toothed cat's story because many of these animals were trapped in the La Brea tar pits in California. The ~~tar~~ tar's ability to preserve body material has provided a rich source of fossils. Probably the animals were drawn to the pits in the first place because ~~mastodons~~ mastodon's bodies had been trapped there.

Practice

Pretend that you have stumbled upon the fossil of an extinct animal. Write a description of your discovery using some plurals and possessives.

Review the description to be sure that your child has:

• used plurals and possessives correctly and without confusion.

• conveyed a sense of drama in finding an important fossil.

• ordered his or her composition chronologically.

Tips for Your Own Writing: Proofreading ···············

Exchange something you have written recently with a partner. Scan for any possessive nouns. Then, be sure that an -' or -'s was added to show possession.

Don't let plurals' pitfalls snag you!

87

Lesson 42

Lesson 42 Usage: Contractions

Here's a hint for identifying contractions: look for the apostrophe and see whether any letters have been omitted.

·············· Did You Know? ··············

A **contraction** is a word formed by combining two words and omitting one or more letters. We show the omission of letters by inserting an apostrophe. One type of contraction combines a pronoun and verb.

she + is = she's	I + am = I'm
who + is = who's	we + are = we're
I + have = I've	he + will = he'll
you + have = you've	they + will = they'll

Another type of contraction combines a verb and the negative word *not*.

are + not = aren't   will + not = won't

Do not confuse contractions with possessive pronouns. For example, the contraction *you're* sounds like the possessive pronoun *your*.

You're sorry that you lost **your** videocassette.

Show What You Know

In the paragraph below, write the contraction for each underlined word or group of words above the word or words.

We're
<u>We are</u> disturbed about plans for the new superhighway. <u>It is</u> supposed to cut
(1)   It's (2)
                                                        won't
through the forest preserve. If the road is built, some animal populations <u>will not</u>
                                                                          (3)
      can't   We've
survive. They <u>cannot</u> tolerate the increased noise and air pollution. <u>We have</u> formed a
            (4)   (5)
                                     Who's
citizen committee to work for a change. <u>Who is</u> interested in becoming a member?
                                       (6)
I'm   don't
<u>I am</u> in charge of next month's meeting. Please <u>do not</u> forget to sign our petition
(7)   (8)
before you leave.

Score: _____   Total Possible: 8

88

Proofread

Read the following tour guide to a historic house. Help the editors make seven corrections. Using the proper proofreading mark, delete each incorrect contraction and write the correction above it.

Example: ~~I~~ I'll be home by dark.

Won't   Your
Welcome to the Elisa Bentley house. ~~Wont~~ you come in? ~~You're~~ first stop is the
vestibule, a small entry room. Notice the hand-painted wallpaper from about the 1800s.
It's   you'll
~~Its~~ really quite rare. Next, ~~youll~~ enter the formal parlor. Of course, this house had no
                     we've
electricity, and ~~weve~~ tried to preserve that feeling by using low lighting. Notice the
                        Isn't   we'll
Regency style of decoration. ~~Isnt~~ it exquisite! The master bedroom is next. Here ~~well~~
see a hand-carved, four-poster bed. Ms. Bentley was most particular about the condition
of her bed. Please return to the front of the house. Your tour has ended.

Practice

Imagine that you will write a guide for your room or some other room that you know well. Follow these steps:

1. Allow yourself time to walk through the room (at least in your mind) and notice details.
2. Decide which details are worth writing about and which ones should be left out.
3. Write the guide to the room just as if you were walking around it, noticing the details.

Review the guide to be sure that your child has:

• used any contractions correctly.

• written the information in his or her guide in a logical order.

• written sentences that make sense and are mechanically correct.

Tips for Your Own Writing: Proofreading ···············

Remember that a contraction stands for two words. It must have an apostrophe. A possessive pronoun never uses an apostrophe.

If you'll try hard, you won't fail to understand contractions.

89

Lesson 43

Lesson
43 Review: Plurals, Possessives, Contractions

A. In each sentence, form the plural of the word in parentheses and write it in the blank to complete the sentence.

1. Today's ____computers____ have a wide variety of software. (computer)
2. Our software usually comes in ____boxes____ that we call *packages*. (box)
3. You can play many ____games____ on the computer. (game)
4. My screen saver shows little ____torpedoes____ gliding through the water. (torpedo)
5. I've also seen screen savers that show ____tomatoes____ exploding. (tomato)
6. Many people used to regard computers as ____toys____. (toy)
7. But ____bosses____ in offices find that software makes workers productive. (boss)
8. Software can teach you fingering for ____banjos____ or tuning for pianos. (banjo)
9. Some do-it-yourself packages tell how to repair ____roofs____ on houses. (roof)
10. Packages even instruct ____beginners____ on building thermal homes. (beginner)
11. And some packages tell farmers how to raise calves and ____geese____! (goose)
12. You could probably tell many more ____stories____ about unusual software. (story)

Score: _____ **Total Possible: 12**

B. In the paragraph below, write the possessive form of each underlined word above it.

I couldn't help laughing at Dad accident. He dabbed red paint on both of his
↑Dad's
sleeves cuffs. He "had a sheep face"—meaning he looked sheepish. I couldn't wait to
↑sleeves' 1 ↑sheep's
see the kids reaction when they came in. "It was my hands fault," said Dad. "They're
2 ↑kids' 3 ↑hands'
clumsy."
4 5

Score: _____ **Total Possible: 5**

90

C. Read this explanation of the naming of the computer object we call a *mouse*. If an underlined possessive or plural noun is used correctly, write C above it. Otherwise, write the correction there.

Have you wondered where computer objects' names come from? A *bug* is
C
so named because a real insect interrupted several circuits electron flow in an
1 ↑circuits' 2
early computer. But perhaps the mouses name is the most humorous. It's not
↑mouse's 3
difficult to guess the name's origin. A computers mouse has a long "tail" and a
C ↑computer's
4 5
smooth, rounded shape. How strange it would be if the computer mouse looked like a
goose. Would we now have "geese-driven" software programs?
C
6

Score: _____ **Total Possible: 6**

D. Read the following science report. It contains eight errors. Using the proper proofreading mark, delete each incorrect contraction and write the correction above it.

won't
Large birds of prey are very territorial. This means that they won't tolerate other
large birds living nearby, especially if the other birds' diets are similar to theirs. They
want to avoid competition with the other birds.

Large crows and owls, for example, do not mix well. The spring is an especially
they're you're
tough time of year, because their trying to raise their young. If you're lucky enough to
live in an uncrowded area that has many large trees, you may see this bird drama
your
played out above you're own head.
don't
Large owls are very powerful creatures, and most birds don't bother them. But
crows are very social—this means that they're accustomed to living closely with each
they'll
other. And they rely on each other, too. When crows feel threatened, they'll call all
We're
other crows within earshot. (Were used to the sound of crows. They're very noisy
it's
birds.) In this way, many crows can gang up on an owl. In the end, is quite possible
for the crows to win.

Score: _____ **Total Possible: 8**

REVIEW SCORE: _____ **REVIEW TOTAL: 31**

91

....

Lesson 44

Lesson
44 Usage: Simple Past Tense

"It was the best of times, it was the worst of times." How do we tell about things that happened in the past?

.... **Did You Know?** ....

Tenses of verbs tell whether an action or a state of being took place in the past, the present, or the future.

We use the **past tense** of a verb to talk or write about something that happened in the past. The <u>simple past tense</u> consists of one word that describes a past action. Many verbs form the simple past tense by adding *-d* or *-ed* to the present tense.

Present Tense	Simple Past Tense
Today they ask.	Yesterday they ask**ed**.
Today they play.	Yesterday they play**ed**.
Today they climb.	Yesterday they climb**ed**.

Other verbs form the simple past tense <u>irregularly</u>: sometimes by changing spellings, sometimes by not changing at all.

Present Tense	Simple Past Tense	Present Tense	Simple Past Tense
make	made	buy	bought
choose	chose	drink	drank
know	knew	hit	hit
feel	felt	cut	cut

Show What You Know
In the blank, write the correct past tense of the verb in parentheses to complete the sentence.

1. Clara ____decided____ to paint her house this summer. (decide)
2. The store manager ____recommended____ a good brand of paint. (recommend)
3. Then Clara ____bought____ many cans of that paint. (buy)
4. Next, she ____scraped____ the old paint off the exterior of her house. (scrape)
5. To reach the high spots, she carefully ____climbed____ on a strong ladder. (climb)
6. Then Clara ____brushed____ the paint on the outside walls. (brush)
7. That evening she ____admired____ her freshly painted home. (admire)

Score: _____ **Total Possible: 7**

92

Proofread
Using the proper proofreading mark, delete each of the twelve incorrect past-tense verbs and write the correct word above it.

asked
Example: Yesterday I was ask to a party.

Last May our town celebrated its centennial, or one-hundredth, anniversary. We
made washed brushed
maked a lot of preparations. A cleanup committee wash and brush all public buildings.
climbed
Members of the fire department climb on high ladders to put up flags and bunting.
asked
At last the celebration started. The high point was when Mayor Lopez ask Olga
remembered
Janssen—at 105, our oldest citizen—what she remember about the old days. "How I
used played
use a churn to make butter and play dominoes with my cousins," said Mrs. Janssen.
drank knew
At the end, we all drunk a ginger ale toast to the town's next century. We knowed
felt
most of us wouldn't be here for the next celebration, but we feel happy to be at this
hit
one. To officially close our celebration, the mayor hitted a large bell with a mallet.

Practice
Rewrite the story in Show What You Know, describing Clara's painting experience. Add descriptive details. When the story is finished, underline all the past-tense verbs.

Review the story to be sure that your child has:
- underlined all the verbs in simple past tense, correctly identifying these verbs.
- expanded the plot of the story.
- written sentences that make sense and are mechanically correct.

Tips for Your Own Writing: Proofreading
If you need help with past-tense verbs, use the dictionary. A dictionary entry for an irregular verb usually lists the past-tense form right after the main entry. For any verbs that give you trouble, write them in your journal or writing folder where you can find them easily.

The only time you can control time is when you change verb tense!

93

Lesson 45

Lesson 45 Usage: Subject-Verb Agreement I

You don't want your subjects and verbs to fight with each other. Make sure they agree!

.... Did You Know? ....

The <u>present tense</u> form of a verb is used to talk or write about something that is happening now. In the present tense of most verbs, the only form that changes is the one used with *he, she,* or *it.* This form adds either *-s* or *-es.* By using the appropriate form of the verb with the subject, we make the subject and verb agree in number. A verb with an *-s* ending is used with *he, she, it,* or other singular subjects, and a verb without an *-s* ending is used with all other subjects.

A <u>conjugation</u> is a table of the forms that a verb takes in a particular tense. Below are conjugations of two verbs in the present tense.

Present Tense of *Live*		Present Tense of *Fix*	
I live	we live	I fix	we fix
you live	you live	you fix	you fix
he, she, it liv**es**	they live	he, she, it fix**es**	they fix

Most verbs ending in *s, sh,* or *ch* add *-es* in the present form for *he, she,* or *it.*

Show What You Know

If the subject and verb in each sentence agree, put a *C* above the underlined verb. If they do not agree, write the correct present-tense form of the verb above the underlined verb.

1. My older sister Karin <u>fixes</u> cars. *(C)*
2. She washes and <u>wax</u> them, too, for a small fee. *(waxes)*
3. Karin <u>works</u> on cars most Saturdays. *(C)*
4. She often <u>start</u> working at 7:00 in the morning. *(starts)*
5. Mom isn't very good with cars, so she sometimes <u>watch</u> Karin. *(watches)*
6. Karin only <u>wish</u> she could make more money fixing cars. *(wishes)*
7. I think Karin is too busy. She <u>dash</u> from one thing to another. *(dashes)*
8. I think she <u>try</u> to do too much between school and her job. *(tries)*

Score: _____ Total Possible: 8

94

Proofread

Rick's report, entitled "How We Depend on Electricity," has five verbs and subjects that do not agree. Using the proper proofreading mark, delete the verb in each error of agreement. Above it, write the verb form that corrects the agreement problem.

Example: That dog ~~bark~~ *barks* too much.

We often don't realize how much we depend on electricity until it ~~stop~~ *stops*. When lightning flashes or a powerful wind ~~blow~~ *blows* down a power line, we're in trouble!

Want to watch TV or listen to that new CD? Not without electricity. Think you'll have some dinner? Try it cold. The family member who ~~fix~~ *fixes* the food will love doing without a stove. You'd like to read a book? Read while the candle ~~melt~~ *melts*!

You feel so thankful when the power ~~come~~ *comes* on again. How did people live without it?

Practice

Look at the picture. It shows one way family and friends entertained themselves at night before electricity. Imagine that you will have to live for a period of several weeks or months without electricity. How will you entertain yourself and others? How will you cope with the nighttime darkness? Write a short description of what you would do.

Review the description to be sure that your child has:

• used correct subject-verb agreement in each sentence.

• combined imagination with a touch of reality in his or her writing.

• written sentences that make sense and are mechanically correct.

Tips for Your Own Writing: Proofreading ....

Select a piece of your own writing and look for verbs in the present tense. Check for agreement with the subject. Just remember: the verb adds *-s* or *-es* when the subject is *he, she, it,* or any singular noun.

Subjects and verbs that work together make strong sentences.

95

. . . .

Lesson 46

Lesson 46 Usage: Subject-Verb Agreement II

Where's the subject? Where's the verb? If you can answer these questions, you're a long way toward understanding this lesson.

.... Did You Know? ....

There are some special problems of agreement between subjects and verbs. In most cases, the subject comes before the verb. However, sometimes we invert, or reverse the order of, subjects and verbs to make a sentence more interesting.

Out of the fog **rises** the **castle**.

Sentences that begin with *here, there,* and *where* put the subject after the verb.

Here **is** the **drawbridge**.
Where **are** the **gates**?

Sometimes a prepositional phrase comes between the subject and the verb.

A **knight** with many servants **arrives** at the castle.

A *compound subject* is made of two or more nouns or pronouns. Compound subjects joined by *and* always take a verb that does not end in *-s.* If the verb is irregular, use the form for plural subjects with a compound subject.

The **knight** and his **squire are** attending the tournament.

Compound subjects joined by *or* or *nor* take a form of the verb that agrees with the subject nearest to the verb.

Either the queen or **her servants have** the secret key.

Show What You Know

If the subject and verb in each sentence agree, put a *C* above the underlined verb. If they do not, write the correct present-tense form of the verb above the underlined verb.

Where <u>is</u> evidence of the Ice Age in North America? Many U.S. states and
¹ *(C)*
Canadian provinces <u>show</u> such evidence. Objects under a glacial mass <u>forms</u> various
² *(C)* ³ *(form)*
land features. Moraines and eskers <u>are</u> types of glacial deposits. From glacial ice <u>come</u>
⁴ *(C)* ⁵ *(comes)*
most of the fresh water on Earth. Glaciers <u>ranges</u> in thickness from 300 to 10,000 feet.
⁶ *(range)*

Score: _____ Total Possible: 6

96

Proofread

Following is a report Tara wrote after a field trip with her science class. Find the six errors of subject-verb agreement. Using the proper proofreading mark, delete each incorrect word and write the correction above it.

Example: There ~~is~~ *are* five science books on the table.

About twenty thousand years ago, the last glacier of the most recent Ice Age retreated northward. As a result, many glacial formations ~~dots~~ *dot* our fertile farmlands. Everywhere ~~is~~ *are* low mounds covered with trees. These mounds in each area ~~tells~~ *tell* a story. On some of them ~~grows~~ *grow* no crops. Farmers don't always ~~plows~~ *plow* the rougher, rockier soil of the glacial mounds. Glaciers have also left behind kettle lakes. A kettle is a bowl-like depression. It remains after a huge chunk of glacial ice has melted. Terminal moraines—long, hilly ridges—also mark the end of glaciers. You can see one if you follow Route 77 westward from Barrytown. But neither kettles nor terminal moraines ~~tells~~ *tell* the entire story of glaciers in the Ice Age. For the whole story, you'll have to study geology.

Practice

Write a paragraph describing the terrain, or land formation, in your area. Is it flat, hilly, or coastal? What kind of vegetation covers the land? Be careful about subject-verb agreement.

Review the paragraph to be sure that your child has:

• used correct subject-verb agreement in his or her sentences.

• used rich vocabulary and precision of description.

• written sentences that make sense and are mechanically correct.

Tips for Your Own Writing: Proofreading ....

The next time you write a story or report, try using some compound subjects. If you join the subjects with *and,* use a verb form that does not end in *-s.* If the subjects are joined by *or* or *nor,* use a verb form that agrees with the nearest subject.

To make verbs and subjects agree, first identify the verbs and the subjects.

97

Lesson 47

Lesson 47 Usage: Verb Agreement—There/Here

Here and there: how do we find the subjects of sentences?

.... **Did You Know?** ....

Sentences that begin with the adverbs *there* or *here* can offer special subject-verb agreement problems. Always use *there is* in the present tense with a singular subject, and *there are* in the present tense with a plural subject.

There is a wonderful **exhibition** at the museum this weekend.
There are always many interesting **exhibitions** at the museum.

Always use *there was* in the past tense with a singular subject and *there were* in the past tense with a plural subject.

Last year, **there was** a special **show** on dinosaurs.
There were two triceratops **skeletons** in that show.

Always use *here is* with a singular subject and *here are* with a plural subject.

Here is my **Uncle Roger**, the curator of the museum.
Here are the **items** I bought at the museum gift shop.
....

Show What You Know

In each blank, write the verb (*is, are, was,* or *were*) that agrees in number with the subject and that is in the proper tense (past or present) for the context of the sentence.

Let's Go to the Museum of Natural History

Here ___is___ my favorite place in town, the Museum of Natural History. What
          1
do they have? Just about everything—come in and find out. First is the Paleontology
Room. Here ___are___ skeletons of dinosaurs, life-size and put back together again.
          2
They give me a thrill because once there ___were___ creatures of this size prowling
          3
Earth! Let's move on to the Geology Room. There ___are___ meteorites, or at least
          4
the remains of them, in this room. And look! There ___is___ a photograph of a
          5
meteorite that crashed right into someone's living room. Gosh, I'm afraid we can't see
any more today. Last week, there ___was___ more time to look.
          6

Score: _____   Total Possible: 6

98

Proofread

Find the five errors of subject-verb agreement in the report on photography. Using the proper proofreading mark, delete each incorrect word and write the correction above it.

                                       are
Example: Here ~~is~~ the answers to our questions.

Some people think that there is nothing more to photography than "point and
                                                    are
shoot." But you can do a lot more. In modern cameras, there ~~is~~ settings to control the
speed of shooting and the amount of light. In an old-fashioned "box" camera, there
were
~~was~~ no such controls. You can also set up a darkroom to develop your own photos.
Here is a place where no light must enter, or the film will be ruined!
                                          is
There ~~are~~ more than just technique to think about, though. Photography ~~are~~ an
aesthetic, or artistic, activity. When taking photos, group objects thoughtfully. From
                                                        Are
your perspective, or view, how do the objects appear? ~~Is~~ they bunched tightly
together? Is the lighting correct? Photography can be especially rewarding.

Practice

Find a photograph that you especially like—a family photo or one from a magazine, for example. Write what you like about it. Consider composition (how the objects are grouped) and tone (whether it is dramatic or humorous, for example). Begin at least three of the sentences with *there* and *here*.

Review the paragraph to be sure that your child has:

• begun at least three sentences with *there* or *here*.

• used correct subject-verb agreement in the sentences.

• written sentences that make sense and are mechanically correct.

Tips for Your Own Writing: Proofreading ....

Choose a piece of your own writing. Do any of your sentences begin with *Here* or *There* followed by *is, are, was,* or *were*? Make sure you used *is* and *was* with singular subjects and *are* and *were* with plural subjects.

Here is a thought: There are a lot of things to keep in mind when using *here* and *there* in sentences.

99

Lesson 48

Lesson 48 Review: Past Tense Verbs, Subject-Verb Agreement

A. In the blank in each sentence, write the past tense of the verb in parentheses.

1. Jamal's teacher ___asked___ him to perform in the piano recital. (ask)

2. He ___chose___ a piece by Chopin called "Valse Brilliante." (choose)

3. When Jamal walked onto the stage, he ___felt___ very nervous. (feel)

4. He ___remembered___ the beginning of his piece, but not the ending. (remember)

5. As Jamal ___touched___ the keys, he felt more confident. (touch)

6. He ___hit___ every single note perfectly. (hit)

7. At the reception, everyone said, "Jamal, you ___played___ very well." (play)

Score: _____   Total Possible: 7

B. In the blank, write the correct ending (*s* or *es*) for each incomplete verb. The completed verb should agree in number with its subject.

Tornadoes are fantastically powerful whirlwinds. A tornado form__s__ along a
                                                                1
front, or narrow zone, between a mass of cool, dry air and a mass of warm, very
humid air. The warm, moist air rise__s__ in rapid updrafts. Soon, a column of air
                                    2
spin__s__. If the updraft is powerful enough, it feed__s__ the growing tornado.
     3   4
Air rush__es__ up the column.
         5
Soon a funnel drop__s__ down from the sky. It touch__es__ down, raising a
                      6   7
black dust cloud. A tornado toss__es__ about debris like paper. It sometimes
                                 8
pitch__es__ automobiles or tractors like softballs. Tornadoes would seem like
       9
pranksters if they weren't so violent. A twister sometimes levels houses on one side of a
street but miss__es__ those on the other side completely. The narrow, whirling
              10
column pass__es__ close to some objects without harming them. Thank goodness
            11
the average tornado live__s__ for only a few minutes!
                          12

Score: _____   Total Possible: 12

100

C. In each pair of verbs in parentheses, underline the verb that agrees in number with the subject.

Out of the shadows (step, _steps_) the king's herald. "I declare, according to His
                            1
Majesty's will," he cries, "that from this day forward the queen and her retinue shall be
kept under guard in the palace." Through the crowd (run, _runs_) a low murmur.
                                                         2
But where (_is_, are) the key to the secret passage under the palace? Does the
          3
queen have it? No, Prince Renaldo (possess, _possesses_) it. He and Princess Angelina
                                                4
(_plot_, plots) to aid the queen.
  5
What is the climax of our story? The queen and her servants (makes, _make_) their
                                                              6
escape. Neither the officials of the court nor the king (find, _finds_) a way to stop them.
                                                              7
Into the free light and air they (_walk_, walks).
                                  8

Score: _____   Total Possible: 8

D. Fill in each blank with *is, are, was,* or *were* so that the subject and the verb agree in tense and number.

Asteroids are rocky chunks that orbit the sun in space. Sometimes an asteroid
comes into Earth's atmosphere and becomes a meteor. Usually, a meteor vaporizes in
the atmosphere. We call the objects that do reach the ground *meteorites*. There
___is___ evidence that meteorites have slammed into Earth. They have left very
   1
large craters. In a few cases, there ___are___ surviving meteorites, too.
                                   2
Meteorites can be very destructive. Scientists believe that there ___was___ a huge
                                                              3
meteorite above Siberia in 1908. It apparently exploded in the air, flattening and
burning forests. Remember that there ___were___ once dinosaurs on Earth. Some
                                    4
scientists think that a massive meteorite hit Earth and raised so much dust that it
changed the climate, killing off the dinosaurs. Here ___is___ something to think
                                                    5
about: What would happen if a very large asteroid was predicted to hit Earth very
soon?

Score: _____   Total Possible: 5

REVIEW SCORE: _____   REVIEW TOTAL: 32

101

Answer Key   **185**

Lesson 49

Lesson 49 Usage: Pronouns—Agreement and Order I

Be a "pro" when using the subject forms of personal pronouns.

Did You Know?

Personal pronouns have subject forms and object forms, in addition to singular, plural, and possessive forms.

The subject form of a pronoun is used as the subject of the sentence or as a pronoun following a linking verb.

A subject pronoun can be used as the subject of the sentence.

He drew the illustrations in the book.

A subject pronoun can be used after a linking verb. You can decide what form of the pronoun to use by inverting the sentence.

The author of the book was **she.**/**She** was the author of the book.

Show What You Know
Read the paragraphs. In each set of parentheses, underline the correct subject pronoun.

In 1804–1806, Captains Meriwether Lewis and William Clark led an expedition across the territory of Louisiana. Today (<u>we</u>, us) know this vast region as the Northern Plains of northwestern U.S.

One woman accompanied the crew—Sacagawea. The courageous daughter of a Shoshone was (<u>she</u>, her). Because Sacagawea helped with communication, the explorers were able to find horses and guides.

The explorers learned much about landforms, wildlife, and Native Americans. (<u>They</u>, Them) spent their first winter in camp with the Mandan and later met the Nez Percé in the northern Rockies. Finally, in November 1805, the expedition reached the Pacific Ocean. (<u>It</u>, Its) was an astonishing sight, according to Captain Clark.

Score: _____ Total Possible: 4

102

Proofread
This imaginary newspaper editorial of 1806 speculates that the members of the Lewis and Clark expedition are lost or dead. The writer used four personal pronouns incorrectly. Draw a delete mark through each mistake and write the correction above it.

Example: ~~Us~~ We have received no mail from them.

We fear that the noble expedition of Captains Lewis and Clark has failed. Consider how many conditions were against ~~they~~ them. The party was last heard from one year ago, when Corporal Warfington rowed into St. Louis. He was a member of the expedition. Since that time, ~~us~~ we have received no word. Yet our ears heard rumors of capture by Spaniards. Some think ~~them~~ they suffered an even worse fate. Whatever the truth about the noble explorers, heroes were ~~them~~ they all.

Practice
Imagine that you are a member of an exploration party in an unknown territory. Write the body of a letter to someone back home—a family member, friend, reporter, or the President. Tell a story about some challenge you have faced. Use at least four subject pronouns.

Review the letter to be sure your child has:

• written an opening and a closing. For example: the opening might say something like "We are quite well. I want to tell you what happened just yesterday."

• organized the narrative section of their letters chronologically.

• used at least four subject pronouns correctly.

Tips for Your Own Writing: Proofreading
In a piece of your own writing, check the forms of the pronouns you used. To choose the correct pronoun form, identify how the pronoun functions in each sentence. If a pronoun is used as a subject or after a linking verb, use the subject form of the pronoun.

The subject of this lesson is subject pronouns as subjects.

103

Lesson 50

Lesson 50 Usage: Pronouns—Agreement and Order II

Be clear about the uses of object pronouns: as direct objects, indirect objects, and objects of prepositions.

Did You Know?

Personal pronouns have singular and plural subject forms, object forms, and possessive forms.

An object pronoun can be used as a <u>direct object</u> of a verb. Notice that a direct object usually comes after the verb and tells what the verb acted upon.

Because Anne's cookies are delicious, she is taking **them** to the bake sale.

An object pronoun can be used as an <u>indirect object</u> in a sentence. Notice that the indirect object comes between the verb and the direct object (*cake*). It tells to or for whom the verb acted. A direct object is necessary in a sentence with an indirect object.

Jim bakes **her** a cake for the birthday party.

An object pronoun can be used as the <u>object of a preposition</u>. Notice that the object of a preposition comes after the preposition *for*.

Ted and Lisa bake bread for **us.**

Show What You Know
Tell how each underlined personal pronoun is used. Is it a direct object, an indirect object, or the object of a preposition? Write DO, IO, or OP above each underlined personal pronoun.

1. "I'll splatter <u>you</u> with this pie," joked the clown. **DO**
2. "Go ahead, entertain <u>us</u>," dared the audience member. **DO**
3. "The Great Miranda" performed for <u>them</u>. **OP**
4. "Give <u>me</u> the ticket," said the lady at the circus box office. **IO**
5. Amazing Amanda the magician sawed <u>him</u> in half. **DO**
6. "I think we pleased <u>them</u>," said the master of ceremonies. **DO**
7. "We always give <u>them</u> their money's worth." **IO**

Score: _____ Total Possible: 7

104

Proofread
The following music review uses seven personal pronouns incorrectly. Draw a delete mark through each incorrect word and write the correction above it.

Example: Please find a seat for ~~we~~ us.

The City Philharmonic played a dazzling concert last night. The conductor was pleased, and so was I. The audience agreed with ~~he~~ him and ~~I~~ me. Mellow as ever, the string section soothed and inspired ~~we~~ us. The horns blared and bounced with agility. (Give ~~they~~ them a hand!) The single brass player blasted his trumpet. (Hats off to ~~he~~ him!) But best of all, percussion player Sara Hue punctuated just the right moments. The audience gave ~~she~~ her a standing ovation! Between you and ~~I~~ me, I think it was one of the orchestra's best concerts ever.

Practice
Write five sentences describing a live performance or movie that you have attended or seen recently. It could be a concert, a sports event, a movie, or a play. Use an object pronoun in each sentence. Try to use an object pronoun as a direct object, as an indirect object, and as the object of a preposition.

Review the sentences to be sure your child has:

• used an object pronoun in each sentence.

• used the pronouns as direct object, indirect object, and object of a preposition.

Tips for Your Own Writing: Proofreading
Reread something that you have written. Identify all of the personal pronouns. Did you use *It's me*? Although that is often used in informal speech, remember that the correct written form is *It is I* because *I* is the subject, not the object. *I* follows a linking verb.

The object of this lesson is to get you to put object pronouns in the right form.

105

Lesson 51

Lesson
51 Usage: Double Negatives

One negative is enough! Avoid the double negative.

.... Did You Know? ....

No, none, not, nobody, and *nothing* are negative words. Using two such negative words in the same sentence is called a *double negative.* Good writers avoid double negatives.

Incorrect: I do **not** like **nothing** in my lunch box today.
Correct: I do **not** like anything in my lunch box today.

Incorrect: You **can't** eat **no** lunch with us.
Correct: You **can't** eat any lunch with us.

The *n't* in *can't* stands for the negative word *not.* To avoid the double negative, watch for *not* in contractions such as *don't, won't, didn't,* and *isn't.*

The words *barely, hardly,* and *scarcely* are also used as negative words. Avoid using the negative word *not* with these words.

Incorrect: I **couldn't hardly** eat after seeing that movie.
Correct: I could **hardly** eat after seeing that movie.

....

Show What You Know
Correct each double negative that is underlined below. Rewrite the words on the line.

1. Teresa couldn't do nothing with her clay. could do nothing/couldn't do anything
2. She hadn't barely started sculpting class. had barely
3. Todd didn't have no clay on his table. had no/didn't have any
4. He wasn't hardly ready to get his hands dirty. was hardly
5. The teacher thought he wouldn't never get Todd to try. wouldn't ever/would never
6. In fact, Todd wouldn't have none of it. wouldn't have any/would have none

Score: _____   Total Possible: 6

106

Proofread
The writer of the following report has overlooked four double negatives. Draw a delete mark through each mistake and write the correction above it.

Example: I don't want ~~none~~ *any*

A true recycler, the hermit crab doesn't believe in ~~no~~ *any* waste. Because it doesn't have ~~no~~ *any* protective covering for its soft stomach, it goes looking for one. It ~~can't~~ *can* hardly wait to find an old shell. A cast-off shell from a shellfish such as a conch will do just fine. The crab pulls itself into its adopted "home." It uses tail hooks to hold the shell in place and guards the opening with crusher claws. Once it is inside, nobody ~~won't~~ *will* bother Mr. or Ms. Hermit Crab!

Practice
Imagine that you are writing a TV ad for a lunch food, such as the one in the picture. Write a description, or write a dialogue between two lunch items, such as a banana and a cookie. Avoid using double negatives.

Review the description to be sure your child has:

• been consistent in his or her selected approach. (For example, if your child wrote dialogue, then he or she should use dialogue throughout.)

• avoided using any double negatives.

Tips for Your Own Writing: Proofreading ....
Select a piece of your own writing. Read aloud any sentences that contain negative words. Do you hear more than one negative word in any of these sentences? Watch particularly for contractions that contain the *n't.*

Remember to use only one negative word in a sentence.

107

....

Lesson 52

Lesson
52 Review: Pronoun Agreement and Double Negatives

A. In the following article, underline the seven subject pronouns.

Maria Mitchell, the daughter of a sea captain in Nantucket, Massachusetts, lived in the 1800s. Maria helped in her father's business. He adjusted navigation instruments for oceangoing ships. They needed to be very accurate instruments. In the meantime, Maria developed an interest in astronomy. She learned how to use a telescope and studied books on astronomy in her free time.

Through careful study and observation, Maria became a very fine astronomer. On October 1, 1847, she noticed a hazy object in the sky. It was an unknown comet. Maria was the first to see it. A famous discoverer was she. Honors came to her, including a medal from the king of Denmark. Later she became professor of astronomy at Vassar College.

Score: _____   Total Possible: 7

B. In each sentence below, identify one object pronoun. If the pronoun is a direct object, draw one line under it. Draw two lines under a pronoun that is an indirect object, and circle a pronoun that is the object of a preposition.

Living things develop defenses against other living things that might eat them. Some plants use poison against their enemies to give them a nasty surprise. If you like the outdoors, poison ivy may be quite familiar to you. Oil from this plant irritates human skin, causing eruptions on it. Eating monkshood, a common garden plant, would probably kill you. But, in fact, poisonous plants can be very useful to us too. Rotenone, from a tropical plant, weakens harmful insects or kills them. Rotenone breaks down quickly in the environment and doesn't harm it. The garden plant foxglove yields a drug, digitalis. Doctors give it to heart patients.

Score: _____   Total Possible: 9

108

C. Underline five sentences with double negatives that you find in this article. Write those sentences correctly on the lines.

In 1974 a discovery was made near Xi'an (Sian) in China. This wasn't no ordinary find. Buried at the tomb of China's first emperor was a life-size army of 7,500 soldiers and horses made of terra cotta, a type of pottery. Hardly any of them weren't broken.

Archaeologists couldn't hardly believe their good luck. (An archaeologist is a scientist who studies objects from past cultures.) The creators of this "army" didn't want no one to disturb the tomb. Some figures were "booby-trapped." For example, moving a particular object may set off the release of a spear or arrow.

Would you like to see the terra-cotta army? If you think you won't never have the chance, you may be wrong. The Chinese government is allowing some of the figures to be displayed outside of China.

Samples answers are given.

This was no ordinary find.

Hardly any of them were broken.

Archaeologists could hardly believe their luck.

The creators of this army didn't want anyone to disturb the tomb.

If you think you won't ever have the chance, you may be wrong.

Score: _____   Total Possible: 5

REVIEW SCORE: _____   REVIEW TOTAL: 21

109

Lesson 53

Lesson 53 Grammar: Nouns

How could we speak or write without the ability to name things? Nouns are essential.

Did You Know?

A **noun** is a word that tells who or what did the action or was acted upon by the verb in the sentence.

Concrete nouns name things that you can see or touch. They can fit in the blank in this sentence: The _____ stood there.

house   star   ice   cloth   horse   woman   child

Abstract nouns name intangible ideas or qualities—things that cannot be seen or touched.

fairness   danger   truth   fear   love   courage   faith

A **common noun** is the general name for someone or something. A **proper noun** is the name of a particular person or place. It may consist of more than one word and begin with capital letters, except for small words such as *of*.

Common Nouns	Proper Nouns
city	Philadelphia
document	Declaration of Independence
author	Thomas Jefferson

Show What You Know

Write *C* or *P* above each underlined noun, identifying it as either a common or a proper noun. Circle any proper noun that is not capitalized.

We expect earthquakes to strike <u>areas</u> (C) along the edges of continental plates. But one of the strongest <u>earthquakes</u> (C) in <u>North America</u> (P) struck along the (mississippi river) (P) in 1811. This is right in the center of the North American plate. During and after the quake, one steamboat captain observed that the <u>river</u> (C) reversed its course and ran backward. An observer in (Kentucky) (P) reported that "the ground waved like a <u>field</u> (C) of corn before the breeze." In northwestern Tennessee, twenty square miles of woodland sank. We know this place today as <u>Reelfoot Lake</u> (P).

Score: _____   Total Possible: 11

110

Practice

The paragraph below is missing all of its nouns. First, read the paragraph and then choose the nouns you wish to add in the blanks. Your paragraph may be serious or humorous.
Sample answers are given.

<u>Candy</u> (1) is the worst <u>taste</u> (2) of the <u>century</u> (3). This unnecessary and irritating <u>mixture</u> (4) is produced when <u>sugar</u> (5) is changed electronically. The first <u>bar</u> (6) was made by mixing <u>things</u> (7) such as <u>chocolate</u> (8) and <u>honey</u> (9). The <u>smell</u> (10) is horrible. I think I like <u>fish</u> (11) better!

Revise

Read the paragraph below. Above each underlined noun, write another noun that is more specific and interesting.

Sample answers are given.

The average bee <u>group</u> (colony) (1) has one important <u>lady</u> (queen) (2), several hundred males, and thousands of young females called workers. By studying these workers, <u>people</u> (scientists) (3) have found that bees are smart, complex, and highly social <u>things</u> (insects) (4). Worker bees have many <u>things</u> (jobs) (5) to do. They clean and protect the <u>home</u> (hive) (6). They also look for <u>juice</u> (nectar) (7) to make honey.

Tips for Your Own Writing: Revising

Review a piece of your writing. Look at the nouns and check to see that you chose the most specific and interesting noun you could in each case. Remember, precise word choice is an important part of effective writing.

Common nouns or proper nouns?—it's a capital difference.

111

Lesson 54

Lesson 54 Grammar: Pronouns

Pronouns take over for nouns.

Did You Know?

A **pronoun** is a word that takes the place of a noun or another pronoun. It keeps language from becoming repetitive.

Without Pronouns: Heinz wanted to make **Heinz's** best shot.
With Pronouns: Heinz wanted to make **his** best shot.

Pronouns can be in the first, the second, or the third person.

First person refers to the person(s) speaking.

Subject	Possessive	Object
I, we	my, our	me, us

Second person refers to the person(s) being spoken to.

Subject	Possessive	Object
you	your	you

Third person refers to a person, animal, or thing being spoken of.

Subject	Possessive	Object
he, she	his, her	him, her
it	its	it
they	their	them

The pronouns *it* and *its* refer to animals or things, never to people.

Show What You Know

Above each underlined pronoun, write *1, 2,* or *3* for first, second, or third person.

<u>I</u> (1) think that Wolfgang A. Mozart was one of the greatest composers who ever lived. <u>He</u> (3) wrote an astounding number of great musical works. Opera fans especially love Mozart's operas. One of the best of <u>them</u> (3) is *The Marriage of Figaro.* In this opera, a woman tries to regain <u>her</u> (3) husband's affection. But Mozart's music is what makes this opera special. <u>It</u> (3) is simply sublime! Mozart composed orchestra and piano pieces, too. Have <u>you</u> (2) ever listened to any of <u>his</u> (3) pieces?

Score: _____   Total Possible: 7

112

Proofread

Mike's story about last night's storm contains five noun repetitions that could be improved by using a pronoun. Two articles will also need to be deleted. Use the proper proofreading mark to delete each repeated noun and the two articles.

Example: Sarah rode ~~Sarah's~~ (her) bike.

Hiss! Crash! Boom! So began last night's terrible thunderstorm. At about eight o'clock, Dad was finishing up his gardening. ~~Dad~~ (He) came running in the house and cried, "This is going to be a big one. Put the awnings down and fasten ~~the awnings~~ (them). ~~Awnings~~ (They) are especially prone to wind damage."

We heard three very loud claps of thunder in a row. On the fourth, the oak tree shuddered and split. ~~The oak tree~~ (It) crashed to the ground. At about that time, we smelled ozone, a pungent chemical. Mom knew what this odor was, because ~~Mom's~~ (her) major in college was meteorology, the study of weather.

Practice

Write four descriptive sentences about a person you know well. You can write about a friend, parent, grandparent, or anyone you're close to. Use at least four pronouns to refer to that person. Avoid repeating nouns awkwardly.

Review the sentences to be sure your child has:

- used either a personal noun or a pronoun to refer to the person he or she has chosen to write about.

- used at least four personal pronouns, each in the correct person and gender.

- avoided awkward noun repetition.

Tips for Your Own Writing: Proofreading

Pronouns have gender. *Masculine gender* refers to male people (*he, him, his*). *Feminine gender* refers to female people (*she, her, hers*). *Neuter gender* refers to animals or things (*it, its*). Find the pronouns in a piece of your writing. Did you use the appropriate form for each gender?

Be pro-pronoun. Use pronouns where they improve your writing.

113

Lesson 55

Lesson 55 Grammar: Verbs

Verbs are the threads that tie language together. How could we speak or write without expressing actions or states of being?

.... **Did You Know?** ....

A <u>verb</u> tells what the person, place, or thing in a sentence is doing, or it links or connects the subject to the rest of the sentence. A verb might tell about being rather than acting.

Many verbs are *action verbs*.

> Hurricane gusts **whipped** the boat.
> The mast of the ship **crashed** to the deck.

Linking verbs express the existence of something or link the subject with a word that renames or modifies it.

> Here **is** a weather chart. *(expresses a state of being)*
> The storm **becomes** a hurricane. *(links the subject to the renaming word)*

Linking Verbs

am	was	become	look	smell
is	were	feel	remain	sound
are	appear	grow	seem	taste

Some verbs can be used either as action verbs or as linking verbs.

> Rena **feels** the wet grass on her bare feet. *(action verb)*
> After walking in the grass, Rena **feels** good. *(linking verb)*

Show What You Know
Underline the verb in each sentence. Then circle each verb that is a linking verb.

Last year, we <u>visited</u> Uncle Taylor's turkey farm. It (is) quite modern. The birds <u>dwell</u> in climate-controlled buildings rather than outdoors. The turkeys' claws hardly ever <u>touch</u> the ground. I <u>imagined</u> majestic, colorful, flying birds. But these turkeys (appear) dull. Only plain, white feathers <u>cover</u> them. Moreover, the turkeys (seem) quite stupid. Nevertheless, they (taste) good at the Thanksgiving feast!

Score: _____ Total Possible: 13

114

Practice
Think about a ride you have enjoyed in an amusement park—a roller coaster, for example. Think of strong action verbs you might use to describe the ride or to express your emotions while on the ride. Write two sentences about the ride, using action verbs.

1. Review sentences to be sure your child has used strong action verbs.
2. Suggestions: *fly, swoop, tear, rip, scream, screech, shake, rattle, clatter.*

Now think of some linking verbs from this lesson that you might use to convey information about the ride. Write two sentences about the ride, using some of these verbs.

1. Review sentences to be sure your child has used linking verbs.
2. The sentences should convey meaningful information. One way to do this when using linking verbs is to use predicate adjectives.

Revise
Read the paragraph below. Above each underlined verb, write another verb that is stronger and more interesting. *Sample answers are given.*

                     select/choose
The Activity Club at Geller School met in September to <u>get</u> a name for our new
                     1   offered   suggested
newspaper. Vance Vedder <u>said</u>, "The Activity Club Journal." Sandra Yee <u>said</u>, "The
             2   debated   3
News and Doers." The club members <u>talked</u> for two hours. We voted three times, and
                                 4   nominated
each time the vote was 4–4. Then Beth Gonzalez <u>said</u>, "The Geller Gazette." On the
                                       5
             was chosen/won
fourth vote, this name <u>was picked</u>.
                6

Tips for Your Own Writing: Revising ....
Select a piece of your own writing. Identify the action verbs that you used. Then, ask yourself, "Are any of these action verbs too vague? Could they be replaced with stronger, clearer action verbs?" Think of other verbs you could use. A thesaurus may help you.

With effort and practice, you can put more verve in your verbs.

115

Lesson 56

Lesson 56 Grammar: Irregular Verbs

Irregular verbs have forms of their own.

.... **Did You Know?** ....

Most English verbs are regular. Regular verbs add *-ed* to form the past tense. The past participle is formed in the same way, but it also uses a helping word such as *is, was, have,* or *had.*

> *Present*—I **walk** a lot. *Past Tense*—I **walked** yesterday.
> *Past Participle*—I **have walked** every day.

Verbs that do not form the past and past participle by adding *-ed* are irregular verbs.

> *Present*—I **sing** a lot. *Past Tense*—I **sang** yesterday.
> *Past Participle*—I **have sung** every day.

For a list of more irregular verbs, see page 159 in the *Writer's Handbook.*

Present Tense	Past Tense	Past Participle	Present Tense	Past Tense	Past Participle (+ helping verb)
catch	caught	caught	make	made	made
do	did	done	ring	rang	rung
eat	ate	eaten	run	ran	run
fall	fell	fallen	speak	spoke	spoken
freeze	froze	frozen	take	took	taken
give	gave	given	teach	taught	taught
go	went	gone	throw	threw	thrown
grow	grew	grown	win	won	won

Show What You Know
Write the correct past tense form of the verb in parentheses to complete each sentence.

Beverly Sills ___grew___ up in New York City. From the time she was very young, she
          1 (grow)
wanted to become an opera singer. She ___began___ her operatic career in 1946. Then she
                           2 (begin)
joined the New York City Opera in 1955. She ___became___ one of the greatest operatic
                                 3 (become)
sopranos of the mid-1900s. She ___won___ fame for her versatile voice and rich tones. Her
                        4 (win)
superior abilities and warm personality ___made___ her popular with audiences and musicians.
                             5 (make)

Score: _____ Total Possible: 5

116

Practice
The paragraph below is missing its verbs. In each blank, write a verb that makes sense in the sentence. *Sample answers are given.*

Opera is a play in which the characters ___sing___ their
                1
lines. It is not a drama where the characters ___read___
                2
their lines. Opera singers must ___wear___ fancy
             3
costumes and ___represent___ their roles. They may also
             4
have to ___learn___ several languages and
          5
___travel___ to other countries to study.
      6

Revise
Read the paragraph below. Above the underlined words, write verbs that make sense in the story and are in the correct form. *Sample answers are given.*

         became   sang
Enrico Caruso <u>got to be</u> a famous opera singer. He first <u>singed</u> at Naples in 1894.
          1   2
     went
Then he <u>gone</u> to London to perform at Covent Garden. In 1903, he <u>sanged</u> at the
         3   4   rang
Metropolitan Opera in New York City. He had a very powerful voice. His notes <u>rung</u>
                                           5
                   became
across the stage and thrilled audiences. He <u>becomed</u> one of the most famous opera
                            6
stars in history.

Tips for Your Own Writing: Revising ....
Review a piece of your writing. Check the verb forms. Use these clues to see that you have used the correct forms of the verbs. Find verbs you have used and put each verb into one of these frames.

> Today I _____. Yesterday I _____. Tomorrow I will _____.

A dictionary can be your best friend when you need to check the forms of irregular verbs.

117

Lesson 57

Lesson

57 Grammar: Adjectives

✏️ *Make your nouns more interesting: modify them with adjectives.*

························ **Did You Know?** ··························

An <u>adjective</u> is a word that modifies a noun. *Modifies* means "describes" or "gives additional information about something."

Some adjectives tell *what kind.*

Jamael's sister is a **brilliant** painter.

Some adjectives tell *how many.*

The band played **many** marches for the crowd.

Some adjectives tell *which one.*

I liked the **third** song.

Articles (*the, a, an*) are a special type of adjective, also called determiners because they signal that a noun follows.

The tune is **an** old favorite.

Adjectives come before the words they modify or after a linking verb.

The **shiny** horn blared. The drummer seems **sleepy.**

A <u>proper adjective</u> is formed from a proper noun. It is always capitalized.

The **Italian** language is used in musical notation.

···

Show What You Know

Underline the adjectives (including articles) in the sentences below. Circle any proper adjectives that should be capitalized.

1. An oceanographer studies many aspects of the seas and oceans.

2. On Earth, the oceans are vast, deep pools of water.

3. But the water in oceans and seas is not drinkable.

4. It contains enormous amounts of common table salt.

5. The Pacific Ocean is the largest ocean on Earth.

6. It has many powerful currents, including the Brazil Current.

Score: _____   Total Possible: 19

118

Practice

Think of a place you like to visit—perhaps the seashore, the lake, or the desert. Close your eyes and picture the place, or a part of it. Think of six adjectives to describe it. The adjectives can describe any aspect of your mental picture—sight, sound, smell, or touch. Write the adjectives on the lines.

Review adjectives to be sure your child has used

descriptive adjectives.

Look for descriptive content (for example, *a sparkling white*

vs. *a nice* beach).

Now think of three adjectives that describe your *feelings* about this place. You can use the sentence form "I feel . . ." to express these feelings. Write the sentence on the lines.

Review adjectives to be sure your child has used descriptive adjectives.

Look for descriptive content (for example, *peaceful* vs. *happy*).

Revise

Revise the paragraph below by adding at least seven adjectives to give more details and make the picture clearer and more interesting to the reader. Write the adjectives above the nouns they modify.

Sample answers are given.

hot, brilliant

The sun alone on the beach and warmed the sand. Waves splashed back and

white

little   rippling   small, red

forth across the cove. Light sparkled on the waves. A boat sailed past in the distance.

wooden

With a snort, a scuba diver rose suddenly to the surface by the pier. People played

fast   crowded   huge

a game of volleyball at one end of the beach while children made sand castles at the

many interesting   best

other end. The sights, sounds, and smells of the beach made it the place to be.

Tips for Your Own Writing: Revising ···············

Choose a piece that you have written. Identify the adjectives that you used. Did you use adjectives like *good, bad,* or *nice* when you might have used a more descriptive adjective? Replace any adjectives that do not give enough detail.

✏️ *Adjectives help people see the world as a colorful, interesting place.*

119

Lesson 58

Lesson

58 Grammar: Articles

✏️ *Know your articles: the, an, and a.*

························ **Did You Know?** ··························

<u>Articles</u> are special adjectives that are used only with nouns. They are also called determiners because they signal that a noun follows.

The definite article *the* is used with a noun when the noun refers to a particular thing.

The Olympic swimmer now speaks at schools.

The indefinite articles *a* and *an* are used with a noun when the noun refers to no particular thing.

We heard **a** swimmer speak about careers in sports.
Next week **an** acrobat will talk to us.

The article *a* is used before a word that begins with a consonant sound: *a speech.*

The article *an* is used before a word that begins with a vowel sound: *an audience.*

···

Show What You Know

Fill in each blank with the appropriate article: *the, an,* or *a.*

Jacques Cousteau was ____an____ important ocean explorer of this century. He
                              1
made many contributions to oceanography, ____the____ science of oceans. Cousteau
                                                  2
developed oxygen tanks for diving. Before divers had these tanks, they had to wear
very heavy, awkward suits. Cousteau's contribution was, therefore, ____a____ very
                                                                          3
important one. Cousteau studied ocean plants and animals that are almost unknown.
He also explored shipwrecks. One of Cousteau's major concerns was pollution. He
opposed ____the____ French government for dumping nuclear wastes at sea.
              4
It is not ____an____ exaggeration to say that Jacques Cousteau popularized
              5
oceanography. His TV specials made millions more aware of ____the____ earth's oceans.
                                                                  6

Score: _____   Total Possible: 6

120

Proofread

Gerry's report on whale music has six mistakes in its use of articles. Use the proper proofreading mark to correct each mistake.

Example: I had a apple for lunch.
                        an

                              an
Whales communicate by a astonishingly rich language. They often use a area of
                                                                          an

the deep sea called the sound channel to send their sound messages over very long

distances. We're not sure what all the whale sounds mean. But whales are known to

                                              a
respond to calls for help from an great distance. Scientists wonder whether the sounds

            an
are produced on a hourly or daily schedule of some kind.

In fact, whales seem to produce two distinct groups of sounds. One group includes

low-pitched barks, whistles, screams, and moans that humans can hear. Whales also

                                          a
make another group of sounds at an high frequency, or pitch, which humans cannot

                                          a
hear. Whales may use these clicks or squeaks like an kind of radar. Perhaps they locate

prey or orient themselves using these sounds.

Practice

Look at the picture. Write three sentences to describe what is happening. Try to use the articles *the* and *a* at least one time each.

1. _____ Review the sentences to be sure your child has:

   • written three complete sentences.

2. _____ • used the articles *the* and *a* at least one time each.

   • described whales playfully in the water.

3. _____

Tips for Your Own Writing: Proofreading ···············

Choose a piece of your own writing. To check that you used the appropriate article with each noun, read your writing aloud. Listening to the beginning sound of each noun will help you know whether you chose the right article.

✏️ *What an article! You needed the articles a, an, and the to complete the lessons.*

121

---

190   Answer Key

Lesson 59 Grammar: Adverbs

✎ *Make your verbs, adjectives, and adverbs more interesting: use adverbs.*

·········· Did You Know? ··········

An <u>adverb</u> is a word that modifies a verb, an adjective, or another adverb. We form many adverbs by adding *-ly* to an adjective. We often change a final *y* to *i* before adding the *-ly*.

quick + -ly = quickly
happy + -ly = happily

When adverbs are used with verbs, they tell *how, when, where,* or *to what extent.*

Brae walked **hurriedly** to the mailbox.
She slammed the door **afterward**.
Then she stomped **upstairs**.
Now Brae relaxed **completely**.

Adverbs that tell *to what extent* can also modify adjectives and other adverbs.

Arturo's house was **almost** invisible.
But now the fog is lifting **very** rapidly.

Show What You Know
Underline each adverb in the article. Draw a line to the word that each adverb modifies.

Listen carefully. You can play a violin correctly. First, hold the instrument securely against the neck and under the chin. Take the bow firmly in the free hand. Apply the bow to the strings so that it barely touches them. Then pull the bow evenly. Do this without breaking contact with the strings. When you very nearly reach the end of the arc, reverse the direction of the bow. Now you push it. The sound you hear may be rather scratchy. But remember, learning to play the violin means practicing regularly.

Score: _____   Total Possible: 22

122

Practice
Write an adverb in each blank in the paragraph. Choose adverbs that tell about the actions of marching bands.
Sample answers are given.

The bass drum ___quickly___ announced the start of
the parade. The beat of the snare drums signaled the steady,
rhythmical pace. The first band played ___smartly___ as it
marched ___precisely___ along the route. Everyone clapped
___loudly___ as the trumpets and trombones blared. The whole town ___proudly___
cheered as the magnificent cars and floats traveled ___slowly___ along the parade route.

Revise
Revise the paragraph below by adding at least four adverbs to give more details and make the picture clearer and more interesting to the reader. Insert carets to show where the adverbs should be added. *Sample answers are given.*

Example: Beat the drum ^slowly

Create your own orchestra. Find some empty pop bottles. Fill them with ^carefully
water at different levels. To "play" them, blow ^softly across their tops. Take a jar with a lid.
Put some dried beans in the jar and close the lid ^tightly. Shake the jar to make a rhythmic
sound. Find some old metal pots and pans and a clean paintbrush. Invert the pans and
"play" them ^briskly with the brush, like a snare drum. If you want to get ^really fancy, make your own
set of wind chimes. Use sticks, string, and small pieces of metal for the "chimes." You
can ^easily make your own music.

Tips for Your Own Writing: Proofreading ··············
Select something from your own writing and find the adverbs. Be sure that you did not use too many adverbs in any one place, as in this sentence: *I read a very, extremely, unbelievably long book.* Like adjectives, adverbs should be used with restraint.

✎ *Here is very useful advice: write quite descriptively with adverbs.*

123

Lesson 60 Grammar: Conjunctions and Interjections

✎ *Use conjunctions to connect words or word groups. Use interjections to express emotion.*

·········· Did You Know? ··········

A <u>conjunction</u> is a word that connects words or groups of words.

Coordinating conjunctions such as *and, but,* and *or* connect related words, groups of words, or sentences.

Meiko **and** Bob go to dance class together.
The recital was entertaining **but** long.
Bob danced in the first dance **and** in the finale.
Meiko forgot the step, **or** her foot slipped.

Correlative conjunctions are conjunctions used in pairs to connect sentence parts.

Neither Tessa **nor** Kato wanted to be first in the lineup.
Trini had to decide **whether** to dance **or** to study piano.
We saw **both** Sharon **and** Quinn in the jazz dance.

An <u>interjection</u> is a word or words that express emotion.

Wow! Your performance in the dance recital was stupendous.
Oh, I want to learn how to dance.

Use either an exclamation point or a comma after an interjection. If the emotion being expressed is strong, use the exclamation point.

Show What You Know
Circle each conjunction and underline each interjection in the paragraph below.

Suddenly I heard, "Yipe! It's a big snake." The poor snake simply wanted peace and quiet. It neither rattled nor hissed. It quietly uncoiled, and then it slithered away. I wanted to follow the snake, but Terri told me to stay away from it. "Look out!" she said. "It's gone under that rock." Both Dr. Herkimer and I are snake scientists. Oh, and we are both afraid of snakes!

Score: _____   Total Possible: 11

124

Practice
Look at the picture of a dog show. Write three sentences that describe the scene. Use conjunctions in at least two of the sentences, perhaps to compare and contrast the owners and their dogs. (Name them if you would like.)

1. _____ Review sentences to be sure your child has:
   _____ • written three complete sentences.
2. _____ • used conjunctions in at least two of the sentences.
   _____ • used correlative conjunctions for comparison
3. _____ and contrast.

Revise
Revise the paragraphs below by adding at least four conjunctions and one interjection to improve the writing. Use proper proofreading marks. *Sample answers are given.*

Example: We called her. ^and We waited for her.

Susan ran home from school. She was very excited ^as she raced in the front door.
She looked for her parents. As soon as she saw her father, she yelled, "^Dad! I won."
Goodness!
"Calm down," said Mr. Campbell. "Tell us what you won."

Susan reported that she had won first place in the science fair. She had gotten a
trophy ^and she had gotten a medal.

Mrs. Campbell congratulated ~~Susan. She~~ ^and hugged Susan. Mrs. Campbell cried, ^but she
did not cry long. Mr. Campbell smiled a lot, ^and he told Susan they were very proud of her.

Tips for Your Own Writing: Revising ··············
Choose a piece of your own writing. Did you use any interjections? If so, did you use them only occasionally? Using too many interjections is like the boy who cried "Wolf!" too often. After a while, the excitement wears off. Save interjections for special occasions.

✎ *Wow! Conjunctions and interjections in the same lesson.*

125

Lesson 61

Lesson
61 Grammar: Prepositions

Use prepositional phrases to modify words in sentences.

.... **Did You Know?** ....

A **preposition** connects a noun or pronoun to the rest of the sentence. The noun or pronoun that follows the preposition is called the **object of the preposition.**

The object, along with the preposition, its object, and any words that modify the object, make up a *prepositional phrase.* This phrase gives more information about the sentence.

We glanced *across* the treacherous river.

A prepositional phrase modifies a noun, pronoun, verb, adjective, or adverb. In the first sentence, the prepositional phrase *along the beach* is an **adverb phrase** that modifies the verb **walked.** In the second sentence, the prepositional phrase *along the beach* is an *adjective phrase* that modifies the noun *walk.*

We walked *along the beach.*
Our walk *along the beach* was enjoyable.

For a list of more prepositions, see page 159 in the *Writer's Handbook.*

Prepositions

about	before	down	of	to
above	behind	for	on	under
across	below	from	over	up
after	beneath	in	since	with
against	beside	like	through	without

Show What You Know
Underline each prepositional phrase. Circle the preposition.

Sweat was running down Matt's face. He couldn't believe that his opponent Marvin would clobber him, even though Marvin was champion of the school district. "Fifteen-love. Thirty-love." The scores were announced over the speaker! Matt tried to remember all he'd been taught: grip the end of the racket, but not too tightly. Stay limber and don't stand in one spot. Keep eyes on the ball. Now a serve was coming across the net. Matt crossed his fingers.

Score: _____ Total Possible: 14

126

Practice
Think of the sights, sounds, feelings, and smells of a storm. It could be a snowstorm, thunderstorm, or hurricane. Write a sentence or poem using as many prepositional phrases as you can.

Example: Rain from the dark clouds in the sky pounded on the roof of the house and pelted the trees in the yard as the lightning flashed across the sky.

Possible beginnings:
Over the trees in the yard
In the dark of night

Review the poem or sentence to be sure your child has used many prepositional phrases and has written descriptively about some of his or her sensory perceptions—sight, sound, feeling, smell.

Revise
Revise the paragraph below by adding at least four prepositional phrases to provide details about the heat, the drought, or the rainy season. Use proper proofreading marks.
Samples answers are given.

In the evening,   under the beautiful elm tree
Example: We sat outside.
In the summer   Under a blue sky
Hot, dry winds sweep across much of southern Asia. The sun bakes the earth, and
in the dry ground   with great eagerness
crops cannot grow. The people wait for the rainy season. The coming of the rain means
in their fields   for their families
that they can plant crops and produce food.

Tips for Your Own Writing: Revising ....
Choose a piece that you have written recently. Look for places to add prepositional phrases to provide additional information or add interesting details to your sentences. Always try to place each phrase next to the word it modifies.

Prepositions add details to your writing.

127

....

Lesson 62

Lesson
62 Review: Parts of Speech

A. Underline the four proper nouns in the article below.

Lucille Ball was one of the most successful comedians of all time. She and her husband, Desi Arnaz, created an incredibly popular TV show in the 1950s. It featured their New York apartment and best friend, "Ethel Mertz."

Score: _____ Total Possible: 4

B. Write a pronoun from the list that best completes each sentence.

you	her	them	we

1. Marla twisted ___her___ ankle on the ice yesterday.
2. Ben and Rae have won the skating match. Let's congratulate ___them___.
3. Can ___we___ join our teams together to put on a bigger skating show?
4. "I know ___you___ will like skating as much as I do," said the champ to her son.

Score: _____ Total Possible: 4

C. Above each underlined verb, write A if it is an action verb and L if it is a linking verb.

                                    A
1. Beavers build lodges in artificial lakes.
              L
2. A lodge is a mound of sticks with an interior chamber.
                                          A
3. As for the artificial lake, the beaver creates that by damming a stream.
       L   A
4. It seems strange that a beaver can make such a difference.

Score: _____ Total Possible: 5

D. Underline fourteen adjectives (including articles) in the report below. Circle one proper adjective.

Pluto is the last planet revolving around the sun. It was discovered in 1930 by American astronomer Clyde Tombaugh. Before this important discovery, astronomers suspected the existence of a ninth planet. They had noticed that a force seemed to pull the seventh planet, Uranus, and the eighth planet, Neptune, off their orbits.

Score: _____ Total Possible: 15

128

E. Fill in each blank with the appropriate article: the, an, or a.

1. Find ___a___ player to pluck the banjo.
2. If you play the harp, then find ___an___ orchestra to play in.
3. This is ___the___ guitar that I played in the concert last year.

Score: _____ Total Possible: 3

F. Underline the adverb in each of the three sentences below.

1. Charles Dickens wrote often about children's hardships.
2. Mrs. Havisham trains Estella to treat all men cruelly.
3. Do you know this story well? It is Dickens's *Great Expectations*.

Score: _____ Total Possible: 3

G. Underline eight conjunctions and circle two interjections.

Have you ever experienced a partial or total eclipse of the sun? Oh, my! It's an exciting experience. The moon passes between the sun and Earth. It casts a shadow on Earth. Not only does the sky darken, but also the air chills. Wow, it feels just like nightfall! Both before and after the deepest part of the eclipse, you have to be careful not to look directly at the sun. To do so could injure your eyes. Whether the eclipse is total or partial, a solar eclipse is something to remember.

Score: _____ Total Possible: 10

H. Underline five prepositional phrases below. Above the phrase, write the part of speech that it modifies (noun, verb, adjective).
                            noun
1. Bread is a staple food for many people.
                                    verb
2. Much of the flour used to make bread comes from wheat.
          noun
3. The wheat heads on the stalk tip provide flour's raw material.
                                      verb
4. To harvest wheat, machines beat the heads against a hard surface.
                      verb
5. The grain is then milled into flour.

Score: _____ Total Possible: 10

REVIEW SCORE: _____ REVIEW TOTAL: 54

129

192 Answer Key

Lesson 63

Lesson
63 Grammar: Sentence Types

Use a different sentence type for each different writing purpose: statement, question, request (or command), and exclamation.

.... Did You Know? ....

Sentences that make statements, *declarative sentences*, usually end with a period.

Rudi goes to see a movie once a week.

Sentences that ask questions, *interrogative sentences*, end with a question mark.

What movie did you see this week?

Sentences that express strong emotions, *exclamatory sentences* or *exclamations*, end with an exclamation point.

I can't wait to see that movie!

Sentences that express commands, requests, or give instructions, *imperative sentences*, have no subject and end with either a period or an exclamation point. To decide which punctuation mark to use, consider the intensity of the emotion in the sentence. Strong emotions call for the exclamation point.

Keep your ticket with you at all times.
Be quiet!

Show What You Know
Write the name of each kind of sentence.

statement	exclamation
question	request

1. This week, our school is having a craft fair.   statement

2. A craft is something made by hand from everyday materials.   statement

3. Do you want to know what I entered as my craft?   question

4. Go to the auditorium of Oak Grove School between 7:00 and 9:00 P.M. request/command

5. Look for the yellow bookcase made of recycled foam packing material. request

6. I won a blue ribbon for best use of materials!   exclamation

Score: _____   Total Possible: 6

130

Proofread
Read Janna's report below. Check for correct end punctuation of sentences. Use proper proofreading marks to correct the eight errors.

Example: Do you know which road to take?

Have you ever seen a dollhouse in a friend's home? Probably so? Most dollhouses are designed to be open on one side so that people can see inside them. Fine dollhouses are carefully furnished. They may even have real wallpaper and light fixtures. They are amazing!

I can't help wondering whether dollhouses are mainly for kids or for adults? Some of these toys are incredibly fancy. Let me tell you what I mean. A German noble in the 1500s hired someone to build a dollhouse castle? He furnished it with precious metals and miniature tapestries, or woven wall hangings. Was this dollhouse ever used by children as a toy? No, the owner kept it so that he could look at it occasionally.

So, are dollhouses for grown-ups or kids? What do you think?

Practice
Imagine that you are attending the Oak Grove School craft fair. You see an exhibit that you especially like. Write four sentences about it. Make sure that one sentence is a statement, one is a question, one is a command or a request, and one is an exclamation.

1. ___ Review sentences to be sure your child has:

   • written complete sentences with proper end punctuation.

2. ___ • written one sentence of each of the following types: declarative, interrogative,

3. ___ imperative, and exclamatory.

4. ___

Tips for Your Own Writing: Revising ....
Select a piece of your own writing. Check to see whether you used different types of sentences. Using a variety of sentence types can make your writing more interesting and effective.

State, ask, request, and exclaim!

131

Lesson 64

Lesson
64 Grammar: Understanding Sentences

Every sentence has a backbone (its subject and verb). Interesting sentences have many details, too.

.... Did You Know? ....

The subject of a sentence tells who or what did something (or occasionally, who *is*). The thing that is done (or that simply is) is the verb or the predicate. In the following sentence, *Carla* tells the "who," and *ran* tells the "thing" that Carla did.

Carla ran.

Most sentences are longer and more complex than *Carla ran.* Writers usually hang details on the sentence backbone. This is because they often want to convey more to listeners and readers. Details can give information about people, places, and things. Or they can tell how, when, where, or to what extent something happens.

My new friend Carla ran fast in the all-state track meet.

Show What You Know
Circle the subject and underline the verb in each question and answer.

1. Why do people think Yosemite National Park is so beautiful? They like the magnificent mountains, deep canyons, and towering waterfalls.

2. Where is Yosemite National Park? The park is located in a wilderness area in California.

3. How many kinds of wildlife live in the park? The park has more than 200 kinds of birds and 60 kinds of other animals.

4. Are there many different plants in the park? Yes, more than 300 kinds of trees and 1,300 kinds of other plants live in the park.

5. What activities can people do in the park? They can go horseback riding, fishing, golfing, hiking, and swimming.

Score: _____   Total Possible: 21

132

Practice
Choose a word or phrase from each column to create a sentence that makes sense. Using this method, make four sentences and write them on the lines.

Subject	Verb	Article/Adjective	Object	Preposition	Object of Preposition
Marcus	painted	the lovely	canvas	under a	concert hall
You	sang	a sorrowful	melody	into the	acrylic paint
They	found	the shiny	kitten	out of the	board
I	pounded	the scared	nail	with	porch
The teacher	touched	the spinning	story	in the	book

1. ___ Some possible sentences:

   Marcus sang a sorrowful melody in the concert hall.

2. ___ You painted the lovely canvas with acrylic paint.

   They found the scared kitten under a porch.

3. ___ I pounded the shiny nail into the board.

   Review the sentences to be sure your child has:

4. ___ • chosen a word or phrase from each column.

   • written complete sentences, correctly punctuated.

Revise
Use information from Show What You Know or an encyclopedia to find additional facts to revise the paragraph below. Use proper proofreading marks. Sample answers are given.

Example: It is a tree.   (magnificent, spreading)

Yosemite National Park is in northern California. The scenery is very pretty with mountains, canyons, and waterfalls. The park has many plants and animals. People visit (Yosemite has several of North America's highest waterfalls.) the park to participate in many activities. Review the paragraphs to be sure your child has added details.

Tips for Your Own Writing: Revising ....
Select a letter you have written. Try to add details to at least two sentences in your letter. Make sure the details are important and needed.

If your sentence backbone is solid, you can hang many details on it!

133

Lesson 65

Lesson 65 Grammar: Combining Sentences I

You can form compound sentences in more than one way.

.... **Did You Know?** ....

Using compounds to combine short sentences can lead to smoother, less choppy writing.

When sentences have the same subject and verb, you can combine them easily.

    Darryl eats apples.   Darryl eats plums.
    Darryl eats **apples and plums.**

When two sentences have the same subject but different verbs and objects, they can also be combined.

    Heather plays soccer.   Heather writes poetry.
    Heather **plays soccer and writes poetry.**

Sentences with the same verb and object but different subjects can also be combined. Many times the form of the verb will change when it becomes plural.

    Diehl goes to summer camp.   Timothy goes to summer camp.
    Diehl and Timothy go to summer camp.

If *I* is one subject in a compound subject, it always comes *last.*

    Timothy and I go to summer camp.

....

Show What You Know

Combine each pair of sentences into one compound sentence.

1. England is in the British Isles. Scotland is in the British Isles.
  England and Scotland are in the British Isles.

2. Aunt Tillie visited England. Aunt Tillie visited Scotland.
  Aunt Tillie visited England and Scotland.

3. She climbed mountains in Scotland. She visited gardens in England.
  She climbed mountains in Scotland and visited gardens in England.

4. Tillie sipped tea in the afternoon. Tillie ate scones in the afternoon.
  Tillie sipped tea and ate scones in the afternoon.

Score: _____   Total Possible: 4

134

Practice

Make a personal profile. First, list four of your physical characteristics such as hairstyle or color, height, and eye color. Next, list four foods that you like. Finally, list four things that you like to do for fun.

Physical Characteristics
_____   _____
_____   _____

Favorite Foods
_____   _____
_____   _____

Things I Like to Do
_____   _____
_____   _____

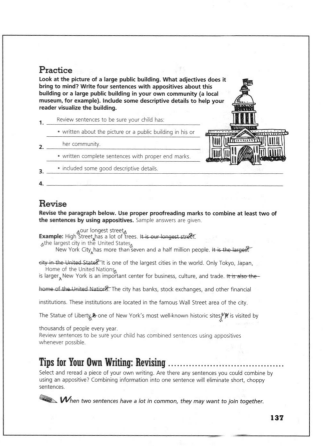

Using the information above, write two compound sentences telling about yourself.

1. _____ Review sentences to be sure your child has written two complete compound sentences

    (e.g., compound subjects, compound objects, or compound predicates, i.e., verbs).

2. _____

Revise

Revise the paragraph below by rewriting at least two sentences as compound sentences. Use proper proofreading marks. Sample answers are given.

    and dogs
Example: Cats are mammals. Dogs are mammals too.

    and crocodiles
Alligators belong to the family *Crocodylidae.* Crocodiles belong to that family, too.

    but
They look a lot alike. Some of the crocodiles' bottom teeth show when they close their

mouths. Alligators' teeth are hidden when they close their mouths. Also, crocodiles

    and
have narrow snouts. Alligators have broad snouts.

Tips for Your Own Writing: Revising ....

Choose a piece of your own writing. Look for short, choppy sentences and see whether combining them will improve your writing. Also, look for sentences that are too long. Sometimes a very long sentence should be divided into two shorter sentences.

Be a joiner! Combine sentences whenever appropriate.

135

Lesson 66

Lesson 66 Grammar: Combining Sentences II

Do two sentences have some words in common? You may be able to combine the sentences by using an appositive.

.... **Did You Know?** ....

Sometimes we can combine two sentences by taking information from one sentence and attaching it to a closely related noun or a phrase in another sentence. Information that is "attached" in this way is called an *appositive.* If it is at the beginning or end of a sentence, you need only one comma after it or before it.

    A river always has a mouth. A mouth is the place where it flows into a larger body of water.
    A river always has a mouth, **the place where it flows into a larger body of water.**

When an appositive adds information but is not necessary to establish the meaning of the sentence, set it off with commas. Delete the appositive and see whether the sentence has the same meaning.

    Our swimming coach teaches summer school. Mrs. Santos is our swimming coach.
    Mrs. Santos, **our swimming coach,** teaches summer school.

When an appositive is needed to clarify something, do *not* use commas.

    Rube and Lou played baseball tonight. Rube and Lou are Hornets team members.
    Hornets team members **Rube and Lou** played baseball tonight.

....

Show What You Know

Use an appositive to combine each pair of sentences below.

1. Every country has a capital. A capital is a city where government is run.
  Every country has a capital, a city where government is run.

2. Rome is full of ancient buildings. Rome is the capital of Italy.
  Rome, the capital of Italy, is full of ancient buildings.

3. A small town is near Rome. The town has many ruins.
  A small town near Rome has many ruins.

Score: _____   Total Possible: 3

136

Practice

Look at the picture of a large public building. What adjectives does it bring to mind? Write four sentences with appositives about this building or a large public building in your own community (a local museum, for example). Include some descriptive details to help your reader visualize the building.

1. _____ Review sentences to be sure your child has:

    • written about the picture or a public building in his or

2. _____ her community.

    • written complete sentences with proper end marks.

3. _____

    • included some good descriptive details.

4. _____

Revise

Revise the paragraph below. Use proper proofreading marks to combine at least two of the sentences by using appositives. Sample answers are given.

    our longest street
Example: High Street has a lot of trees. It is our longest street.

    the largest city in the United States,
New York City has more than seven and a half million people. It is the largest

city in the United States. It is one of the largest cities in the world. Only Tokyo, Japan,

    Home of the United Nations,
is larger. New York is an important center for business, culture, and trade. It is also the

home of the United Nations. The city has banks, stock exchanges, and other financial

institutions. These institutions are located in the famous Wall Street area of the city.

The Statue of Liberty, one of New York's most well-known historic sites, is visited by

thousands of people every year.
Review sentences to be sure your child has combined sentences using appositives whenever possible.

Tips for Your Own Writing: Revising ....

Select and reread a piece of your own writing. Are there any sentences you could combine by using an appositive? Combining information into one sentence will eliminate short, choppy sentences.

When two sentences have a lot in common, they may want to join together.

137

Lesson 67

Lesson 67 Grammar: Combining Sentences III

Do two sentences have related ideas? Are they of equal importance? If the answer to these questions is yes, you may want to form compound sentences.

.... **Did You Know?** ....

Similar sentences can be combined when they have closely related ideas of equal importance. We can form such compound sentences by using the coordinating conjunctions *and, but,* or *or.* Place a comma after the first sentence and before the conjunction.

Use *and* to join sentences that have equal importance and similar ideas.

Mr. Raeford will bake pies. Ms. Tasco will prepare salads.
Mr. Raeford will bake pies, **and** Ms. Tasco will prepare salads.

Use *but* to join sentences that have equal importance and contrasting ideas.

We had a picnic on Memorial Day. We stayed indoors on Independence Day.
We had a picnic on Memorial Day, **but** we stayed indoors on Independence Day.

Use *or* to join sentences that have equal importance and that offer a choice.

Play games with the children. Talk to the adults.
Play games with the children, **or** talk to the adults.

Show What You Know

Use *and, but,* or *or* to form a compound sentence from each pair of sentences. Make sure you punctuate the sentences correctly.

1. We make homemade ice cream. Our neighbors enjoy sharing it with us.
   We make homemade ice cream, and our neighbors enjoy sharing it with us.

2. I like pistachio ice cream. My sister prefers strawberry ice cream.
   I like pistachio ice cream, but my sister prefers strawberry.

3. You can have homemade ice cream with us. You can go to the movie with them.
   You can have homemade ice cream with us, or you can go to the movie with them.

Score: _____ Total Possible: 3

138

Practice

Think of holiday parties that your family has. Many families have celebrations at Thanksgiving or the Fourth of July. Use one of your family's special holiday celebrations in this writing assignment.

Write three sentences to describe the holiday celebration. Try to use each of the conjunctions *and, but,* and *or* at least one time.

1. _____ Review sentences to be sure your child has:
   • written about a holiday celebration.
2. _____ • written complete sentences with proper end
      punctuation.
3. _____ • used *and, but,* and *or* at least one time each in the sentences.

Revise

Revise the paragraph below by combining at least two sentences. Use proper proofreading marks to add the conjunctions *and, but,* and *or.* Sample answers are given.

Example: I like toppings on my ice cream, ^but^ My brother doesn't.

Ice cream is made from milk products, sugar, and flavorings. It is a popular dairy treat. Ice cream is eaten alone, ^or^ It can also be eaten with cake or pie. It is the main ingredient in milk shakes, sodas, and sundaes. The most popular flavor is vanilla, ^and^ Chocolate is the next most popular flavor. Ice cream can be found in many parts of the world, ^but^ Americans eat more ice cream than people in any other country.

Tips for Your Own Writing: Revising ....

Select a piece of your own writing. Did you use the conjunctions *and, but,* and *or* to join sentences that have similar ideas? If the sentences do not have similar ideas, then you should not try to combine them.

When two sentences have a lot in common, they may belong together as one.

139

Lesson 68

Lesson 68 Grammar: Combining Sentences IV

Do two clauses have related ideas? Is one of the clauses more important than the other? This may be a place for a subordinating conjunction.

.... **Did You Know?** ....

These two clauses can be combined using a subordinate conjunction.

Granddad fed the livestock. He went to school each day.
Granddad fed the livestock **before** he went to school each day.

A sentence part that can stand on its own as a complete sentence is a *main clause.* A sentence part that cannot stand on its own is a *subordinate clause.*

If the subordinate clause comes first in the sentence, insert a comma before the main clause.

Unless you feed them on schedule, the cows won't give milk.

Subordinating Conjunctions			
after	how	though	whenever
as	once	unless	where
as if	since	until	while
because	than	when	why

Show What You Know

Draw lines to match main and subordinate clauses and form complex sentences. Add commas where needed.

Although the temperature is above freezing — so that we could dress properly.
No one measured the chilling effect of wind — bundle up in layers.
The Weather Service developed the scale — when it is exposed to cold winds.
Your flesh can freeze very fast — the air feels like it's freezing.
If you expect to be in wind on a cold day — until we had a wind chill scale.

Score: _____ Total Possible: 7

140

Practice

Look at the picture. On a farm, people have chores to do early in the morning. Think how you would feel if you had to get up early in the morning to do chores. Write four sentences describing how you think it would feel. Use a subordinate clause with a subordinating conjunction in at least one sentence.

1. _____ Review sentences to be sure your child has:
   • written about the picture.
2. _____ • written four complete sentences with proper
      end punctuation.
3. _____ • used a subordinate clause with a subordinating conjunction in at least one sentence.
4. _____

Revise

Revise at least four sentences in the paragraphs below to include subordinate clauses. Use proper proofreading marks to use subordinating conjunctions such as *after, although, because, even though, while,* and *when.* Sample answers are given.

Example: ^Because^ My mom received her teaching certificate last year, ^when^ She can teach at my school now.

America lost a great pilot ^When^ Amelia Earhart's plane vanished in 1937. ^While^ Earhart was making a trip around the world, ^Her^ plane went down near the Howland Islands in the Pacific Ocean. Some people think her plane crashed in the ocean ^because^ It ran out of fuel. No one knows what really happened ^because^ No trace of her or her plane has ever been found.

^After^ Earhart got her pilot's license in 1922, ^She^ began to fly in meets. She became the first female pilot to fly alone across the Atlantic in 1932. She was the first woman to be awarded the Distinguished Flying Cross. Her aviation career was full of "firsts," ^even though^ It was cut short by her disappearance.

Tips for Your Own Writing: Revising ....

Select a report you have written. Look for sentence fragments. A *sentence fragment* is a subordinate clause that has been left to stand on its own. Join it with a main clause.

Use subordinating conjunctions such as after, before, since, until, and while to join sentences.

141

Lesson 69 Grammar: Combining Sentences V

Use relative pronouns such as who, whose, that, and which to introduce dependent sentence parts known as relative clauses.

.... Did You Know? ....

You can form a complex sentence by combining two short sentences with a relative pronoun.

> Spring rains are good for tulips. Spring rains can begin in March.
> Spring rains, **which** can begin in March, are good for tulips.

In the combined sentence—"Spring rains, . . . are good for tulips"—is the main clause. It can stand alone. The other part of the sentence—"which can begin in March"—is a relative clause that is introduced by the relative pronoun *which*. It cannot stand alone. Some relative pronouns are *who, what, whom, whose, that,* and *which.*

A relative clause can function as an adjective or a noun.

> The girl **who sat next to me** is my new neighbor.
> We found **what we wanted** at the garden center.

Set off a relative clause with commas *only* if it adds information that is not necessary to the sentence. Read the sentence without the clause and see whether the sentence has the same meaning.

Show What You Know
Build a complex sentence using the provided sentence parts. Omit any words in brackets. Write your sentence on the line.

1. [The story] made my skin crawl.   Mr. Gates told a frightening tunnel story   that
   Mr. Gates told a frightening tunnel story that made my skin crawl.

2. I have been in a tunnel on my   [The tunnel] cuts through the Smoky   which
   way to New York.   Mountains.
   I have been in a tunnel, which cuts through the Smoky Mountains, on my way to New York.

3. He told you [something] about tunnels.   [It] is not true.   what
   What he told you about tunnels is not true.

Score: _____   Total Possible: 3

142

Proofread
Read Ferris's report below about hailstorms. Use proper proofreading marks to add four needed commas and to delete three commas that are not needed.

Example: The man who is wearing a red hat is my uncle, whom you have met.

A hailstorm is one of the strangest kinds of weather that I can think of. Hailstones, which are lumps of ice, fall out of thunderstorm clouds.

One of the worst hailstorms in recent times struck Cheyenne, Wyoming, in August 1985. After the storm, people who lived there found six inches of ice on the ground! Their calendars told them it was summer, but the scene looked like winter.

What causes this freakish weather? A thunderstorm piles clouds up very high in the atmosphere. Strong, moist winds rush up to great heights. There, water droplets freeze into tiny ice pellets which get many additional coatings of ice. Finally, the hailstones become so heavy that they fall to the ground. Hailstones, which are usually smaller than a marble, can become as large as grapefruits. You wouldn't want one of those to fall on your head!

Practice
Write three sentences about a bridge or a tunnel. Use a relative clause in two of the sentences.

1. _____ Review sentences to be sure your child has:
   • written about the required topic: a bridge or a tunnel.
2. _____ • written complete sentences with proper end punctuation.
3. _____ • included properly constructed and punctuated relative clauses in two sentences.

Tips for Your Own Writing: Revising ....

Select a story you have written. Did you begin any relative clauses with *who* or *whom?* Check to see whether you used them correctly.
The woman **who** gave me the coat is my aunt. (subject)
The woman **whom** I visited last summer is my aunt. (object)

Hooray for all of your relatives—relative pronouns and clauses, that is.

143

Lesson 70 Grammar: Combining Sentences VI

*Words derived from verbs, called **participles**, give us yet another way to combine sentence parts.*

.... Did You Know? ....

You can change the verb of one sentence into a participle to combine two sentences as shown.

> Ted's kite soared and dived. Ted's kite was flying in the wind.
> Ted's kite soared and dived, flying in the wind.

You can combine these sentences as shown.

> Val was slowed by the wind. Val made little progress on her bike.
> Slowed by the wind, Val made little progress on her bike.

A *present participle* is a form of a verb that usually ends in *-ing,* and a *past participle* usually ends in *-ed.* They both act like adjectives. Irregular verbs do not follow this pattern for past participles.

Verb	Present Participle	Past Participle
knock	knocking	knocked
find	finding	found
see	seeing	seen

A phrase containing a participle is called a *participial phrase.*

Show What You Know
Choose one word in each column to write four sentences that make sense on the lines below.

Participle	Adverb	Prepositional Phrase	Subject	Verb	Object
Speaking	yesterday	on the platform	Alfredo	recited	my fingers
Racing	often	in our town	the player	made	attention
Seen	slowly	in the street	the kitten	wanted	the salt
Held	tightly	in my hand	the ice cream	froze	a goal
Found	around	on the field	the deer	licked	the poem

1. _____ Review sentences to be sure your child has chosen a word or phrase from each column and
2. _____ has written four sentences that make sense and have correct punctuation.
3. _____ Possible answers: Speaking slowly on the platform, Alfredo recited the poem.
4. _____ Racing around on the field, the player made a goal. Found yesterday in the street, the kitten licked my fingers. Seen often in our town, the deer wanted attention.

Score: _____   Total Possible: 4

144

Proofread
Combine four sentences in the paragraphs below by using proper proofreading marks to change one sentence into a participial phrase and adding it to another sentence. Sample answers are given.

Example: *Seeing* We saw Jessica on her bike. We waved to her.

Waiting The cyclists waited at the starting line. *the cyclists* They were ready to go. The starter checked their positions at the line. Then he sounded his horn. That was the starting signal. The cyclists pushed off on their bicycles, beginning the first leg of the Tour de France. *the cyclists* The cyclists were bunched together at first. Then they began to spread out. The faster ones put some distance between themselves and the rest of the pack. *Struggling* They struggled up the hills. They seemed to barely move. But on flat stretches, they whizzed past the spectators. *watching* The spectators watched the race from the sides of the road. At last, the finish line was in sight.

Practice
Sometimes things we do, such as riding a bike, seem easy. But at other times, the same activity may seem difficult. Look at the picture. Why is this girl having such a hard time riding her bike? Have you ever had this experience? Write four sentences with participial phrases about riding your bike under difficult conditions.

1. _____ Review sentences to be sure your child has:
2. _____ • written about riding a bike under adverse conditions.
3. _____ • written four complete sentences with proper end punctuation.
4. _____ • used participial phrases in their sentences.

Tips for Your Own Writing: Proofreading ....

Choose something that you have written recently. Look to see whether you used any participial phrases. Make sure you used a comma after a participial phrase that comes at the beginning of a sentence.

Using participial phrases, you can combine sentences to add variety to your writing.

145

Lesson 71

Lesson

71 Grammar: Combining Sentences VII

When combining sentences, use any and all methods you can. Often, there is more than one way to combine sentences.

.... Did You Know? ....

A big part of the writer's job is *selection*, that is, deciding which details to include (and which ones to leave out).

There is more than one way to combine the following sentences.

> Mom just planted that rosebush.
> The rosebush was full of blossoms.
> We cut the rose.
> The rose smelled very fragrant.
> The rose had a bright red color.

> We cut the bright red, fragrant rose from Mom's new rosebush, which was full of blossoms.

You could also write:

> Planted recently by Mom, the rosebush yielded a bright red, fragrant rose, which we cut.

Show What You Know

Combine each set of sentences to create a new sentence. Write the new sentence on the line.
Sample answers are given.

1. I recently read a new book.   Elbert Baze wrote it.
   The book is *Dinosaur Music*.   It is an entertaining book.
   I recently read an entertaining new book, Dinosaur Music, by Elbert Baze.

2. I didn't know that the book signing was scheduled for Tuesday.
   I made other plans with Bert and Ernie.
   Not knowing that the book signing was scheduled for Tuesday, I made other
   plans with Bert and Ernie.

Score: _____   Total Possible: 2

146

Practice

At a book signing, an author greets people and signs copies of his or her latest book. Think about your favorite author. Imagine that you are going to this author's book signing. Write four sentences that you might say to the author.

1. _Review sentences to be sure your child has:_
   • written about what he or she will say to his or her
2. _favorite author at a book signing._
   • written complete sentences with proper end
3. _punctuation._

4. _____

Revise

Combine sentences in the paragraphs below using any of the methods you have learned. Use proper proofreading marks. Sample answers are given.

Example: I like to cook. Cooking takes time. My favorite recipe is spaghetti sauce.

To make this pasta salad, you will need 1/2 lb of vermicelli. Vermicelli are very thin, long Italian noodles. Add 1/2 tsp. of salt to rapidly boiling water. Add the vermicelli to rapidly boiling water. Boil the vermicelli until tender. Drain them in a colander. Rinse them in cold water. Toss the noodles with a little oil. The noodles will stay separated. Chop up 1/2 cup of black olives. Chop up 1/2 cup of green onions. Cut up 1/4 lb of provolone. Provolone is a mild Italian cheese. Mix the vermicelli, olives, onions, and cheese. Add mayonnaise. Add Italian dressing instead. Use salt, pepper, and garlic. Season the salad. Cover the salad. Refrigerate it for at least two hours.

Tips for Your Own Writing: Revising ....

Look at a piece of your own writing. Did you write many long sentences? Good writers use sentences of different lengths—both short and long—to add variety and interest to their writing.

Don't be afraid of combining. Put those sentences together!

147

Lesson 72

Lesson

72 Review: Understanding and Combining Sentences

A. Choose a word or phrase from each column to build a sentence that makes sense. Using this method, make three sentences and write them on the lines.

Subject	Verb	Object	Preposition	Object
Benny	likes	the letters	in	her aunt
We	planted	sunshine	to	the clay pot
Courtney	mailed	a flower	for	the summer

1. _Review sentences to be sure your child has chosen a word or phrase from each_
2. _column, written complete sentences with correct punctuation, and written sentences_
3. _that make sense. Possible answers: Benny planted a flower in the clay pot. We_
   mailed the letters to her aunt. Courtney likes sunshine in the summer.

Score: _____   Total Possible: 3

B. Combine the sentences using *and, but,* or *or.* Write the sentences on the lines.

1. Oranges have vitamin C. Grapefruits have vitamin C.
   Oranges and grapefruits have vitamin C.

2. Go camping with Gene. Go to the movies with Leslie.
   Go camping with Gene, or go to the movies with Leslie.

3. We go to the movies frequently. We often see Leslie there.
   We go to the movies frequently, and we often see Leslie there.

Score: _____   Total Possible: 3

C. Combine the following sentences, using an appositive. Write the sentence on the line.

Mrs. Tanaka is our librarian.   Mrs. Tanaka helps us with our research papers.
Mrs. Tanaka, our librarian, helps us with our research papers.

Score: _____   Total Possible: 1

148

D. In each sentence, underline the subordinate clause and circle the main clause.

1. If you like my model ship, (I'll make you one.)
2. (I think I can build it myself) unless the kit is very complicated.

Score: _____   Total Possible: 4

E. Build a sentence using the provided sentence parts. Write the sentence on the line.

the green butterfly made a comeback   no one had seen in years   which
The green butterfly, which no one had seen in years, made a comeback.

Score: _____   Total Possible: 1

F. Combine the sentences using a participial phrase.

June was feeling sick.   June lay down and closed her eyes.
Feeling sick, June lay down and closed her eyes.

Score: _____   Total Possible: 1

G. Combine the three sentences. Write the combined sentence on the line.
Sample answer is given.
1. Berne is a new student.   2. He has red hair.   3. Berne is good at swimming.
Berne, the new student with red hair, is good at swimming.

Score: _____   Total Possible: 1

H. Decide whether each sentence is a statement, question, exclamation, or request. Then write the correct punctuation on the line.

1. What time does Reeva get home from work this evening _?_
2. Last night Janice got home at 8:30 _./!_
3. Don't stay out too late _./!_

Score: _____   Total Possible: 3

REVIEW SCORE: _____   REVIEW TOTAL: 17

149

Proofreading Marks

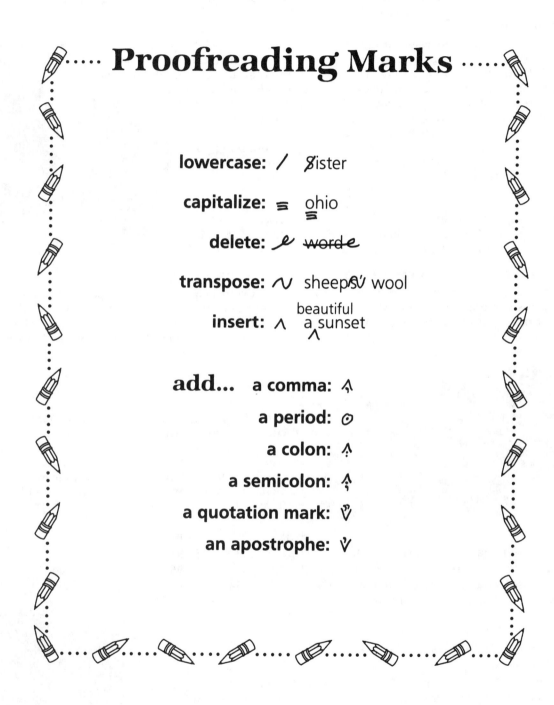

lowercase: / Sister

capitalize: ⹀ ohio

delete: ℯ word̶e̶

transpose: ⌒ sheeps⁀ wool

insert: ∧ a beautiful sunset

add... a comma: ⌄

a period: ⊙

a colon: ⌃

a semicolon: ⌃

a quotation mark: ⱽ

an apostrophe: ⱽ

McGraw-Hill Consumer Products

The skills taught in school are now available at home!
These award-winning software titles meet school guidelines and are based on
The McGraw-Hill Companies classroom software titles.

MATH GRADES 1 & 2

These math programs are a great way to teach and reinforce skills used in everyday situations. Fun, friendly characters need help with their math skills. Everyone's friend, Nubby the stubby pencil, will help kids master the math in the Numbers Quiz show. Foggy McHammer, a carpenter, needs some help building his playhouse so that all the boards will fit together! Julio Bambino's kitchen antics will surely burn his pastries if you don't help him set the clock timer correctly! We can't forget Turbo Tomato, a fruit with a passion for adventure, who needs help calculating his daredevil stunts.

Math Grades 1 & 2 use a tested, proven approach to reinforcing your child's math skills while keeping him or her intrigued with Nubby and his collection of crazy friends.

TITLE	ISBN	PRICE
Grade 1: Nubby's Quiz Show	1-57768-321-8	$9.95
Grade 2: Foggy McHammer's Treehouse	1-57768-322-6	$9.95

Available in jewel case only (no box included)

MISSION MASTERS™ MATH AND LANGUAGE ARTS

The Mission Masters™—Pauline, Rakeem, Mia, and T.J.—need your help. The Mission Masters™ are a team of young agents working for the Intelliforce Agency, a high-level cooperative whose goal is to maintain order on our rather unruly planet. From within the agency's top secret Command Control Center, the agency's central computer, M5, has detected a threat...and guess what—you're the agent assigned to the mission!

MISSION MASTERS™ MATH
GRADES 3, 4, & 5

This series of exciting activities encourages young mathematicians to challenge themselves and their math skills to overcome the perils of villains and other planetary threats. Skills reinforced include: analyzing and solving real-world problems, estimation, measurements, geometry, whole numbers, fractions, graphs, and patterns.

TITLE	ISBN	PRICE
Grade 3: Mission Masters™ Defeat Dirty D!	1-57768-323-5	$9.95
Grade 4: Mission Masters™ Alien Encounter	1-57768-324-2	$9.95
Grade 5: Mission Masters™ Meet Mudflat Moe	1-57768-325-0	$9.95

Available in jewel case only (no box included)

MISSION MASTERS™ LANGUAGE ARTS
GRADES 3, 4, & 5

This series invites children to apply their language skills to defeat unscrupulous characters and to overcome other earthly dangers. Skills reinforced include: language mechanics and usage, punctuation, spelling, vocabulary, reading comprehension, and creative writing.

TITLE	ISBN	PRICE
Grade 3: Mission Masters™ Freezing Frenzy	1-57768-343-9	$9.95
Grade 4: Mission Masters™ Network Nightmare	1-57768-344-7	$9.95
Grade 5: Mission Masters™ Mummy Mysteries	1-57768-345-5	$9.95

Available in jewel case only (no box included)

BASIC SKILLS BUILDER K to 2 – THE MAGIC APPLEHOUSE

At the Magic Applehouse, children discover that Abigail Appleseed runs a deliciously successful business selling apple pies, tarts, and other apple treats. Enthusiasm grows as children join in the fun of helping Abigail run her business. Along the way they'll develop computer and entrepreneurial skills to last a lifetime. They will run their own business – all while they're having bushels of fun!

TITLE	ISBN	PRICE
Basic Skills Builder –The Magic Applehouse	1-57768-312-9	$9.95

Available in jewel case only (no box included)

TEST PREP – SCORING HIGH

This grade-based testing software will help prepare your child for standardized achievement tests given by his or her school. Scoring High specifically targets the skills required for success on the Stanford Achievement Test (SAT) for grades three through eight. Lessons and test questions follow the same format and cover the same content areas as questions appearing on the actual SAT tests. The practice tests are modeled after the SAT test-taking experience with similar directions, number of questions per section, and bubble-sheet answer choices.

Scoring High is a child's first-class ticket to a winning score on standardized achievement tests!

TITLE	ISBN	PRICE
Grades 3 to 5: Scoring High Test Prep	1-57768-316-1	$9.95
Grades 6 to 8: Scoring High Test Prep	1-57768-317-X	$9.95

Available in jewel case only (no box included)

SCIENCE

Mastering the principles of both physical and life science has never been so FUN for kids grades six and above as it is while they are exploring McGraw-Hill's edutainment software!

TITLE	ISBN	PRICE
Grades 6 & up: Life Science	1-57768-336-6	$9.95
Grades 8 & up: Physical Science	1-57768-308-0	$9.95

Available in jewel case only (no box included)

REFERENCE

The National Museum of Women in the Arts has teamed with McGraw-Hill Consumer Products to bring you this superb collection available for your enjoyment on CD-ROM.

This special collection is a visual diary of 200 women artists from the Renaissance to the present, spanning 500 years of creativity.

You will discover the art of women who excelled in all the great art movements of history. Artists who pushed the boundaries of abstract, genre, landscape, narrative, portrait, and still-life styles; as well as artists forced to push the societal limits placed on women through the ages.

TITLE	ISBN	PRICE
Women in the Arts	1-57768-010-3	$29.95

Available in boxed version only

Most titles for Windows 3.1™, Windows '95™ & '98™, and Macintosh™.

Visit us on the Internet at:

www.MHkids.com

Or call 800-298-4119 for your local retailer.

McGraw-Hill Consumer Products

All our workbooks meet school curriculum guidelines and correspond to
The McGraw-Hill Companies classroom textbooks.

SPECTRUM SERIES

DOLCH Sight Word Activities

The DOLCH Sight Word Activities Workbooks use the classic Dolch list of 220 basic vocabulary words that make up from 50% to 75% of all reading matter that children ordinarily encounter. Since these words are ordinarily recognized on sight, they are called *sight words*. Volume 1 includes 110 sight words. Volume 2 covers the remainder of the list. Over 160 pages.

TITLE	ISBN	PRICE
Grades K-1 Vol. 1	1-57768-429-X	$9.95
Grades K-1 Vol. 2	1-57768-439-7	$9.95

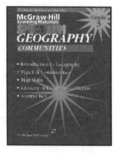

GEOGRAPHY

Full-color, three-part lessons strengthen geography knowledge and map reading skills. Focusing on five geographic themes including location, place, human/environmental interaction, movement, and regions. Over 150 pages. Glossary of geographical terms and answer key included.

TITLE	ISBN	PRICE
Gr 3, Communities	1-57768-153-3	$7.95
Gr 4, Regions	1-57768-154-1	$7.95
Gr 5, USA	1-57768-155-X	$7.95
Gr 6, World	1-57768-156-8	$7.95

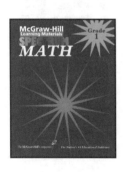

MATH

Features easy-to-follow instructions that give students a clear path to success. This series has comprehensive coverage of the basic skills, helping children to master math fundamentals. Over 150 pages. Answer key included.

TITLE	ISBN	PRICE
Grade 1	1-57768-111-8	$7.95
Grade 2	1-57768-112-6	$7.95
Grade 3	1-57768-113-4	$7.95
Grade 4	1-57768-114-2	$7.95
Grade 5	1-57768-115-0	$7.95
Grade 6	1-57768-116-9	$7.95
Grade 7	1-57768-117-7	$7.95
Grade 8	1-57768-118-5	$7.95

PHONICS

Provides everything children need to build multiple skills in language. Focusing on phonics, structural analysis, and dictionary skills, this series also offers creative ideas for using phonics and word study skills in other language arts. Over 200 pages. Answer key included.

TITLE	ISBN	PRICE
Grade K	1-57768-120-7	$7.95
Grade 1	1-57768-121-5	$7.95
Grade 2	1-57768-122-3	$7.95
Grade 3	1-57768-123-1	$7.95
Grade 4	1-57768-124-X	$7.95
Grade 5	1-57768-125-8	$7.95
Grade 6	1-57768-126-6	$7.95

READING

This full-color series creates an enjoyable reading environment, even for below-average readers. Each book contains captivating content, colorful characters, and compelling illustrations, so children are eager to find out what happens next. Over 150 pages. Answer key included.

TITLE	ISBN	PRICE
Grade K	1-57768-130-4	$7.95
Grade 1	1-57768-131-2	$7.95
Grade 2	1-57768-132-0	$7.95
Grade 3	1-57768-133-9	$7.95
Grade 4	1-57768-134-7	$7.95
Grade 5	1-57768-135-5	$7.95
Grade 6	1-57768-136-3	$7.95

SPELLING

This full-color series links spelling to reading and writing and increases skills in words and meanings, consonant and vowel spellings, and proofreading practice. Over 200 pages. Speller dictionary and answer key included.

TITLE	ISBN	PRICE
Grade 1	1-57768-161-4	$7.95
Grade 2	1-57768-162-2	$7.95
Grade 3	1-57768-163-0	$7.95
Grade 4	1-57768-164-9	$7.95
Grade 5	1-57768-165-7	$7.95
Grade 6	1-57768-166-5	$7.95

WRITING

Lessons focus on creative and expository writing using clearly stated objectives and pre-writing exercises. Eight essential reading skills are applied. Activities include main idea, sequence, comparison, detail, fact and opinion, cause and effect, and making a point. Over 130 pages. Answer key included.

TITLE	ISBN	PRICE
Grade 1	1-57768-141-X	$7.95
Grade 2	1-57768-142-8	$7.95
Grade 3	1-57768-143-6	$7.95
Grade 4	1-57768-144-4	$7.95
Grade 5	1-57768-145-2	$7.95
Grade 6	1-57768-146-0	$7.95
Grade 7	1-57768-147-9	$7.95
Grade 8	1-57768-148-7	$7.95

TEST PREP
From the Nation's #1 Testing Company

Prepares children to do their best on current editions of the five major standardized tests. Activities reinforce test-taking skills through examples, tips, practice, and timed exercises. Subjects include reading, math, and language. Over 150 pages. Answer key included.

TITLE	ISBN	PRICE
Grade 1	1-57768-101-0	$8.95
Grade 2	1-57768-102-9	$8.95
Grade 3	1-57768-103-7	$8.95
Grade 4	1-57768-104-5	$8.95
Grade 5	1-57768-105-3	$8.95
Grade 6	1-57768-106-1	$8.95
Grade 7	1-57768-107-X	$8.95
Grade 8	1-57768-108-8	$8.95

LANGUAGE ARTS

Encourages creativity and builds confidence by making writing fun! Seventy-two four-part lessons strengthen writing skills by focusing on parts of speech, word usage, sentence structure, punctuation, and proofreading. Each level includes a *Writer's Handbook* at the end of the book that offers writing tips. This series is based on the highly respected SRA/McGraw-Hill language arts series. More than 180 full-color pages. *Available March 2000.*

TITLE	ISBN	PRICE
Grade 2	1-57768-472-9	$7.95
Grade 3	1-57768-473-7	$7.95
Grade 4	1-57768-474-5	$7.95
Grade 5	1-57768-475-3	$7.95
Grade 6	1-57768-476-1	$7.95

CERTIFICATE OF ACCOMPLISHMENT

THIS CERTIFIES THAT

HAS SUCCESSFULLY COMPLETED

SPECTRUM
Language Arts
Grade 6
WORKBOOK

CONGRATULATIONS AND KEEP UP THE GOOD WORK!

McGraw-Hill
Consumer Products

A Division of The McGraw-Hill Companies

_____

Publisher